Data Sharing Regulation in Europe

This book provides a comprehensive examination of data sharing within the EU, exploring the regulatory challenges and opportunities created by EU frameworks and policies.

As data becomes a critical resource across sectors, EU regulators, policymakers and scholars face the urgent task of crafting frameworks that support data sharing while ensuring fairness, competition and protection of personal data. Through its chapters, the book adopts a holistic approach, analyzing data sharing from the perspectives of EU law, intellectual property, competition law, data protection and governance. It addresses the impact of recent EU legislation – including the Digital Markets Act (DMA), Digital Services Act (DSA), Data Governance Act and Data Act – on enabling or limiting data-sharing practices, particularly in the private sector. Each chapter offers policy recommendations and insights, collectively building a robust theoretical framework for responsible data sharing.

This book serves as a valuable resource for researchers, practitioners and students of EU law, competition law, data protection, intellectual property and governance, offering timely insights and a nuanced exploration of the evolving EU data-sharing landscape.

Laura Zoboli is an Assistant Professor at the University of Brescia and the Scientific Coordinator of the Centre for Antitrust and Regulatory Studies at the University of Warsaw, where she started her academic tenure. She is the Co-Director of the ASCOLA Center Europe Chapter. Laura earned her PhD from Bocconi University, where she currently teaches Data Law. Among her research experiences, she has been a research fellow at the Berkman Klein Center at Harvard University and the Max Planck Institute for Innovation and Competition. Her research focuses on the overlaps between competition law, intellectual property and regulation within data economy.

Maciej Bernatt is a Professor of Law at the University of Warsaw, Poland. He holds the Chair in European Economic Law at the Faculty of Management, and serves as the Director of the Centre for Antitrust and Regulatory Studies. He is the Co-Director of ASCOLA Central Europe Chapter. Maciej holds a Habilitation, PhD and MA titles in law and a second MA title in international relations. He held visiting appointments at the Bocconi University, the University of Chicago and the University of Melbourne, among others. Maciej's research interests lie at the intersections of competition law with constitutional law and EU law.

Routledge Research in Information Technology and E-Commerce Law

Titles in this series include:

International Internet Law
Joanna Kulesza

The Domain Name Registration System
Liberalisation, Consumer Protection and Growth
Jenny Ng

Law of Electronic Commercial Transactions, 2nd Edition
Contemporary Issues in the EU, US and China
Faye Fangfei Wang

Cyberthreats and the Decline of the Nation-State
Susan W Brenner

Balancing Privacy and Free Speech
Unwanted Attention in the Age of Social Media
Mark Tunick

Social Networks as the New Frontier of Terrorism
#Terror
Laura Scaife

Global Cybersecurity and International Law
Antonio Segura Serrano

Platform Neutrality Rights
AI Censors and the Future of Freedom
Hannibal Travis

Data Sharing Regulation in Europe
Edited by Laura Zoboli and Maciej Bernatt

Data Sharing Regulation in Europe

Edited by Laura Zoboli and Maciej Bernatt

Routledge
Taylor & Francis Group
LONDON AND NEW YORK

First published 2025
by Routledge
4 Park Square, Milton Park, Abingdon, Oxon OX14 4RN

and by Routledge
605 Third Avenue, New York, NY 10158

Routledge is an imprint of the Taylor & Francis Group, an informa business

British Library Cataloguing-in-Publication Data
A catalogue record for this book is available from the British Library

ISBN: 978-1-032-16371-0 (hbk)
ISBN: 978-1-032-16372-7 (pbk)
ISBN: 978-1-003-24825-5 (ebk)

DOI: 10.4324/9781003248255

Typeset in Times New Roman
by Deanta Global Publishing Services, Chennai, India

Contents

Contributors

Marco Botta is a Professor at the European University Institute in Florence (Italy), where he is the Scientific Coordinator of the Centre for a Digital Society. In addition, he is an External Lecturer at the Law Faculty University of Vienna and Visiting Professor at the Central European University in Vienna (Austria). In the past, he was Senior Research Fellow at the Max Planck Institute for Innovation and Competition (MPI) in Munich (Germany). Marco's research interests lie at the intersection of competition policy and sector regulation in the context of the digital economy.

Björn Lundqvist is Professor of European Law with a focus on competition law at Stockholm University, Sweden. He is the Chair of the Swedish Network of European Legal Studies, Director of the European Law Institute and Director of Ascola Nordic. Björn is a well-renowned European Competition Law scholar and has published extensively, both books and articles, on Competition, Data and IP Law and Policy-related issues. His latest book has been available since April 2023, titled *Regulating Access and Transfer of Data* by Cambridge University Press.

Mariateresa Maggiolino is a Professor of Antitrust Law and the Director of the Integrated Master of Arts in Law at Bocconi University, Milan. She is an expert in Competition Law and Regulation, serving as a Professor at Bocconi University, where she is also the Director of the five-year Master's program in Law. With three monographs to her name and numerous publications in top international and national journals, her work spans the critical intersections of competition law, intellectual property, banking law and data law, making her an important voice in these dynamic fields.

Joanna Mazur, Doctor of Law, Assistant Professor in the Department of European Economic Law, Faculty of Management, University of Warsaw. From 2019 to 2022, she was pursuing a National Science Centre Prelude grant entitled "Automated decision-making and the prohibition of discrimination under European law". In 2022 she was awarded the START scholarship (Foundation for Polish Science) and in 2023 the scholarship of the Ministry of Education and Science for outstanding young scientists. Her research focuses on European Union Law concerning new technologies.

Maria Lillà Montagnani is an Associate Professor of Commercial Law at Bocconi University in Milan, Italy, and Director of the Bocconi LLM Program in European and Social Law. She is currently a Transatlantic Technology Law Fellow (Stanford Law School). Lillà holds a PhD in Competition Law and an LLM in IP Law (Queen Mary University of London). In recent years, she has been a NYU Global Research Fellow at NYU Law School, Visiting Professor at Peking University School of Transnational Law (China) and Haifa University (Israel), and a Faculty Associate at the Berkman Klein Center of Harvard University.

Acknowledgments

The book was prepared as part of the research project "Business-to-Business Data Sharing within the EU Digital Market", financed by the Polish National Science Centre (Opus grant, 2018/31/B/HS5/01192) and conducted at the Centre for Antitrust and Regulatory Studies, which is part of the Faculty of Management at the University of Warsaw, Poland.

The editors express their gratitude to all those involved in the research project, particularly to Joanna Mazur, Maria Lillà Montagnani, Monika Woźniak-Cichuta and Marcin Zieliński, as well as to Maciej Janik and Monika Gac.

The editors are also thankful for the comments received during the book's roundtable, which was part of the international conference "Business-to-Business Data Sharing within the EU Digital Market", hosted by the Centre for Antitrust and Regulatory Studies in Warsaw, Poland, on 14 and 15 September 2023.

Introduction

Maciej Bernatt and Laura Zoboli

0.1 Context: Data Sharing as a Challenge for the EU Economy

In today's digital age, data has become a crucial asset, often compared to "oil" for its transformative impact on the 21st-century economy.[1] The ability to collect and analyze "Big Data" is essential for businesses seeking to enhance customer experiences, lower production costs and gain a competitive edge. The rapid growth of online platforms and the proliferation of Internet of Things (IoT) devices, which gather extensive data through embedded sensors, underscore the increasing importance of data.[2] This data is pivotal for training Artificial Intelligence (AI) algorithms, which in turn improve decision-making and operational efficiency.[3]

For the European Union (EU), enabling effective data sharing goes beyond regulatory compliance; it is a strategic necessity vital for driving innovation and economic advancement. Data sharing holds significant promise for augmenting data value, stimulating economic activity and lowering entry barriers for emerging market players. Developing efficient data-sharing mechanisms is crucial for realizing the full potential of data and fostering innovation.

The value of Business-to-Business (B2B) data sharing is profound. When companies exchange data, they unlock new avenues for value creation rather than merely exchanging information. The European Political Strategy Centre (EPSC) highlights that the benefits derived from data can differ greatly between the data provider and the data user.[4] A dataset held by one organization may not be fully

1 Shannon Tellis, 'Data is the 21st Century's Oil, says Siemens CEO Joe Kaeser' (*The Economics Times*, 24 May 2018) https://economictimes.indiatimes.com/magazines/panache/data-is-the-21st-centurys-oil-says-siemens-ceo-joe-kaeser/articleshow/64298125.cms?from=mdrlast accessed 25 January 2024.

2 McKinsey, 'Internet of Things: Catching Up to an Accelerating Opportunity' (*McKinsey Digital*, 1 June 2015) https://www.mckinsey.com/~/media/mckinsey/business%20functions/mckinsey%20digital/our%20insights/iot%20value%20set%20to%20accelerate%20through%202030%20where%20and%20how%20to%20capture%20it/the-internet-of-things-catching-up-to-an-accelerating-opportunity-final.pdf last accessed 25 January 2024.

3 Ajay Agrawal, Joshua Gans and Avi Goldfarb, *Prediction Machines: The Simple Economics of Artificial Intelligence* (Harvard Business Review, 2018).

4 EPSC Strategic Notes, *Enter the Data Economy, EU Policies for a Thriving Data Ecosystem* (Issue 21, 2017) 5–7.

DOI: 10.4324/9781003248255-1

utilized, while another organization could repurpose this data to generate substantial new insights and innovations.[5] This ability to create additional value from existing data illustrates a core feature of the data economy. Moreover, businesses can further benefit by monetizing data that has already been fully leveraged within their operations.[6]

The impact of data sharing extends beyond the immediate stakeholders to the broader economy. Effective B2B data sharing can spur innovation across industries, create new business models and lower barriers for start-ups. These start-ups, which often excel in data analysis but lack resources to acquire large datasets, can gain significantly from shared data.[7] Companies seeking data can engage in various activities, including collaborations, data purchases through marketplaces or accessing data from public and private sources. Data Service Providers, such as data marketplaces and industrial data spaces, play a critical role in facilitating these transactions within a controlled environment. These intermediaries function similarly to social media platforms and online marketplaces, shaping the data market ecosystem.

Despite the growing importance of data, the EU's data economy lags behind the United States market. Research indicates that improving data access could boost firm competitiveness and economic growth. For example, the OECD estimates that data sharing might contribute to GDP growth of 0.1% to 1.5% from public sector data and 1% to 2.5% from private sector data.[8] Yet, many firms remain hesitant to share data, with large portions of industrial data going unused. The EU Commission's 2020 Data Strategy highlights these issues, noting that while data sharing is prevalent in high-tech, utilities and financial sectors, it remains limited in public agencies, pharmaceuticals and healthcare.[9]

Key challenges to effective data sharing include interoperability issues, regulatory barriers and security concerns.[10] Additionally, the lack of a robust data market creates incentive problems: firms often struggle to assess the value of their data,

5 D Daniel Sokol and Roisin Comerford, 'Does Antitrust Have a Role to Play in Regulating Big Data?' in Roger D Blair and D Daniel Sokol (eds), *Cambridge Handbook of Antitrust, Intellectual Property and High Tech* (Cambridge University Press 2017) 6–7.

6 Francesco Mezzanotte, 'Access to Data: The Role of Consent and the Licensing Scheme' in Sebastian Lohsse, Reiner Schulze and Dirk Staudenmayer (eds), *Trading Data in the Digital Economy: Legal Concepts and Tools* (Hart/Nomos 2017) 160.

7 European Commission Communication, *Towards a common European data space* (COM/2018/232 final) 9–10; Terrell McSweeny and Brian O'Dea, *Data, Innovation, and Potential Competition in Digital Markets – Looking Beyond Short-Term Price Effects in Merger Analysis* (CPI Antitrust Chronicle, vol 2, 2018) 7.

8 OECD, 'Enhancing Access to and Sharing of Data: Reconciling Risks and Benefits for Data Re-Use across Societies' (2019) 59–64. The text of the report is available at: https://www.oecd.org/en/publications/enhancing-access-to-and-sharing-of-data_276aaca8-en.html last accessed 25 January 2024.

9 European Commission Communication, *A European strategy for data* (COM/2020/66 final) 6.

10 Richard Feasey and Alexandre de Streel, 'Data Sharing for Digital Markets' Contestability: Towards a Governance Framework' (CERRE Report, 2020) 15 https://cerre.eu/publications/data-sharing-digital-markets-competition-governance last accessed 25 January 2024.

leading to either open access without compensation or a reluctance to share.[11] To address this "data-sharing paradox", the EU has introduced a new legal framework designed to tackle these issues. This framework comprises two main components: the development of Common European Data Spaces to address technical, privacy and security challenges and a suite of cross-sector legislative proposals.[12]

These legislative proposals include the Data Act (DA),[13] the Open Data Directive (ODD),[14] the Data Governance Act (DGA),[15] and the Digital Markets Act (DMA).[16] Together, they aim to enhance data sharing across various sectors, provide legal clarity and address specific market failures and public interest concerns. The framework covers B2B, Government-to-Business (G2B) and Business-to-Government (B2G).

In summary, navigating the complexities and opportunities presented by data-sharing regulations is crucial for the EU's economic strategy. By implementing a robust and cohesive regulatory framework, the EU has the potential to fully harness its data economy and drive innovation throughout the digital landscape.

0.2 Approach and Methodology

Navigating the regulatory landscape for data sharing within the EU reveals a complex interplay of legal frameworks that shape and constrain data-sharing practices. This book aims to deepen understanding of how existing regulations influence data sharing and highlights areas ripe for improvement. By critically assessing and comparing the current legal environment, it seeks to provide valuable insights for policymakers, businesses and academics, ultimately contributing to a more effective and innovative data economy across Europe.

The challenge of creating a regulatory environment that both promotes data sharing and upholds individual rights, fosters competition and respects IP protections

11 Deloitte, *Study on Emerging Issues of Data Ownership, Interoperability, (Re-)Usability and Access to Data and Liability* (European Commission, 2018) 56. https://op.europa.eu/en/publication-detail/-/publication/74cca30c-4833-11e8-be1d-01aa75ed71a1/language-en last accessed 25 January 2024.

12 European Commission, *Staff Working Document on Common European Data Spaces* (SWD/2022/45 final). https://digital-strategy.ec.europa.eu/en/library/staff-working-document-data-spaces last accessed 25 January 2024.

For further information concerning the development of the Common European Data Spaces initiative *see* http://dataspaces.info/common-european-data-spaces/ last accessed 25 January 2024.

13 Regulation (EU) 2023/2854 of the European Parliament and of the Council of 13 December 2023 on harmonized rules on fair access to and use of data and amending Regulation (EU) 2017/2394 and Directive (EU) 2020/1828 (Data Act) [2023] OJ L 2023/2854.

14 Directive (EU) 2019/1024 of the European Parliament and of the Council of 20 June 2019, on open data and the re-use of public sector information [2019] OJ L172/56.

15 Regulation (EU) 2022/868 of the European Parliament and of the Council of 30 May 2022 on European data governance and amending Regulation (EU) 2018/1724 (Data Governance Act) [2022] OJ L152/1.

16 Regulation (EU) 2022/1925 of the European Parliament and of the Council of 14 September 2022 on contestable and fair markets in the digital sector, amending Directives (EU) 2019/1937 and (EU) 2020/1828 (Digital Markets Act) [2022] OJ L265/1.

is intricate and multifaceted. Therefore, it is crucial to reflect on how to harmonize these frameworks to support a balanced and forward-thinking data economy.

The EU's legislative efforts, including the Data Act, the Open Data Directive, the Data Governance Act, the Digital Services Act and the Digital Markets Act, underscore the commitment to advancing data sharing while fostering an environment conducive to innovation. These regulations aim to tackle issues related to data access, interoperability and fairness, striving to build a robust and inclusive digital market across Europe. However, significant gaps persist, especially in B2B data sharing.

This book intends to highlight how B2B data sharing, despite its potential to drive innovation and create value, is hindered by considerable legal limitations and obstacles that affect business competitiveness and innovation. More specifically, the analysis carried out in the book underscores the need for focused attention and strategic interventions to unlock the full potential of data-driven collaboration among businesses. While current regulations have a significant added value, they often lack coherence and fail to fully address the complexities of B2B data sharing. Moreover, the interplay between competition law, IP law and data protection law presents both limitations and opportunities. IP laws, while safeguarding innovation, can restrict data flow. Competition law, aimed at preventing anti-competitive practices, can sometimes obstruct collaborative data-sharing efforts. Data protection laws prioritize privacy and security but may create barriers to data access. Balancing these interests is essential for developing a coherent data-sharing regime that encourages innovation while respecting legal and ethical boundaries.

A further and significant challenge is the need for greater coherence among the EU's new data-sharing regulations. Although the regulatory framework is robust, the overlapping and occasionally conflicting nature of these laws can create uncertainty and impede effective implementation. This book offers insights into how these regulations can be better integrated to facilitate data sharing, particularly among private entities.

Against this backdrop, the development of Common European Data Spaces presents a promising solution to harmonize these frameworks, addressing technical, privacy and security barriers. Data spaces could effectively balance regulatory frameworks by providing structured environments that align with fundamental interests and rights while promoting data sharing. They aim to enhance data flow within specific strategic sectors by establishing common interoperability standards and sectoral governance rules. Continued support for the development of these data spaces, through EU funding and regulatory guidance, could help overcome existing barriers and improve data-sharing practices.

The original idea behind the book relates to a significant gap in the literature regarding comprehensive analyses of B2B data-sharing policies within the EU. Existing studies often focus on isolated aspects of data regulation or examine the theoretical implications of data sharing without addressing the practical realities and interactions of regulatory frameworks. There is a need for a holistic assessment that explores the systemic challenges, regulatory shortcomings and potential solutions for optimizing B2B data sharing.

This need has been tackled within the research project "Business-to-Business Data Sharing within the EU Digital Market", financed by the Polish National Science Centre (Opus, 2018/31/B/HS5/01192) and pursued within the Centre for Antitrust and Regulatory Studies, part of the Faculty of Management at the University of Warsaw, Poland (hereinafter the "Research project").[17] This book is the outcome of the Research project.

As EU regulators, policymakers and scholars confront the evolving landscape of data sharing, there is indeed a pressing need for a cohesive and thorough understanding of the associated barriers and incentives. This book is designed to fill in this gap by offering an in-depth analysis of data-sharing initiatives within the EU. It investigates the regulatory frameworks that influence these initiatives, emphasizing the principle of technological neutrality. This principle advocates for regulations that focus on the desired outcomes rather than the specific technologies involved, thereby promoting a more adaptable and forward-looking legal framework.

In light of the above, the overarching aim of this book is to assess the impact of EU policies on data sharing and to explore how these policies can be optimized to foster innovation and competition. By adopting a holistic approach, this book seeks to clarify the interplay between general EU regulations, data protection laws, intellectual property law and competition law. In other words, the book integrates the perspectives of general EU data regulation, data protection, competition law and intellectual property. It uses this multi-disciplinary approach to address the complex interactions between different legal frameworks and to propose solutions that promote effective data sharing in the EU. The book combines rigorous legal analysis with interdisciplinary approaches. Each chapter draws upon a wide range of sources, including primary legal texts, policy documents and reports, case-law and scholarly literature.

0.3 Book Structure and Its Key Themes

This book is structured to provide a comprehensive and cohesive exploration of data sharing within the European Union. Recognizing the complexity of the subject, the book is divided into two main parts, each addressing critical aspects of data sharing from foundational regulatory frameworks to their interactions with competition and intellectual property concerns. The aim is to offer a holistic view that reflects the various layers of data-sharing regulation studies within the mentioned Research project, while ensuring a seamless flow through the research process.

More specifically, the structure of the book reflects an integrative approach, designed to guide the reader through the multifaceted nature of data-sharing

17 More information about the project and the project's open access research reports are available here: https://cars.wz.uw.edu.pl/en/research-and-expertise/research-projects/583-9-research-project-business-to-business-data-sharing-within-the-eu-digital-market-2019-2021-financed-by-the-polish-national-science-centre-opus-grant-2018-31-b-hs5-01192.html. The editors are grateful to all those involved in the Research project, in particular to Joanna Mazur, Maria Lillà Montagnani, Monika Woźniak-Cichuta and Marcin Zieliński as well as to Maciej Janik and Monika Gac.

regulations. The two-part division mirrors the systematic progression of the Research project: starting with the fundamental concepts and regulations in Part I and moving towards the specific interactions with competition and intellectual property in Part II.

This sequential approach ensures that the reader builds a solid understanding of the regulatory landscape before delving into more specialized topics. By addressing foundational regulatory frameworks first, the book sets the stage for a nuanced discussion of how these frameworks intersect with and impact competition and intellectual property rights.

The book closes with "Part III: Conclusions" which contains Chapter 7, focusing on the interplay of data protection, competition law, IP law and data sharing.

0.4 Part I: Categorization of Data and Regulation of Data

Part I of the book lays the groundwork for understanding data sharing by categorizing different types of data and analyzing the regulatory frameworks that govern their sharing. This section is crucial for establishing a comprehensive background, which informs the subsequent analysis of competition and intellectual property concerns.

0.4.1 Types of Data and Stakeholders in Data Sharing (Chapter 1)

Chapter 1 provides a thorough examination of data categories, and the diverse stakeholders involved in data sharing, with a primary focus on business-to-business (B2B) contexts. This chapter explains key concepts that underpin the Research project's exploration of the regulatory frameworks impacting data sharing within the EU. It addresses several critical aspects, including:

Nature of Data:

- **Non-Rivalrous and Multifunctional**: data stands out as a non-rivalrous resource, meaning it can be utilized by multiple entities simultaneously for various purposes, often generating new data in the process. This multifunctional and dynamic nature of data differentiates it from most natural resources and underscores the necessity of broad access and incentivized sharing. Such characteristics are essential for maximizing social welfare and enhancing the EU data economy.

Data Categories:

- **Blurring Boundaries**: traditional distinctions between personal, non-personal, private and public data are increasingly overlapping. The highest value from data often arises from combining datasets from diverse sources to develop new data-oriented products and services. This fluidity highlights the evolving nature of data and the need for adaptable regulatory frameworks.

Data in Practice:

- **Practical Applications**: in practical applications, such as in a smart city, data integration across sectors like telecommunications, transportation and healthcare can significantly enhance public services and operational efficiencies. For instance, improved data sharing could revolutionize areas like traffic management, urban planning and public health, leading to more effective and responsive service delivery.

Transition of Data Categories:

- **Dynamic Nature**: data's categorization is not static. Processes like anonymization can transform personal data into non-personal data, and private data may become public, reflecting the versatile nature and broad applications of data. This aspect emphasizes the need for flexible approaches to data regulation.

Stakeholder Roles:

- **Business-to-Business (B2B)**: involves data exchange between commercial entities, fostering collaboration, innovation and value creation within and across industries;
- **Business-to-Government (B2G)**: entails the provision of data from private sector entities to government bodies for purposes such as regulatory compliance, public service delivery and policy formulation;
- **Government-to-Government (G2G)**: concerns data sharing between different governmental bodies, which facilitates interagency coordination, information sharing and decision-making;
- **Government-to-Business (G2B)**: refers to the dissemination of public sector data to private entities, aimed at driving innovation, fostering transparency and supporting economic growth.

In conclusion, Chapter 1 lays the essential groundwork for understanding data-sharing dynamics by outlining the diverse types of data and the roles of various stakeholders. This foundational knowledge is critical for comprehending the regulatory frameworks and broader implications of data sharing discussed in subsequent chapters. The insights provided here set the stage for a deeper exploration of how data is regulated, protected and leveraged across different sectors and contexts.

0.4.2 General and Sectoral Regulations Impacting Data Sharing (Chapter 2)

Chapter 2 addresses the complex interaction between various EU legal frameworks that regulate data access, transfer and sharing. As the EU introduces a slew of new regulations, the legal landscape governing data sharing has become increasingly intricate, with overlapping rules across different sectors. This chapter examines these regulations, highlights areas of overlap and inconsistency and explores how these complexities impact legal certainty and coherence. In doing so, Chapter 2 provides the reader with a unique systematization of the EU regulations affecting data sharing and sets the stage for understanding the fragmented nature of these regulations and their implications for businesses navigating multiple legal systems. In particular, Chapter 2 addresses:

EU General Regulations:

- **Data Act (DA)**: it delves into the Data Act, which aims to standardize data access and sharing across various sectors. It examines how the Act establishes general principles for data handling and its interaction with other regulations;
- **Digital Markets Act (DMA)**: the DMA's focus on regulating digital gatekeepers and ensuring fair competition is analyzed, particularly how it influences data-sharing practices;
- **Digital Services Act (DSA)**: the DSA's impact on data sharing is reviewed, especially in terms of content moderation and platform responsibilities;
- **Open Data Directive (ODD)**: this directive's role in promoting transparency and access to public sector data is discussed, highlighting its implications for data sharing;
- **Data Governance Act (DGA)**: the DGA's provisions for data access and data-sharing services are examined. This section also considers the Act's approach to facilitating data sharing and establishing data intermediaries.

EU Sectoral Regulations:

- **Data Spaces**: the chapter explores the European Commission's Data Spaces initiative, which aims to create sector-specific data-sharing frameworks;
- **Health Data Space**: analysis of regulations governing the sharing of health data, focusing on privacy, security and access issues;
- **Directive on Payment Services II (PSD2)**: this section covers data-sharing requirements within the financial sector, including implications for payment services;
- **Vehicle Data for Independent Repair Shops**: the regulation concerning vehicle data and its impact on independent repair shops is examined. A reflection on emerging regulations for in-vehicle data sharing and their implications for industry stakeholders is also made;
- **Other Sectoral Legal Systems**: review of additional sector-specific regulations mandating data sharing, highlighting variations and commonalities.

In conclusion, Chapter 2 consolidates the key findings from the analysis of both general and special sectoral regulations. It provides an overview of the regulatory landscape and identifies areas where overlaps and inconsistencies arise. The chapter concludes by advocating for the introduction of a unified set of rules for data access and transfer. It argues that a general regulatory framework could mitigate the challenges posed by disparate and overlapping regulations, thereby enhancing legal certainty and coherence across the EU.

0.4.3 Personal Data Protection and Its Influence on Data Sharing (Chapter 3)

Chapter 3 delves into how personal data protection laws, especially the General Data Protection Regulation (GDPR), shape the regulatory framework for data sharing. In an era where the economic value of data is widely recognized, this chapter emphasizes the critical importance of data protection. It explores how GDPR principles, including consent, transparency and data subject rights, impact data-sharing practices. Additionally, it addresses the ongoing challenges and tensions between safeguarding personal data and facilitating data flows. In doing so, the chapter opens with a discussion on the significance of data protection amidst the growing economic reliance on data. Despite heightened awareness and calls for reform, major tech companies often continue practices that raise concerns about data protection. This sets the stage for a closer examination of the boundaries established by data protection laws for data sharing. In particular, Chapter 3 systematically addresses several critical aspects, including:

Data Protection Framework:

- **General Data Protection Regulation (GDPR)**: the GDPR serves as the focal point of the analysis, detailing its influence on data-sharing practices. The chapter reviews key GDPR provisions and relevant decisions from national data protection authorities (DPAs);
- **International and Regional Laws**: the chapter briefly references other significant legal instruments, such as the European Convention on Human Rights (ECHR) and Convention 108+, as well as regional trade agreements that include data protection provisions.

Data Categorization and Processing:

- **Types of Data**: the chapter clarifies the scope of GDPR by discussing categories such as personal data, pseudonymization and anonymization. It also examines special categories of data, including sensitive data and data related to minors, highlighting how these classifications affect data protection rules;
- **Purpose of Processing**: the chapter specifically addresses the importance of processing purposes under GDPR and how the lawful basis for processing impacts data sharing. It explores how specific purposes can dictate the permissibility of data use and sharing.

Principles of Data Processing:

- **Core Principles**: the chapter delves into GDPR's core principles – such as data minimization, accuracy and accountability – and their implications for data sharing. These principles set limits on what is permissible in terms of data processing and sharing;

- **Data Subject Rights**: the chapter examines the rights of data subjects, including access, rectification and erasure, and how these rights influence data-sharing practices. The chapter highlights how compliance with these rights can complicate data-sharing arrangements.

Data Transfers:

- **International Data Transfers**: the chapter discusses the mechanisms and restrictions on transferring personal data outside the EU, including the role of adequacy decisions, Standard Contractual Clauses (SCCs) and Binding Corporate Rules (BCRs). It explores how these regulations ensure that data protection standards are maintained across borders.

Balancing Data Protection and Data Flow:

- **Facilitating Data Movement**: the chapter considers the GDPR's dual objective of protecting personal data while enabling data flow. It reviews provisions like data portability, which aim to support data movement within the EU while upholding strong protection standards;
- **Regulatory Tensions**: the chapter discusses the tension between robust data protection and the need for free data flows, proposing strategies for balancing these priorities.

In conclusion, Chapter 3 provides a detailed exploration of how GDPR and related data protection laws influence data sharing and offers guidance on evaluating GDPR provisions when planning data-sharing operations. In doing so, it assesses the significance of various GDPR requirements for both data protection and the free movement of personal data, suggesting ways to navigate these rules effectively.

0.4.4 Compensation Mechanisms for Data Sharing (Chapter 4)

Chapter 4 investigates the mechanisms through which stakeholders are compensated for data sharing, focusing on various compensation models such as financial remuneration and alternative forms of value exchange. It assesses how these mechanisms affect stakeholders' willingness to share data and the overall efficacy of data-sharing initiatives. The chapter addresses the prevalent issue of insufficient incentives for data sharing and explores the new EU regulatory framework designed to tackle these challenges. As a premise of the analysis, the chapter outlines the paradox of data sharing in the modern economy. Despite the increasing value of data, obstacles like lack of interoperability, regulatory barriers and security concerns hinder data sharing. The primary issue is the incentive problem: firms struggle to evaluate the value of their datasets, leading them to either avoid sharing data or to adopt open-access approaches without compensation. Against this backdrop, Chapter 4 examines the essential components needed to complement general data regulations with respect to private-sector compensation for data sharing. In particular, Chapter 4 addresses:

Need for Compensation:

- **Incentivizing Data Sharing**: the chapter emphasizes that compensation is essential to motivate data sharing. Without compensation, data holders lack the incentive to share their datasets, resulting in fewer data-sharing agreements and missed opportunities for data-driven innovation.

Data Sharing Business Models:

- **Business-to-Business (B2B) Models**: the chapter explores various B2B data-sharing models, including financial transactions and non-monetary exchanges of value. It examines how these models influence the willingness of businesses to share their data;
- **Government-to-Business (G2B) and Business-to-Government (B2G) Models**: the chapter also discusses G2B and B2G models, highlighting how data sharing is incentivized through mechanisms like data prizes, civic data sharing and data philanthropy. These models often focus on public interest rather than direct economic gain.

Benefits of Data Sharing:

- **Economic and Strategic Advantages**: the chapter outlines the benefits of data sharing, such as enhanced innovation, improved decision-making and increased efficiency. It underscores how effective compensation mechanisms can amplify these benefits by encouraging more stakeholders to participate in data-sharing initiatives.

Obstacles to Data Sharing:

- **Technical Barriers**: the chapter discusses technical challenges, including interoperability issues and data integration difficulties, that impede data sharing;
- **Market Failures**: it explores the market failures affecting data sharing, such as the lack of a functioning market for data valuation;
- **Lack of Trust**: the chapter highlights how trust issues between data holders and data users can obstruct data-sharing efforts.

EU Regulatory Framework on Compensation:

- **Overview of EU Legislation**: the chapter provides an in-depth analysis of the EU's new regulatory framework designed to address data-sharing compensation. It reviews key legislative acts already framed in Chapters 2 and 3 and in particular:
    - **Open Data Directive (ODD)**: this directive aims to promote data sharing between public authorities and the private sector;

- **Data Governance Act (DGA)**: introduces a governance framework to encourage both G2B and B2B data sharing;
- **Data Act (DA)**: recent legislation that mandates B2B data sharing and addresses data sharing during public emergencies (B2G);
- **Digital Markets Act (DMA)**: mandates data-sharing obligations for digital gatekeepers and includes sector-specific rules for industries like chemicals, banking and automotive;
- **General Data Protection Regulation (GDPR)**: the right to data portability under GDPR is discussed as part of the EU data-sharing framework, facilitating B2B transactions.

- **Compensation Rules**: the chapter examines how the EU framework provides general rules on compensation, allowing parties to negotiate compensation based on data quality and value. It assesses whether these rules create a consistent legal framework or leave too much flexibility for individual agreements.

In conclusion, Chapter 4 offers a thorough examination of compensation mechanisms for data sharing, delving into the challenges and regulatory responses within the EU context. It evaluates various business models, assesses the benefits and obstacles associated with data sharing and reviews the newly established legislative framework. The chapter illuminates how to effectively incentivize data sharing and tackle the paradox of high data value versus reluctance to share. By providing critical insights, it aims to assist stakeholders and policymakers in enhancing data-sharing practices and overcoming existing barriers. In its conclusion, the chapter evaluates the effectiveness of the EU data-sharing acquis, focusing on the impact of compensation mechanisms. It assesses whether the new regulatory framework has effectively resolved incentive issues and offers recommendations for further improvements.

0.5 Part II: Competition, Intellectual Property and the Balance of the Regulatory Frameworks

Part II shifts the focus to the competition and intellectual property dimensions of data sharing, analyzing how data sharing intersects with antitrust concerns and intellectual property rights. This section explores the balance between promoting competition and protecting intellectual property, providing insights into the broader implications for data sharing.

0.5.1 Competitive Impacts of Data Sharing and Antitrust Response (Chapter 5)

Chapter 5 investigates the impact of data sharing on market competition and the antitrust responses necessary to address these effects. It explores how data sharing can influence competitive dynamics, both positively and negatively, and examines the role of competition law in regulating such practices. The chapter provides a thorough analysis of situations where data sharing may undermine competition and discusses how antitrust authorities can balance these concerns with the benefits of data sharing. More specifically, Chapter 5 underscores the dual nature of data sharing, which can either enhance or hinder competition depending on the context. In particular, Chapter 5 addresses:

Data Sharing and Collusion:

- **Facilitating Cartels**: the chapter examines how data sharing among competitors can facilitate collusion by reducing uncertainty and enabling firms to sustain anti-competitive practices such as price fixing. It highlights the need for antitrust interventions to prevent such harmful effects.

Exploitation through Data Sharing:

- **Unilateral Exploitation**: the chapter explores scenarios where unilateral data sharing allows a firm to exploit its competitors. It discusses how access to data can be used to harm rivals, creating an imbalance in the competitive landscape.

Refusal to Share Data:

- **Competitive Disadvantage**: the chapter assesses the impact of data refusal by dominant firms or groups of firms. It considers how such refusal can disadvantage competitors and whether it constitutes an antitrust violation.

Intersection with Data Protection Laws:

- **Balancing Competition and Privacy**: the chapter also addresses the interaction between competition law and data protection regulations, such as the GDPR. It examines how the need to protect personal data intersects with competition concerns, especially when data-sharing practices involve personal information.

In conclusion, Chapter 5 evaluates the current antitrust frameworks' effectiveness in addressing the challenges posed by data sharing. It emphasizes that while data sharing can offer significant competitive benefits, it also poses risks that need to be managed through appropriate regulatory measures. Chapter 5 recommends that competition authorities adopt a nuanced approach, carefully assessing the competitive impacts of data sharing and intervening only when necessary to prevent anti-competitive practices. Additionally, it highlights the importance of integrating competition law with data protection regulations to ensure a balanced and fair market environment.

0.5.2 Intellectual Property Rights and Data-Sharing Obligations (Chapter 6)

Chapter 6 explores the intricate relationship between intellectual property (IP) rights and data-sharing obligations, focusing on how IP laws influence data-sharing practices. As data becomes a critical asset in the digital age, the chapter examines how IP rights like patents, copyrights and trade secrets intersect with data sharing, assessing whether these rights facilitate or obstruct data access and sharing. It highlights the evolving EU regulatory framework and its impact on balancing IP protection with the need for data flow, offering insights into the ongoing shifts in data-sharing policies. In particular, Chapter 6 addresses:

Data and IP Relationship:

- **Patents and Data**: the chapter examines how patents interact with data, stating that data itself, as an output of a patented process, usually does not qualify for patent protection due to its descriptive nature and lack of originality;
- **Copyright and Data**: the chapter explores the role of copyright in protecting data, particularly how copyright laws impact the accessibility and sharing of data. While databases can receive protection if they show intellectual creation, raw data often lacks the required originality. The EU Directive 96/9/EC provides a two-tier system, offering copyright protection for original databases and *a sui generis* right for those with significant investment but lacking originality. This protection focuses on the structure of databases rather than their contents;
- **Trade Secrets and Data**: the chapter assesses how trade secrets laws protect proprietary data and the implications for data sharing. While trade secret protection is relevant, it is complex due to the often non-secret nature of data and the challenge of maintaining secrecy. The focus on trade secrets in the Data Governance Act (DGA) and the Data Act (DA) reflects the ongoing need to balance secrecy with data-sharing obligations;
- **The Data Producer's Right**: this part reviews the failed attempt to establish a semi-property right on data, known as the data producer's right, and its implications for data sharing.

Paradigmatic Shift in the EU Approach:

- **DGA and Data Sharing**: the chapter discusses the Data Governance Act (DGA), which promotes data sharing while considering IP rights protection. It introduces mechanisms for data intermediaries and common data spaces to facilitate data flow while respecting IP rights;
- **DA and Data Flow**: the Data Act (DA) is examined for its role in enabling data access and flow, particularly how it interacts with existing IP rights. It focuses on reducing barriers to data sharing while maintaining IP protection;
- **Role of Data Intermediaries**: data intermediaries and common data spaces are explored as tools to support data sharing and flow. The chapter assesses how these mechanisms work within the EU regulatory framework to balance IP protection with the need for accessible data.

Change in EU Approach: the chapter also considers the shift in the EU's approach from reinforcing IP rights to encouraging data access and flow. It reflects on how the DGA and DA illustrate this change and assesses the current role of IP rights in the EU regulatory framework for data sharing.

In conclusion, Chapter 6 highlights the complex interplay between IP rights and data-sharing obligations, illustrating how IP laws can both support and hinder data sharing. The analysis reveals a significant shift in EU policies from emphasizing IP protection to encouraging data flow, as seen in the Data Governance Act and the Data Act. This evolving regulatory landscape aims to reconcile the need for data accessibility with the protection of IP rights, ultimately fostering a more dynamic and inclusive data economy. In general terms, Chapter 6 underscores the importance of this balance in advancing data-driven innovation while respecting intellectual property considerations.

0.6 Part III: Conclusions

0.6.1 Balancing Data Protection, Competition Law and Intellectual Property and the Coherence of EU Data Law (Chapter 7)

Chapter 7 is the conclusive chapter that delves into the complex relationships between data protection, competition law and IP rights, analyzing how these legal frameworks can be harmonized with pro-data-sharing regulation to promote the advancement of the EU data economy. In doing so, the chapter explores the challenges and opportunities presented by these regulatory areas and proposes strategies for balancing innovation, competition and privacy while facilitating data sharing. In particular, Chapter 7 assesses:

Limitations Imposed by IP, Competition and Data Protection Laws:

- **IP Perspective**: IP laws, which safeguard proprietary information and incentivize innovation through exclusivity, can restrict the free flow of data. These laws present challenges to data-sharing efforts by prioritizing the protection of IP over the sharing of data. Additionally, the absence of copyright and patent protections specifically for data limits the ability to enforce and strengthen the position of data holders, thereby complicating data sharing;
- **Competition Law Perspective**: Competition law, designed to prevent anti-competitive practices, can inadvertently hinder data-sharing initiatives. The application of Article 101 TFEU (which addresses anti-competitive agreements) may complicate data sharing between firms. Furthermore, competition law can restrict data sharing if it leads to potential violations of Article 102 TFEU, which addresses the abuse of market dominance. For instance, a dominant firm may face antitrust scrutiny if it pressures its business customers or individual consumers to share their data;

- **Data Protection Perspective**: data protection laws, particularly GDPR, prioritize the privacy and security of individuals' data. These laws ensure that data subjects maintain control over their information but can also impose significant restrictions on how data can be shared and utilized, affecting collaborative data-sharing initiatives.

Fostering Data Sharing Through Regulatory Frameworks:

- **IP Laws:** despite their restrictive nature, IP laws can facilitate data sharing through mechanisms such as licensing agreements. These agreements allow controlled data sharing while protecting intellectual property rights. Additionally, IP protection on data can in specific cases extend to trade secrets, and, under certain conditions, to copyright and *sui generis* rights on databases, providing residual protection that can support data-sharing initiatives;
- **Competition Law**: competition law can promote data sharing by ensuring that market practices do not suppress collaborative efforts. Article 101(3) TFEU provides potential exemptions for certain data pooling, standardization or research and development agreements. Furthermore, merger scrutiny under competition law can prevent excessive data concentration, encouraging a more balanced and competitive data-sharing environment;
- **Data Protection Laws**: data protection laws can facilitate data sharing through secure data-sharing mechanisms and frameworks. Compliance with GDPR and other data protection regulations can be achieved by implementing robust privacy safeguards and data-sharing protocols.

Coherence of EU Data-Sharing Acquis:

- The chapter examines the coherence of the EU's data-sharing regulations, which are often complex and overlapping. While new regulations are designed to enhance data sharing, their integration and practical application remain challenging. The chapter emphasizes the need for a more coherent regulatory framework to provide legal certainty and effectively stimulate data sharing.

Data Spaces as a Harmonizing Solution:

- Data spaces are presented as a potential solution to balance horizontal and vertical regulatory frameworks. These spaces aim to create structured environments for data sharing while aligning with fundamental rights and interests. By establishing common standards and governance rules, data spaces could overcome existing barriers and promote data-driven innovation in strategic sectors.

In conclusion, Chapter 7 provides a comprehensive analysis of how data protection, competition law and intellectual property rights interact and influence data-sharing practices and regulations. It identifies critical gaps in the regulatory framework and proposes strategies for creating a more balanced and coherent approach to data sharing. The chapter highlights the importance of aligning regulatory frameworks to support data-driven innovation while safeguarding privacy, promoting competition and respecting IP protections. The development of Common European Data Spaces represents a promising approach to harmonizing these frameworks and addressing the challenges faced by businesses in the digital age.

In summary, this book contributes to the discourse on data governance by advocating for a more integrated and coherent regulatory approach. It offers valuable insights and strategies for enhancing data sharing while ensuring that competition, innovation and privacy are maintained. By addressing the complexities of the current regulatory framework and proposing actionable solutions, this work aims to support a more effective and innovative data economy in Europe. Moving forward, fostering collaboration and aligning regulatory frameworks will be crucial for unlocking the full potential of data-driven innovation and shaping the future of the digital economy.

Part I

Categorization of Data and Regulation of Data

1 Players and Interests at Stake in Data Sharing

Laura Zoboli

1.1 Introduction

Data sharing is more than a mere exchange of information; it is a dynamic process where data transcends its traditional role as an output to become a catalyst for innovation.[1] Imagine a scenario: one company holds a dataset, while another gains access to and reimagines its possibilities.[2] What is important is that each entity may detect the value of this data differently. While the former may view it as a valuable but exploited asset, the latter might see it as a wellspring of untapped potential.[3]

As mentioned in the introductory chapter, the European Union, recognizing the transformative power of data sharing, has embarked on a journey to facilitate its widespread adoption. Yet, this path is fraught with challenges. Trust issues, lack of control over shared data and regulatory complexities pose significant hurdles, particularly in private sector interactions.[4] Despite these obstacles, the EU has taken proactive steps, issuing guidelines, reports and legislative proposals to foster an environment conducive to data sharing and pooling.[5]

Amidst this evolution, EU regulatory intervention regarding data has become increasingly pervasive, impacting public, private, personal and non-personal data.[6] The EU strategy aims not only to enhance data availability and utilization but also to cultivate a robust market for data-driven products and services. In exploring

1 In this sense, data is not only an *output* – i.e. as a product generated through a process – but also as an *input*, capable of generating and/or improving processes, products and services.

2 D Daniel Sokol and Roisin Comerford, 'Does Antitrust Have a Role to Play in Regulating Big Data?' in Roger D Blair and D Daniel Sokol (eds), *The Cambridge Handbook of Antitrust, Intellectual Property, and High Tech* (Cambridge University Press 2017). In fact, the ability to create additional value by using the same data for other purposes is noted as one of the defining aspects of the data economy – on this point *see* G Cattaneo and others, How the Power of Data Will Drive EU Economy. First Report On Policy Conclusions (2018).

3 Francesco Mezzanotte, 'Access to Data: The Role of Consent and the Licensing Scheme' in Sebastian Lohsse, Reiner Schulze and Dirk Staudenmayer (eds), *Trading Data in the Digital Economy: Legal Concepts and Tools* (Nomos/Hart 2017).

4 Laura Zoboli, 'Fueling the European Digital Economy: A Regulatory Assessment of B2B Data Sharing' (2020) 31(4) European Business Law Review 9.

5 Björn Lundqvist, 'Competition and Data Pools' (2018) 7(4) Journal of European Consumer and Market Law 146.

6 European Commission Communication, *A European strategy for data* (COM/2020/66 final) 26.

DOI: 10.4324/9781003248255-3

this multifaceted landscape, it is essential to first examine the scope of the types of data – public and private, personal and non-personal data – and their interplay, thus turning the spotlight on the EU's efforts to mandate the sharing of public data, to incentivize the sharing of private data while respecting the autonomy of operators in deciding whether and how to share their data (with a few exceptions as in the Data Act), and to balance the imperative need to safeguard the protection of personal data with the goal of not hindering innovation.

Before delving into the various types of data, it is crucial to recognize their common features.[7] Data is a non-rivalrous, multifunctional and highly dynamic resource.[8] Unlike most natural resources, data can be used concurrently by multiple users for different purposes, generating new data in the process. From an economic standpoint, maximizing social welfare involves allowing everyone who values data to consume it, incentivizing data sharing to enhance the value of the EU data economy.[9]

Labeling data also poses challenges as distinctions between public, private, personal and non-personal data blur.[10] In the global data-driven economy, the highest value often arises from creating data-oriented products and services utilizing mixed datasets from various sources. Consider the landscape of a smart city: an expansive array of services seamlessly integrated into its grid – encompassing telecommunications, transportation, healthcare, security, finance and more. Enhanced collaboration among providers within this grid could markedly improve service delivery.[11] For instance, the unrestricted sharing of data related to traffic management, urban planning, air quality monitoring, street lighting regulation and smart parking could vastly enhance public transportation, health monitoring systems, the efficiency of smart vehicles and the responsiveness of emergency services. Furthermore, widening access to data maintained by private entities is widely acknowledged as pivotal for fostering the development of innovative data-driven applications.[12] Moreover, data can transition between these categories as it undergoes processing. For instance, personal data can be anonymized, thereby transforming into non-personal data; anonymized and processed private data can become public data; public sector data might be the basis for private-driven initiatives, etc.

7 *See*, also, Marcin Zieliński, 'Business-to-Business Data Sharing within the EU Digital Market (2019–2021): Categorization of Data and Actors Involved in Data Sharing Operations' (2023). Available at SSRN: https://ssrn.com/abstract=4462295 or http://dx.doi.org/10.2139/ssrn.4462295.

8 ALI & ELI, *ALI-ELI Principles for a Data Economy: Data Transactions and Data Rights* (2019) 6. Available at: https://europeanlawinstitute.eu/projects-publications/publications/ali-eli-principles-for-a-data-economy-data-transactions-and-data-rights/.

9 Brett M Frischmann, *Infrastructure: The Social Value of Shared Resources* (OUP 2013) 28.

10 Pierre Trudel, 'Privacy Protection on the Internet: Risk Management and Networked Normativity' in Serge Gutwirth, Yves Poullet, Paul de Hert, Cécile de Terwangne and Sjaak Nouwt (eds), *Reinventing Data Protection?* (Dordrecht, Springer 2009) 327.

11 Mariateresa Maggiolino and Laura Zoboli, 'Smart Mobility and Technological Compatibility from an Antitrust Perspective' in Michèle Finck, Matthias Lamping, Valentina Moscon and Heiko Richter (eds), *Smart Urban Mobility: Law, Regulation, and Policy* (Springer 2020).

12 European Commission Communication, *Artificial Intelligence for Europe* (COM/2018/237 final). https://eur-lex.europa.eu/legal-content/EN/TXT/PDF/?uri=CELEX:52018DC0237

Beyond the types of data involved in sharing operations, that will be analyzed in the next sections, data sharing dynamics are influenced by a diverse array of stakeholders spanning various sectors and institutional domains. These stakeholders – as it will be better framed by Marco Botta in Chapter 4 – engage in different types of data sharing arrangements, each serving unique purposes and objectives. Business-to-business (B2B) data sharing involves the exchange of data between commercial entities, fostering collaboration, innovation and value creation within and across industries. On the other hand, business-to-government (B2G) data sharing entails the provision of data from private sector entities to governmental agencies for regulatory compliance, public service delivery and policy formulation purposes. Conversely, government-to-government (G2G) data sharing involves the exchange of data between different governmental bodies at local, national or international levels, facilitating interagency coordination, information sharing and decision-making processes. Lastly, government-to-business (G2B) data sharing refers to the dissemination of public sector data to private sector entities for commercial, research or public interest purposes. These data sharing arrangements enable businesses to access valuable information resources, drive innovation and create new products and services while promoting transparency, accountability and economic growth.

1.2 Public Data

Public data constitutes a cornerstone of modern governance and societal functioning, encompassing a vast array of information generated and/or collected by public entities. At its core, public data refers to any data generated, compiled or maintained by *public sector bodies*. This encompasses a broad spectrum of information, ranging from census data and weather forecasts to legislative records and transportation schedules. Thus, the scope of public data extends far beyond mere governmental statistics, encompassing datasets generated by publicly funded research institutions, educational establishments and other entities operating in the public domain. These datasets often hold immense value for various stakeholders, including researchers, policymakers, businesses and the general public. Indeed, they provide crucial insights into societal trends, scientific advancements and governmental operations, fostering transparency, accountability and innovation.

The delineation of public data is not always clear-cut, as it intersects with other categories such as personal and proprietary data. Therefore, complexities linked to data control, access rights, privacy concerns and third parties' rights, often arise, necessitating robust governance frameworks to ensure responsible stewardship and equitable access to public data resources. This is even more true as societies continue to embrace data-driven decision-making and open governance principles. The definition and scope of public data is evolving, presenting both opportunities and challenges in the quest for greater transparency and societal progress.

What is of particular interest in this analysis is that public data stands as the initial category for which the EU legislator has constructed a framework to encourage broader sharing, sparking discussions on the potential benefits of reusing such data.[13] Nonetheless, it can be argued that the current regulatory framework falls short of maximizing the openness of public data. To delve into this assertion, this section – also considering that the book does not feature a chapter devoted to public data – will provide an overview of the open data policies enacted at the EU level over the past two decades.

The current EU regulatory framework features the Open Data Directive 2019/1024/EU (ODD)[14] and the Data Governance Act (DGA),[15] the latter aiming to broaden the availability of public data for re-use by stipulating conditions for its use, especially in cases where data falls under existing protections like commercial confidentiality, intellectual property rights or data protection. From a chronological standpoint, the first Directive concerning the re-use of public sector information (the PSI Directive) was enacted in 2003,[16] underwent revision in 2013,[17] and was subsequently supplanted by the ODD in 2019,[18] that has recently been supplemented by the DGA.

Directive (EC) 2003/98 thus stands as the inaugural legislative framework establishing regulations for the re-use of public data by imposing minimum requirements on Member States regarding the accessibility of PSI for re-use.[19] It aimed to alleviate some of the barriers impeding PSI re-use across the Union by introducing the option – though not yet the obligation – for Public Sector Bodies (PSBs) to make their held data available for re-use. The 2003 PSI Directive already included provisions regarding the protection of personal data and, in delineating its scope, asserted that it would not in any way compromise the level of protection afforded to individuals concerning the processing of personal data.[20]

13 European Commission, Directorate-General for the Information Society and Media, Wendy Carrara, Wae San Chan, Sander Fischer, Eva van Steenbergen, 'Creating Value Through Open Data: Study on the Impact of Re-Use of Public Data Resources' (Publications Office, 2015) Available at: https://data.europa.eu/doi/10.2759/328101.

14 Directive (EU) 2019/1024 of the European Parliament and of the Council of 20 June 2019 on open data and the re-use of public sector information (recast) [2019] PE/28/2019/REV/1, OJ L172/56.

15 Regulation (EU) 2022/868 of the European Parliament and of the Council of 30 May 2022 on European data governance and amending Regulation (EU) 2018/1724 (Data Governance Act) [2022] OJ L152/1 1–44.

16 Directive 2003/98/EC of the European Parliament and of the Council of 17 November 2003 on the re-use of public sector information [2003] OJ L345/90.

17 Directive 2013/37/EU of the European Parliament and of the Council of 26 June 2013 amending Directive 2003/98/EC on the re-use of public sector information [2013] OJ L175/1.

18 Directive (EU) 2019/1024/EU of the European Parliament and of the Council of 20 June 2019 on open data and the re-use of public sector information [2019] OJ L172/56.

19 *See* Georg Aichholzer and Herbert Burkert (eds), *Public Sector Information in the Digital Age* (Cheltenhan, UK – Northampton, MA, USA, Edward Elgar 2004); Katleen Janssen, *The Availability of Spatial and Environmental Data in the European Union* (Wolters Kluwer 2010); Josef Drexl, 'The Competition Dimension of the European Regulation of Public Sector Information and the Concept of an Undertaking' in Josef Drexl and Vicente Bagnoli (eds), *State-Initiated Restraints of Competition* (Cheltenhan, UK – Northampton, MA, USA, Edward Elgar 2015) 64, 77; Björn Lundqvist, '"Turning Government Data Into Gold": The Interface Between EU Competition Law and the Public Sector Information Directive' (2013) 44(1) IIC 79. https://colab.ws/articles/10.1007%2Fs40319-012-0007-0

20 Article 1(4), Directive 2003/98/EC.

Aligned with the objective of expanding the pool of public data available for re-use, each subsequent amendment to the PSI legislative framework has aimed at broadening the concept of public data while introducing more sophisticated mechanisms for sharing them. Notably, the 2013 revision introduced a pivotal change by requiring PSBs to make information within their possession accessible for re-use, provided such re-use complied with applicable data protection laws and safeguarded third-party rights.[21] The 2013 Directive underwent recasting in 2019, primarily to align its provisions with technological advancements and further dismantle remaining barriers to developing PSI data markets.[22] The overarching aim of the 2019 ODD is to establish an 'open by default' principle as a standard rule across all Member States and to eliminate cross-border discrimination, thereby enabling third parties to create products and services based on data available within the internal market.[23] Specifically, the ODD extends the scope of the obligation to re-use public data by encompassing public undertakings and broadening the category of PSI to include data from utilities and transportation sectors, irrespective of their public or private nature, provided they receive full or partial public funding.[24] The same principle applies to research data resulting from public funding, which, even when managed by private organizations, are subject to the obligation of access and re-use outlined in the Directive.[25] Additionally, the ODD facilitates real-time data access and reduces re-use costs by mandating access and re-use through the adoption of application programming interfaces (APIs).[26] This allows third parties to dynamically integrate data from public transport bodies, for example, into their service offerings, such as transportation applications. Subsequent to the modernization of the PSI framework through the ODD,[27] the DGA, which came into effect in June 2022, aims to further expand the re-use of

21 Article 3, Directive 2013/37/EU. On this profile, *see* also Article 29 Data Protection Working Party, 'Opinion 06/2013 on open data and public sector information (PSI') reuse' (1021/00/EN WP207, 2013) 3, 2; Mauro Alovisio, 'Criticità Privacy nel riuso dei dati pubblici' (2011) 1–2 Informatica e Diritto 46. https://eur-lex.europa.eu/legal-content/EN/TXT/?uri=CELEX:52018SC0127

22 *See* the *Impact Assessment Accompanying the document Proposal for a Directive of the European Parliament and of the Council on the re-use of public sector information* (SWD/2018/127 final) 32.

23 On this aspect, *see* Sara Gobbato, 'Open Science and the Reuse of Publicly Funded Research Data in the New Directive (EU) 2019/1024' (2020) 2(2) Journal of Ethics and Legal Technologies 145.

24 Heiko Richter, 'Exposing the Public Interest Dimension of the Digital Single Market: Public Undertakings as a Model for Regulating Data Sharing' (2020) Max Planck Institute for Innovation and Competition Research Paper, no 20–03 7.

25 Member States are required to develop policies for open access to publicly funded research data, while harmonized rules on re-use will apply to all publicly funded research data made accessible through repositories. *See* Article 10, Directive (EU) 2019/1024/EU.

26 More specifically, public sector bodies are no longer allowed to charge more than the marginal cost for re-using their data, except in very limited cases. On this aspect, *see* Article 6, Directive (EU) 2019/1024/EU.

27 A better interplay between data protection and public open data and an enlargement of the (personal) data available for re-use was crucial to unlock the potential of public sector information; *see* Groupement Français de l'Industrie de l'Information, Paris, 'Position Paper, Key Issues for Successful PSI Policies in Europe: Improve the Articulation with GDPR and Enhance Data Quality' (2018).

public data by focusing on categories of data subject to third-party rights, such as commercial confidentiality, intellectual property or data protection.[28] Specifically, the DGA envisions establishing a legal regime complementary to the ODD, which applies to PSI excluded from the ODD.[29]

Therefore, as of today, the primary impediment to achieving openness in public data across Member States appears to stem from the insufficient resources and infrastructure available to public bodies. This deficiency not only jeopardizes uniformity in the pace of openness among states but also underscores a greater reliance on resource allocation rather than the regulatory framework governing their operations. In other words, the still predictable variance in openness levels across states may be more attributable to disparities in resource availability and infrastructure than to differences in the regulatory environment.

1.3 Private Data

In contrast to public data, private data pertains to information held or controlled by non-governmental entities, typically for commercial or proprietary purposes. Private data encompasses a diverse range of datasets, including customer records, financial transactions or proprietary algorithms. Unlike public data, which is generated or maintained for public use, private data is often considered confidential, requiring protection against unauthorized access or disclosure.

The scope of private data extends across various sectors and industries, reflecting the breadth of modern economic activities. From multinational corporations to small businesses, entities collect and utilize vast amounts of data to drive decision-making, enhance operational efficiency and gain competitive advantages. This includes customer data used for targeted marketing campaigns, supply chain data optimizing logistical operations and research and development data fueling innovation.

However, the proliferation of private data also raises significant ethical, legal and societal concerns, regarding for example data exclusivity, data security, privacy rights and algorithmic bias. The commodification and monetization of personal data, in particular, have sparked debates surrounding consent, transparency and individual rights in the digital age. As regulatory frameworks evolve to address these challenges, stakeholders must navigate complex landscapes of data governance, balancing innovation and economic interests with privacy and consumer protection imperatives.

It is in this context that the greatest weakness of the EU data economy lies: as mentioned in the introduction, there is a scarcity of business-to-business (B2B)

28 The DGA also prohibits public entities from granting exclusive rights on data. Furthermore, if a public body grants or refuses access for data re-use, it must ensure that the terms of such access (or refusal) are non-discriminatory, proportionate and objectively justified, and it must make those terms available to the public.

29 Article 3(1)d, DGA.

data sharing activities.[30] This weakness is particularly detrimental considering that there is a recognized causal relationship between data sharing within companies and innovation, suggesting that sharing data can lead to the creation of new or significantly improved products or processes, which differ substantially from previous ones and are made available to users or implemented by the company.[31] To provide some illustrative data, at the end of 2017, the Commission reported that 78% of data in the EU was classified as closed, only 2% as open, and 20% had been shared at least once, including through company acquisitions and joint ventures.[32] Furthermore, empirical evidence indicates that EU companies with large datasets generally prefer to handle data processing in-house rather than outsourcing it. Even when data analysis is subcontracted, it rarely results in further re-use of the data. The report "Competition Policy for the Digital Era", drafted for the European Commission and published in April 2019, emphasizes the importance of data sharing between private entities. It states that access to data is increasingly crucial for the competitiveness and innovation potential of firms.[33] More recently, the public consultation on the Data Act conducted between June and September 2021 revealed that engaging in data-sharing practices with other companies is a common practice among stakeholders.[34] However, they face numerous challenges, including technical issues like data interoperability and transfer mechanisms, barriers to data access such as denied access due to competition concerns, prohibitive

30 "Data Economy measures the overall impacts of the data market on the economy as a whole. It involves the generation, collection, storage, processing, distribution, analysis elaboration, delivery and exploitation of data enabled by digital technologies"; IDC & Open Evidence, 'Final Report, European Data Market' (SMART 2013/0063, February 2017) 123. From an economic perspective, *see* Wolfgang Kerber & Jonas Frank, 'Data Governance Regimes in the Digital Economy: The Example of Connected Cars' (2017). Available at https://ssrn.com/abstract=3064794; Wolfgang Kerber, 'Rights on Data: The EU Communication "Building a European Data Economy" from an Economic Perspective' in Sebastian Lohsse, Reiner Schulze and Dirk Staudenmayer (eds), *Trading Data in the Digital Economy: Legal Concepts and Tools* (Hart/Nomos 2017) 109.

31 OECD & Eurostat, 'The Measurement of Scientific, Technological and Innovation Activities in Oslo Manual 2018, Guidelines for Collecting, Reporting and Using Data on Innovation' (4th edn, 2018) 20. On innovation and the sharing economy, *see* Sofia Ranchordás, 'Does Sharing Mean Caring? Regulating Innovation in the Sharing Economy' (2015) 16(1) Minnesota journal of law, science & technology 17–27.

32 The latter two qualify as data transfer. Colin Blackman & Simon Forge, *In-depth Analysis Realized for the European Parliament ITRE Commitee, Data Flows – Future Scenarios* (IP/A/ITRE/IC/2017–04, 2017) 12. However, considering the sample analyzed by Deloitte in the study ordered by the EU Commission, only 6.3% of companies in the EU take active part in B2B data sharing and re-use initiatives; Deloitte, *Study on Emerging Issues of Data Ownership, Interoperability, (Re-) Usability and Access to Data, and Liability* (European Commission, 2018) 31.

33 European Commission, Directorate-General for Competition, Jacques Crémer, Yves-Alexandre de Montjoye, Heike Schweitzer, *Competition Policy for the Digital Era* (Publications Office, 2019). *See* also Angelika Pauer, Lars Nagel, Thomas Fedkenhauser, Dr. Yvonne Fritzsche-Sterr and Aleksei Resetko, *Data Exchange as a First Step Towards Data Economy* (PricewaterhouseCoopers 2018).

34 'Public Consultation on the Data Act, June–September 2021' (European Commission, 3 June 2021). https://digital-strategy.ec.europa.eu/en/consultations/public-consultation-data-act last accessed 30 January 2024.

prices and abuse of contractual imbalances. Consequently, the consultation highlighted the need to provide greater certainty to stakeholders by establishing fair, transparent and non-discriminatory conditions for accessing and sharing data.

Looking at the EU's intervention, it adopted a more cautious approach towards private data, still aimed at increasing the availability, use and demand for data and data-driven products and services. For a long period, it primarily issued non-binding strategic documents for the private sector. Notably, the 2018 "Guidance on Sharing Private Sector Data" (the "Guidance") was a key document in this context.[35] In a nutshell, the Guidance aimed to level the playing field for stakeholders by outlining key principles and providing legal, business and technical tools for data sharing. The Guidance emphasizes transparent data access, recognition of multiple contributors, protection of commercial interests, fair competition and minimizing data lock-in. It also details various B2B data-sharing models, from data monetization to industrial data platforms and technical enablers. By offering this framework, the EU tried to boost confidence in data sharing among private parties, ensuring they understand the conditions and models for secure and effective data exchange. While the Guidance is a valuable resource, its impact on the free flow of data is limited compared to personal data portability provisions or public data access mandates. Nonetheless, it represented an important – as mentioned not binding – first step in fostering private data sharing.

In the last couple of years, as discussed in more detail in the book and in particular by Björn Lundqvist in Chapter 2, the Commission has launched ambitious regulatory projects as part of its digital and data strategies, including the Digital Services Act (DSA)[36] and the Digital Markets Act (DMA),[37] aimed at creating thriving and inclusive European digital and data markets.[38]

The DSA introduces uniform rules on intermediaries' obligations and accountability across the single market. The DMA imposes data-sharing obligations on large online platforms, known as gatekeepers, to reduce their exclusive control over the data they collect and decrease their market leverage.[39] These obligations aim to eliminate market distortions within the platform, including self-reporting

35 European Commission, *Staff Working Document on Guidance on sharing private sector data in the european data economy Accompanying the document Communication on "Towards a Common European Data Space"'* (SWD/2018/125 final). last accessed 30 January 2024. https://eur-lex.europa.eu/legal-content/EN/TXT/?uri=celex:52018SC0125

36 Regulation (EU) 2022/2065 of the European Parliament and of the Council of 19 October 2022 on a Single Market For Digital Services and amending Directive 2000/31/EC (Digital Services Act) [2022] OJ L277/1 1–102.

37 Regulation (EU) 2022/1925 of the European Parliament and of the Council of 14 September 2022 on contestable and fair markets in the digital sector and amending Directives (EU) 2019/1937 and (EU) 2020/1828 (Digital Markets Act) [2022] OJ L265/1 1–66.

38 Laura Zoboli, 'Fueling the European Digital Economy: A Regulatory Assessment of B2B Data Sharing' (2020) 31(4) European Business Law Review 665. last accessed 30 January 2024.

39 A gatekeeper is a provider of a core platform that: has a significant impact on the internal market; operates a core platform service which serves as an important gateway for business users to reach end users; and enjoys an entrenched and durable position in its operations or it is foreseeable that it will enjoy such a position in the near future.

and information asymmetries between the platform and its commercial users, as well as distortions between competing platforms.[40]

Additionally, the Commission adopted the Data Act,[41] a new horizontal legislative proposal that completes the EU legislative framework within the data realm. Its objective is to create an equitable data economy by ensuring access to and use of data and enhancing B2B and B2G (business-to-government) sharing mechanisms.[42] The Data Act provides opportunities for data re-use and measures to remove barriers to data sharing, promote fair and equitable access to data and enhance interoperability. Key provisions include increasing legal certainty for consumers and businesses accessing data from connected products and related services; establishing general rules for data holders obliged to make data available; addressing unfair contractual terms; and setting essential requirements for operators of data spaces to facilitate interoperability and data sharing. Specifically, as discussed in more detail in the book, the major innovation of the Data Act is its shift towards a binding approach. It introduces rules requiring businesses ("data holders") to make data available to other businesses ("data recipients") when legally obligated under EU or national law, primarily in the context of IoT data.

1.4 Personal Data

We will now distinguish between personal and non-personal data, highlighting how most datasets are mixed. Indeed, the need to protect personal data often leads to subjecting the entire mixed dataset to regulations, particularly the GDPR, as it will be better framed by Joanna Mazur in Chapter 3.[43]

Pursuant to Article 4, point (1), the GDPR,

> 'personal data' means any information relating to an identified or identifiable natural person ('data subject'); an identifiable natural person is one who can be identified, directly or indirectly, in particular by reference to an identifier such as a name, an identification number, location data, an online identifier or to one or more factors specific to the physical, physiological, genetic, mental, economic, cultural or social identity of that natural person.

40 Luis Cabral, Justus Haucap, Geoffrey Parker, Georgios Petropoulos, Tommaso Valletti, Marshall Van Alstyne, 'The EU Digital Markets Act' (JRC Publications Repository, Publications Office, 2021), publications.jrc.ec.europa.eu/repository/handle/JRC122910.

41 Regulation (EU) 2023/2854 of the European Parliament and of the Council of 13 December 2023 on harmonized rules on fair access to and use of data and amending Regulation (EU) 2017/2394 and Directive (EU) 2020/1828 (Data Act) [2023] OJ L, 2023/2854.

42 'Public Consultation on the Data Act' June–September 2021' (European Commission, 3 June 2021) https://digital-strategy.ec.europa.eu/en/consultations/public-consultation-data-act last accessed 30 January 2024.

43 Regulation (EU) 2016/679 of the European Parliament and of the Council of 27 April 2016 on the protection of natural persons with regard to the processing of personal data and on the free movement of such data, and repealing Directive 95/46/EC (General Data Protection Regulation) [2016] OJ L119/1 1–88.

Therefore, personal data is any information that relates to an identified or identifiable living individual. Different pieces of information, when collected together, can lead to the identification of a particular person and thus also constitute personal data. More specifically, personal data that has been de-identified, encrypted or pseudonymized but can still be used to re-identify a person remains personal data and falls within the scope of the GDPR.

Personal data constitutes a cornerstone of individual privacy and data protection frameworks, encompassing information that relates to an identified or identifiable natural person. This includes not only direct identifiers such as names and addresses but also indirect identifiers like IP addresses, biometric data and online identifiers. The scope of personal data extends to any information that, either alone or in combination with other data, can be used to identify or distinguish an individual.

In today's data-driven society, personal data is ubiquitous, permeating virtually every aspect of daily life. From social media profiles and online purchases to healthcare records and employment histories, individuals generate vast amounts of personal data through their interactions with various digital and physical environments. This data fuels targeted advertising, personalized services and decision-making processes across public and private sectors.

However, the widespread collection and processing of personal data raise profound concerns regarding privacy, autonomy and individual rights. The unauthorized use or disclosure of personal data can lead to identity theft, discrimination and other forms of harm, underscoring the need for robust data protection regulations and enforcement mechanisms. As governments and organizations grapple with the complexities of personal data governance, ensuring transparency, consent and accountability remains paramount in safeguarding individuals' privacy and dignity.

1.5 Non-Personal Data

Defining "non-personal data" is not straightforward, as it relies on the absence of characteristics defining personal data. According to the Regulation on the free flow of non-personal data,[44] non-personal data refers to data other than personal data. Therefore, non-personal data constitutes a distinct category of information unrelated to or identifying specific individuals. Instead, it encompasses data relating to entities, objects or phenomena other than natural persons. This includes anonymized data, aggregated data, machine-generated data and other forms lacking personal identifiers or attributes.

The scope of non-personal data is broad and diverse, spanning datasets generated by sensors, devices, applications and automated processes. From environmental sensor readings and traffic flow patterns to market trends and scientific research

44 Regulation (EU) 2018/1807 of the European Parliament and of the Council of 14 November 2018 on a framework for the free flow of non-personal data in the European Union [2018] OJ L303/59 59–68.

findings, non-personal data offers valuable insights for informed decision-making and innovation. Unlike personal data, which faces stringent privacy regulations and consent requirements, non-personal data enjoys greater flexibility in use and dissemination. However, this flexibility does not negate ethical or societal considerations. Issues such as data quality, interoperability and algorithmic bias can still affect the reliability and fairness of non-personal data-driven systems, highlighting the need for responsible data stewardship and governance frameworks.

As the volume and variety of non-personal data expand rapidly, stakeholders must address complex challenges related to data ownership, access and control. Collaborative approaches promoting data sharing, interoperability and innovation while respecting privacy and security concerns are crucial for unlocking the full potential of non-personal data in driving societal progress and economic prosperity.

In abstract terms, both the GDPR and Regulation (EU) 2018/1807 on the free flow of non-personal data could potentially apply to mixed datasets, which contain both personal and non-personal data. However, Article 2, paragraph two of Regulation (EU) 2018/1807 specifies that when personal and non-personal data in a set are inseparably linked, the GDPR should take precedence.[45] Consequently, the GDPR fully applies to the entire mixed dataset, even if personal data constitute a small and secondary part, provided they cannot be distinguished or separated.

The concept of "inextricably linked" is not explicitly defined in the regulations, but the Commission, in its Guidance on EU Regulation 2018/1807, suggests that it refers to situations where separating personal and non-personal data would be practically impossible, economically inefficient or technically unfeasible for the data controller.[46] Thus, the decision on whether data are inseparable largely rests with the data controller, who must weigh the costs of distinguishing the data against the potential reduction in the value of resulting datasets.[47]

45 The guidance states: "if the non-personal data part and the personal data parts are 'inextricably linked', the data protection rights and obligations stemming from the General Data Protection Regulation fully apply to the whole mixed dataset, also when personal data represent only a small part of the dataset". *See* Communication from the Commission to the European Parliament and the Council Guidance on the Regulation on a framework for the free flow of non-personal data in the European Union COM/2019/250 final, 8. On the legal distinction between personal and non-personal data, *see* also Simon Forge, *Optimal Scope for Free-Flow of Non-Personal Data in Europe* (Directorate-General for Internal Policies, PE 618.988, 2018).

46 Francesca Casalini & Javier López González, *Trade and Cross-Border Data Flows*, OECD Trade Policy Papers, no 220, 33–34 (2019). In particular, "respondents to the business questionnaire overwhelmingly reported that separating data was likely to be costly or very costly, a response consistent across most sectors" (sample of 165 companies from different sectors, e.g. trade, agriculture, transport, insurance, manufacturing).

47 Francesca Casalini & Javier López González, *Trade and Cross-Border Data Flows*, OECD Trade Policy Papers, no 220, 34 (2019). In particular, "respondents to the business questionnaire overwhelmingly reported that separating data was likely to be costly or very costly, a response consistent across most sectors" (sample of 165 companies from different sectors, e.g. trade, agriculture, transport, insurance, manufacturing).

Furthermore, as mentioned, non-personal data are defined in contrast to personal data,[48] leading to uncertainty among business players regarding the precise boundaries between the two.[49] The expansive interpretation of personal data by case law further complicates matters,[50] making it challenging to exclude the application of the GDPR or identify relevant rules for specific situations.[51] Consequently, the scope of the GDPR may limit cases where the Regulation on the free flow of non-personal data applies, making truly non-personal data rare.[52]

In summary, the costs and technical challenges of separating data,[53] coupled with the uncertainty surrounding data classification, make it extremely difficult to differentiate data categories within a dataset. Neither regulation requires businesses to make such distinctions within datasets they control or process. Therefore, as recognized by the Commission, mixed datasets are generally subject to the GDPR. This entails fulfilling all obligations of data controllers and processors, as well as the rights of data subjects, for any data-sharing operation involving mixed databases.[54] For instance, both the sharing and receiving companies must ensure

48 Article 1 of Regulation (EU) 2018/1807, *supra* note 44. In particular, the non-personal data can be categorized by origin as: "Firstly; data which originally did not relate to an identified or identifiable natural person, such as data on weather conditions generated by sensors installed on wind turbines or data on maintenance needs for industrial machines. Secondly; data which were initially personal data, but were later made anonymous. The 'anonymization' of personal data is different to pseudonymization (*see* above), as properly anonymised data cannot be attributed to a specific person, not even by use of additional data16 and are therefore non-personal data". Commission COM/2019/250 final, *supra* note 45, 5–6.

49 On the debate concerning the difficulties to distinguish between personal and non-personal data, *see* also Josef Drexl, 'The Changing Role of Personal and Non-Personal Data' (2018) Max Planck Institute for Innovation and Competition Research Paper, no 18–23.

50 In particular, in the *Nowak* case, the Court of Justice has attributed an extended meaning to the concept of personal data, including any information regardless of its objective or subjective nature, or its sensitive or private content. Such information of whatever nature or content is personal if, by reason of its content, purpose or effect, is related to a person. *See* Case C-434/16 *Peter Nowak v Data Protection Commissioner* [2017] ECLI:EU:C:2017:994. This orientation is in line with the Working Group 29 in WP136; Article 29 Data Protection Working Party, 'Opinion 4/2007 on the concept of personal data' (01248/07/EN, WP136, 2007). It should also be borne in mind that the Court of Justice, in the *Breyer* case, stated that it is not necessary for all information enabling the identification of the person concerned to be in possession of one single entity. Case C-582/14 *Patrick Breyer v Bundesrepublik Deutschland* [2016] ECLI:EU:C:2016:779.

51 Nadezhda Purtova, 'The Law of Everything. Broad Concept of Personal Data and Future of EU Data Protection Law' (2018) 10(1) Law, Innovation and Technology. last accessed 30 January 2024. https://doi.org/10.1080/17579961.2018.1452176

52 European Economic and Social Committee, *Guidance on the free flow of non-personal data*, (TEN/699-EESC-2019-03048-00-00-AC-TRA 2018).

53 The alternative is the anonymization of personal data, which still requires the distinction of data and entails a cost for the data holder. In addition, one should consider the risk of liability if the anonymization is not correct. Data rendered anonymous in an appropriate manner may not be attributed to a specific person, even by the use of additional information. *See* Commission COM/2019/250 final, *supra* note 45, at 6. On the complexities of anonymization, *see* Paul Ohm, 'Broken Promises of Privacy: Responding to the Surprising Failure of Anonymization' (2010) 57 UCLA Law Review; Ira S. Rubinstein & Woodrow Hartzog, 'Anonymization and Risk' 91 Washington Law Review 703 (2016) NYU School of Law, Public Law Research Paper no 15–26 530.

54 *See* Commission COM/2019/250 final, *supra* note 45, at 10.

adequate security levels for the entire dataset, as per Article 5 (f) of the GDPR. Consequently, the application of the GDPR to most data-sharing operations involving mixed datasets presents a significant hurdle and effectively inhibits companies from initiating data-sharing initiatives.

1.6 Conclusions

This chapter aimed to enlighten the intricate landscape of data sharing, encompassing various types of data and stakeholders across different sectors and domains. From public data governed by regulatory frameworks to private data driven by commercial interests, and from personal data safeguarded by privacy regulations to non-personal data fostering innovation, the data-sharing phenomenon is multifaceted and dynamic.

The EU's efforts to promote data sharing through legislative initiatives such as the Open Data Directive, the Data Governance Act, the Digital Services Act, the Digital Markets Act and the Data Act underscore the importance of creating a conducive environment for data-driven innovation while upholding principles of transparency, accountability and privacy. These regulatory projects seek to address challenges related to data access, interoperability and fairness, aiming to foster thriving and inclusive digital and data markets in Europe.

However, amidst these efforts, a critical gap persists at least in the realm of B2B data sharing. Despite its recognized potential to drive innovation and create value, B2B data sharing activities remain limited, with significant implications for the competitiveness and innovation potential of firms. The scarcity of B2B data-sharing initiatives underscores the need for focused attention and strategic interventions to unlock the full potential of data-driven collaboration among businesses.

2 General and Sectoral Regulations of Data Sharing

Björn Lundqvist

2.1 Introduction

This chapter deals with the interaction between EU laws that impact data-sharing initiatives. The tsunami of new regulations introduced in Brussels regulating data access, transfer and sharing on a sector-specific basis has created a complicated system of rules that overlaps in several aspects.

The chapter describes the wholeness of the system by analysing several different legal acts originating from the EU,[1] while pointing at areas where the overlaps

1 Regulation (EU) 2023/2854 of the European Parliament and of the Council of 13 December 2023 on harmonised rules on fair access to and use of data and amending Regulation (EU) 2017/2394 and Directive (EU) 2020/1828 [2023] OJ L, 2023/2854 (hereinafter Data Act); Regulation (EU) 2022/1925 of the European Parliament and of the Council of 14 September 2022 on contestable and fair markets in the digital sector and amending Directives (EU) 2019/1937 and (EU) 2020/1828 [2022] OJ L265/1 (hereinafter Digital Markets Act); Regulation (EU) 2022/2065 of the European Parliament and of the Council of 19 October 2022 on a Single Market For Digital Services and amending Directive 2000/31/EC [2022] OJ L277/1 (hereinafter Digital Services Act); Directive (EU) 2019/1024 of the European Parliament and of the Council of 20 June 2019 on open data and the re-use of public-sector information [2019] OJ L172/56 (hereinafter Open Data Directive); Regulation (EU) 2022/868 of the European Parliament and of the Council of 30 May 2022 on European data governance and amending Regulation (EU) 2018/1724 [2022] OJ L152/1 (hereinafter Data Governance Act); For the European Commission, *Proposal for a Regulation of the European Parliament and of the Council on the European Health Data Space*, COM(2022) 197 final, 3.5.2022. For the latest version from the EU Parliament, *see* the Provisional agreement, https://www.europarl.europa.eu/meetdocs/2014_2019/plmrep/COMMITTEES/CJ43/AG/2024/04-09/1299790EN.pdf (hereinafter EHDS); Directive (EU) 2015/2366 of the European Parliament and of the Council of 25 November 2015 on payment services in the internal market, amending Directives 2002/65/EC, 2009/110/EC and 2013/36/EU and Regulation (EU) No 1093/2010, and repealing Directive 2007/64/EC [2015] OJ L337/35 (hereinafter PSD II); Regulation (EU) 2018/858 of the European Parliament and of the Council of 30 May 2018 on the approval and market surveillance of motor vehicles and their trailers, and of systems, components and separate technical units intended for such vehicles, amending Regulations (EC) No 715/2007 and (EC) No 595/2009 and repealing Directive 2007/46/EC [2018] OJ L151/1; Regulation (EC) No 1907/2006 of the European Parliament and of the Council of 18 December 2006 concerning the Registration, Evaluation, Authorisation and Restriction of Chemicals (REACH), establishing a European Chemicals Agency, amending Directive 1999/45/EC and repealing Council Regulation (EEC) No 793/93 and Commission Regulation (EC) No 1488/94 as well as Council Directive 76/769/EEC and Commission Directives 91/155/EEC, 93/67/EEC, 93/105/EC and 2000/21/EC [2006] OJ L396/1; Directive (EU) 2019/944 of the European Parliament and of the

DOI: 10.4324/9781003248255-4

create problems in reference to coherence and legal certainty. What rules apply at a given situation when sharing data? Which legal system is *lex generalis* in reference to more sector- specific legal rules, i.e. *lex specialis*? If *lex specialis* does not provide a coherent answer, can rules stipulated in *lex generalis* be used? And, when can other *lex specialis* be used by analogy, i.e. with respect to a different sector than the legal system was drafted to regulate?

The chapter is divided into two large subchapters focusing firstly on presenting the access and sharing rules for data in several general regulations, starting with the Data Act, Digital Markets Act, Digital Services Act and thereafter the Open Data Directive and the Data Governance Act. The regulations are general in the sense that they apply to several sectors, industries and markets. Thereafter sector-specific regulations and rules in reference to access to data are discussed. Initially, by discussing the data space initiative of the European Commission and then by discussing health data, payment and financial data, vehicle data and finally other laws that mandate data sharing. The chapter does not discuss in detail the GDPR, nor the competition law intellectual property law interface, since these issues will be discussed extensively in Chapter 3 and the second part of the book, respectively. In the end, the chapter concludes by suggesting that general rules for data access and transfer should be introduced instead of the system of disparate rules.[2]

2.2 General Sectoral Regulations of Data Sharing

2.2.1 The Data Act

The Data Act has in December 2023 been enacted and it will come into force in 2025. The Data Act applies to different industries and sectors. If the product or service is connected through a sensor to the internet, it applies. It applies to all sectors and industries and works as *lex generalis,* leaving room for sector-specific solutions for separate markets and industries. Any *lex specialis* may thus go beyond the Data Act and implement a different equilibrium between the power of platforms, or as they are called in the Data Act, data holders,[3] and users. The main objective

---

Council of 5 June 2019 on common rules for the internal market for electricity and amending Directive 2012/27/EU [2019] OJ L158/125; Directive (EU) 2018/1972 of the European Parliament and of the Council of 11 December 2018 establishing the European Electronic Communications Code (EECC) [2018] OJ L321/36; Directive 2008/6/EC of the European Parliament and of the Council of 20 February 2008 amending Directive 97/67/EC with regard to the full accomplishment of the internal market of Community postal services [2008] OJ L52/3; For the European Commission, *Proposal for a Regulation of the European Parliament and of the council on a framework for Financial Data Access and amending Regulations (EU) No 1093/2010, (EU) No 1094/2010, (EU) No 1095/2010 and (EU) 2022/2554* (FIDA) COM(2023) 360 final, 28.6.23.

2 For further discussion regarding a general data access and transfer right in reference to sector-specific regulation and competition law, cf. Björn Lundqvist, *Regulating Access and Transfer of Data* (CUP 2023).

3 The definition of data holder is very broad including both products and services catering to IoT, *see* Article 3 of the Data Act "'data holder' means a legal or natural person who has the right or obligation, in accordance with this Regulation, applicable Union law or national legislation implementing

of the Data Act in reference to data and IoT is to generally facilitate access to and the use of data by consumers and businesses, while preserving incentives to invest in ways of generating value through data.[4]

That objective can be divided into four subsidiary objectives.[5] Firstly, empowerment of consumers and businesses to have more control over the use of their IoT data, and to benefit from more, better and cheaper products and services on secondary markets. The benefit will be derived from more intense competition. According to the Explanatory Memorandum,[6] a high level of consumer protection is reinforced with the new right to access user generated data in IoT situations. Ownership, or as the Commission puts it, the "right to use and dispose of lawfully acquired possessions"[7] is reinforced with a right to access data generated from the use of an IoT object. "This way, the owner may benefit from a better user experience and a wider range of, for example, repair and maintenance services".[8] A second sub-objective, is the dissemination of data: more data shall be available to businesses, especially for more innovation (unlocking the wealth of existing data). The second subsidiary objective is to empower or create a level playing field both horizontally and vertically among undertakings. This is in line with the third sub-objective, fairness in the allocation of data and the value from data among actors in the data economy, while still preserving incentives of manufacturers of IoT products, data holders and others to invest in ways of generating value from data which should still be considered the fourth sub-objective.

Even though the Impact Assessment Report drafts the application of the Data Act more narrowly, limiting the effect within the digital ecosystems and enhancing competition on aftermarkets only, the objectives found in the Explanatory Memorandum and the legal text of the Data Act have a broader application.[9] That application is to create a level playing field across the board, not only vertically or within ecosystems, but also horizontally between ecosystems.

The basic structure of the Data Act for meeting these objectives is the introduction of an obligation in Article 3 that

---

Union law, or in the case of non-personal data and through control of the technical design of the product and related services, the ability, to make available certain data".

4 Recital 40 Data Act.

5 Wolfgang Kerber, 'Governance of IoT Data: Why the EU Data Act Will not Fulfill Its Objectives' (2022) . Available at SSRN: https://ssrn.com/abstract=4080436 or http://dx.doi.org/10.2139/ssrn.4080436.

6 *See* For the European Commission, *Proposal for a Regulation of the European Parliament and of the Council on harmonised rules on fair access to and use of data* (Data Act), COM(2022) 68 final, 23.2.2022.

7 Ibid.

8 Ibid.

9 Josef Drexl, Carolina Banda, Begoña Gonzalez Otero, Jörg Hoffmann, Daria Kim, Shraddha Kulhari, Valentina Moscon, Heiko Richter and Klaus Wiedemann, 'Position Statement of the Max Planck Institute for Innovation and Competition of 25 May 2022 on the Commission's Proposal of 23 February 2022 for a Regulation on Harmonised Rules on Fair Access to and Use of Data (Data Act)' 15 *et seq.*

> products shall be designed and manufactured, and related services shall be designed and provided, in such a manner that product data and related service data, including the relevant metadata necessary to interpret and use those data, are, by default, easily, securely, free of charge, in a comprehensive, structured, commonly used and machine-readable format, and, where relevant and technically feasible, directly accessible to the user.

An issue is whether the obligation is strict in the sense that violation renders a repercussion and whether private action is available. The obligation is accompanied by a right for users to access and share the (raw) data that they have generated through their use of IoT devices (Articles 4 and 5).[10] It is uncertain whether the right in Article 4 of the Data Act is applicable when the data is directly accessible under Article 3 of the Data Act, and whether the right to access data is without restrictions and *erga omnes*, for example vis-à-vis purchasers of the database originally set up by the manufacturer of the IoT device.

The right under Article 4 does not distinguish between consumers and businesses. All users of IoT devices (B2C and B2B) should be empowered by the rights and can get access to all data they have created. According to recital 30, the user should be free to use the data for any lawful purpose. According to Article 5, the user also has the right to share the generated data with third parties (firms or other actors), who can use the data for those purposes that are agreed upon with the users, while the third party still needs to negotiate and enter an agreement with the data holder according to Article 8 of the Data Act, and will often have to pay a fee to the data holder according to Article 9 of the Data Act. The agreement needs to be constructed on fair and reasonable terms, while the terms and conditions need to meet the requirements of Articles 8 and 13 of the Data Act. Article 13 stipulates a general rule against unfair contract terms.[11] However, according to Articles 5, 6 and 7, the user and data recipient is severely restricted to be able to compete vis-à-vis the data holder, and to innovate. Indeed, the Data Act stipulates a broad non-compete obligation, intricate rules regarding adherence to trade secret restrictions and data processing restrictions in reference to personal data. Moreover, the Data Act also restricts the data holder to use data in competition with third parties.[12] Thus, as a general rule, *lex generalis* does not oblige the data holder to create a levelled playing field vis-à-vis users or third-party data recipients. To some extent the Data Act

10 Wolfgang Kerber, 'Governance of IoT Data: Why the EU Data Act Will not Fulfill Its Objectives' (2022) Available at SSRN: https://ssrn.com/abstract=4080436 or http://dx.doi.org/10.2139/ssrn.4080436.

11 According to Regulation 1/2003, unfair competition rules have until recently been regulated predominantly on a national level.

12 Article 5(6) Data Act reads "A data holder shall not use any readily available data to derive insights about the economic situation, assets and production methods of, or the use by, the third party in any other manner that could undermine the commercial position of the third party on the markets in which the third party is active, unless the third party has given permission to such use and has the technical possibility to easily withdraw that permission at any time".

creates the basis for the data holder and the third-party data recipients to agree not to compete, i.e. enable them to prevent competition.

According to recital 15, the scope of data the rights stipulated in Articles 4 and 5 cover is raw data, i.e. the unprocessed data directly generated by the user. Derived data and inferred data are not encompassed by the rights, or the Data Act as such. Only access to raw data is the default setting, and that sector-specific regulations, such as the Digital Markets Act, will go beyond and also require access to raw data as well as derived or inferred data.

Article 3 of the Data Act addresses, in an unsatisfactory manner, the delicate issue of how the manufacturer or data holder gains legal control over the data in the first place. Article 3 provides that before concluding a contract for the purchase, rent or lease of a product or a related service, certain topics or points of information shall be provided to the user. These points will make the user aware of the collection and use of data conducted by the product or service purchased or used by the user.

The unsatisfying issue is that Article 3 does not require the contract to include that the user give up or sell the right to be monitored, it only requires the user to be informed. Accordingly, Article 3 indirectly identifies the original data holder (often the manufacturer of the device or part that includes the sensor). The third-party data holder can be the purchaser of the product that includes the sensor that is monitoring the user or when the user purchases the product directly, the purchaser of the contractual right to monitor the user through the sensor. Although not explicitly discussed, the contract between the user and the data holder, be it the manufacturer or a third party, could be identified as a data mining or monitoring agreement.[13] The data mining or monitoring agreement can thus be traded, while still the Data Act does not mention the issue of whether the user entering into this contract has a "right" that the user can licence out or trade to the original data holder in the first place. This is unsettling and the legislator needs to identify the subject of the contract between the monitoree and the monitor. In its essence, it looks like a licence agreement, even though the preamble indicates that the data holder should not gain any further rights based on the Data Act.[14]

Moreover, Article 3 of the Data Act circumvents the delicate issue of exhaustion in reference to the product that includes the sensor picking up the data. The right to the data collected from a sensor would, at least if there is no right held by the user/the monitoree, be transferred in an exhaustive sale of a product to the purchaser of the product, and without having such a licence agreement as envisioned in Article 3, the data holder would not – under the rules of exhaustive sales – have access to the sensor and the data originating from the sensor. Indeed, Article 3 of the Data Act opens up the possibility to trade the access right to purchaser, renter or lessor

13 Wolfgang Kerber, 'Governance of IoT Data: Why the EU Data Act Will not Fulfill Its Objectives' (2022) Available at SSRN: https://ssrn.com/abstract=4080436 or http://dx.doi.org/10.2139/ssrn.4080436.

14 Preamble 5 Data Act.

of the product and the right to access separately, while Articles 4 and 5 give an underdeveloped right to access and transfer the generated raw data for the benefit of the user.

The Data Act does not directly address the issue of whether the user is licencing the manufacturing the right to collect user generated data shows that a major problem with the Data Act is that it accepts the notion that the collector of the data, i.e. the firm with the *de facto* technical possibility to exclude others from mining the sensor, is the rightful "owner" of the data. Thus, even the commentators that find the outcome of the Data Act attractive, should recognise that the starting point for said rules should be that the owner of the sensor should be able to collect the data, while others could be given a right to access and transfer the data collected, as stipulated in Articles 4 and 5. Thus, the data generated by the users should as a *default* be in the control of the holder of the property right of the sensor and the user, which may be the same person. Indeed, the right of the user should be on an equal level as the data holder. This should have been recognised in Articles 3, 4, 5 and 11, which restricts the right for the user to utilise the data and guarantee the data holder to contractually restrict the user and the possibility to make use of technical protection measures (TPMs) under Article 6 of the Directive on the harmonisation of certain aspects of copyright and related rights in the information society[15] (InfoSoc) to prevent access to the sensor.[16]

The data holder could make a successful claim, for example, that TPMs under Article 6 InfoSoc (or the copyright protections of the API[17]) are available, irrespective of an obligation to grant access and the possibility to port data under Article 5 of the Data Act.

Moreover, Articles 5 and 8 of the Data Act put forward the notion of contractual negotiations with the data holder and third parties that convey the message that it is the system leaders and gatekeepers that will oversee the data flows and can use the bilaterally contractual negaotiations to influence, to shape, the data structure. Indeed, the third party according to Article 5 should be bound to FRAND commitments, remunerating the data holder.

Article 43 of the Data Act stipulates that the *sui generis* right does not apply to data obtained from or generated by the use of a product or a related service that are covered by the Data Act. The database *sui generis* protection cannot be invoked by data holders as a defence for not fulfilling their obligations under Articles 4 and 5,

15 Directive 2001/29/EC of the European Parliament and of the Council of 22 May 2001 on the harmonisation of certain aspects of copyright and related rights in the information society [2001] OJ L167/10.

16 The Data Act emphasises that these user rights do not diminish in any way the rights of data subjects from EU data protection law regarding personal data but complement them. This also implies that the DA *de facto* extends these rights on personal data, e.g. with respect to continuous and real-time data access and data sharing (if applicable). *See* recital 31, discussed in Wolfgang Kerber 'Governance of IoT Data: Why the EU Data Act Will not Fulfill Its Objectives' (2022) 6. Available at SSRN: https://ssrn.com/abstract=4080436 or http://dx.doi.org/10.2139/ssrn.4080436.

17 It is highly uncertain that APIs are covered by copyright in the EU.

without the risk of liability.[18] If they still refuse access, liability under the Data Act can be expected, while the *sui generis* database right cannot be overridden, since the Data Act is not enacting a system of countervailing rights, unless a countervailing right is hidden in Article 4. It is uncertain whether injunctions for accessing data are available under the Data Act for the benefit of the user. The Data Act could be regarded as *lex specialis* vis-à-vis the database directive, yet such a conclusion is strained given that the Data Act has been presented as a *lex generalis* for IoT. As regards EU law, before the legislative development reflected in the Data Act and Digital Markets Act, only competition law provided a means to limit the availability of intellectual property remedies. To be able to grant injunction for accessing data vis-à-vis a holder of a database implies that the Data Act may trump the right based on the database directive.[19]

On the other hand, Article 11(1) confirms that the data holder can make use of TPMs (e.g. Article 6 InfoSoc), which are an additional means to enable and safeguard *de facto* data control [*see* also Article 5(5)]. In reference to technical means to enable data access, the Commission mentions application programming interfaces (APIs) in the preamble. However, the Data Act leaves open how this should work, if the APIs are protected by intellectual property law.[20]

Article 5(3) of the Data Act includes a rule that seeks to exclude platform providers that have been declared gatekeepers according to the Digital Markets Act from benefitting from the application of Article 5(1), i.e. gaining access through agreement with users. In reference to the larger picture of Article 5, the provision constitutes a limitation of the right of the user to freely choose the third party to

18 Josef Drexl, Carolina Banda, Begoña Gonzalez Otero, Jörg Hoffmann, Daria Kim, Shraddha Kulhari, Valentina Moscon, Heiko Richter and Klaus Wiedemann, 'Position Statement of the Max Planck Institute for Innovation and Competition of 25 May 2022 on the Commission's Proposal of 23 February 2022 for a Regulation on Harmonised Rules on Fair Access to and Use of Data (Data Act)' 90 *et seq*.

19 Josef Drexl, Carolina Banda, Begoña Gonzalez Otero, Jörg Hoffmann, Daria Kim, Shraddha Kulhari, Valentina Moscon, Heiko Richter and Klaus Wiedemann, 'Position Statement of the Max Planck Institute for Innovation and Competition of 25 May 2022 on the Commission's Proposal of 23 February 2022 for a Regulation on Harmonised Rules on Fair Access to and Use of Data (Data Act)' 37. A very similar provision can be found in both the Data Governance Act, which in Article 5(7) states that "[t]he right of the maker of a database as provided for in Article 7(1) of Directive 96/9/EC shall not be exercised by public-sector bodies in order to prevent the re-use of data or to restrict re-use beyond the limits set by this Regulation". And in Article 1(6) of the 2019 Open Data Directive which contains the same language as the Data Governance Act.

20 Josef Drexl, Carolina Banda, Begoña Gonzalez Otero, Jörg Hoffmann, Daria Kim, Shraddha Kulhari, Valentina Moscon, Heiko Richter and Klaus Wiedemann, 'Position Statement of the Max Planck Institute for Innovation and Competition of 25 May 2022 on the Commission's Proposal of 23 February 2022 for a Regulation on Harmonised Rules on Fair Access to and Use of Data (Data Act)' 81 *et seq*. *See* also Jörg Hoffmann and Begoña Gonzalez Otero, 'Demystifying the Role of Data Interoperability in the Access and Sharing Debate' (29 September 2020) Max Planck Institute for Innovation & Competition Research Paper no 20–16. Available at: https://ssrn.com/abstract=3705217 or http://dx.doi.org/10.2139/ssrn.3705217.

which the data should be made available for the provision of added value services.[21] However, users can make data available to gatekeepers in their capacity as cloud providers, or as data processing service providers.[22]

As will be shown below, the Data Act, the Digital Markets Act and the Directive on Payment Services II share a similar structure in reference to establishing a legal system of access and transfer of data. The owner of the sensor or platform collects the data, while users are given a limited right to access and transfer the data collected back to its own servers or to third parties. In the system, the Data Act acts as *lex generalis,* in reference to, for example the Digital Markets Act and the Directive on Payment Services II. However, it fails to integrate the regulation of public-sector information. According to the preamble, data collected when the data holder or user is a public-sector body should not be available for re-use under Open Data initiative.[23] However, what about devices purchased by the public, should manufacturers be able to harvest data from such devices? The Data Act does not seem to take this into consideration, while the public-sector bodies need to address this issue under public procurement.

Indeed, the Data Act acts as *lex generalis* in the new system being developed. It is the fallback option should sector-specific regulations for some reason not provide a suficient answer. However, public data is treated differently and should not be encompassed by the system.

2.2.2 Digital Markets Act

The Digital Markets Act provides *ex ante* rules for so-called "gatekeepers" to abide by. Specifically, three main cumulative criteria determine whether a company falls within the scope of the Digital Markets Act, while it also must be providing a so-called "core platform service" to be able to qualify as a "gatekeeper":

(i) A size that impacts the internal market: this is presumed to be the case if the company achieves an annual turnover in the European Economic Area (EEA) equal to or exceeding EUR 7.5 billion in the three preceding financial years, or where its average market capitalisation or equivalent fair market value amounted to at least EUR 75 billion in the most recent financial year, and it provides a core platform service in at least three Member States;
(ii) The control of an important gateway for business users towards final consumers: this is presumed to be the case if the company operates a core platform service with more than 45 million monthly active end users established or located

21 Josef Drexl, Carolina Banda, Begoña Gonzalez Otero, Jörg Hoffmann, Daria Kim, Shraddha Kulhari, Valentina Moscon, Heiko Richter and Klaus Wiedemann, 'Position Statement of the Max Planck Institute for Innovation and Competition of 25 May 2022 on the Commission's Proposal of 23 February 2022 for a Regulation on Harmonised Rules on Fair Access to and Use of Data (Data Act)' 34.

22 Recital 41 Data Act.

23 Preamble 70 Data Act.

in the EU and more than 10,000 yearly active business users established in the EU in the most recent financial year;

(iii) An (expected) entrenched and durable position: this is presumed to be the case if the company fulfilled the other two criteria in each of the past three financial years.

The core platform services include: (i) Online intermediation services (incl. for example marketplaces, app stores and online intermediation services in other sectors, such as mobility, transport or energy); (ii) Online search engines; (iii) Social networking; (iv) Video-sharing platform services; (v) Number-independent, interpersonal, electronic communication services;[24] (vi) Operating systems;[25] (vii) Cloud services; and (viii) Advertising services, including advertising networks, advertising exchanges and any other advertising intermediation services, where these advertising services are related to one or more of the other core platform services mentioned above. In addition, during the negotiations with the Parliament and the Council, two more services were added to the list, virtual assistants and web browsers. Some services, i.e. cloud services, operating systems and advertising services connected to platforms are included in the Digital Markets Act, but could also possibly be identified as related services under Article 3 of the Data Act or otherwise fall inside the Data Act (cf. for example chapter 6 in reference to cloud services).

The relevant prohibitions to abide by for the Gatekeepers are listed in Article 5 to 7 of the Digital Markets Act. Of interest for this chapter, paragraphs two, nine and ten of Article 6 of the Digital Markets Act (DMA), when read in combination, may – with the help of end users – provide an access and portability right for business users. However, in comparison with the Data Act, the DMA does not stipulate a stand-alone access and portability right for the benefit of business users vis-à-vis gatekeepers.[26] Article 6 stipulates obligations for the gatekeepers that are the prerogative of the Commission to enforce. Notwithstanding this, the CJEU may still utilise for example the doctrine of direct effect, so as to identify that the business users have a right to access and port data under the DMA. Moreover, the end user may bring the data from the gatekeeper to the business user and by doing

24 For a definition, *see* para 7 of Article 2 of Directive (EU) 2018/1972: "'number-independent interpersonal communications service' means an interpersonal communications service which does not connect with publicly assigned numbering resources, namely, a number or numbers in national or international numbering plans, or which does not enable communication with a number or numbers in national or international numbering plans". (Most OTT services will fall within this category.) For these, at least one natural person must be involved, and the recipients must be taken from a finite number of recipients chosen by the sender. This includes services where the remuneration is data instead of money and excludes broadcast-style services. There is still confusion as to whether services such as Facebook/Twitter fall within this definition.

25 According to Article 2 para 10 DMA, "Operating system" means a system software which controls the basic functions of the hardware or software and enables software applications to run on it.

26 This is also reflected in the updated recital 54, which does not contain the notion of portability.

so eliminate the gatekeeper's access to the same data. The use of the notion of portability should imply that the gatekeeper cannot keep a copy of said data. The provisions state that the platform provider is *de facto* not allowed to use the data generated by the business user on the platform in competition with the business user [*see* also Article 5(2) in the Regulation]. Interestingly, the obligation in Article 6(2) compared to the obligations in Articles 9 and 10 reflects that business users have some sort of preferential right to the data generated, vis-à-vis the platform provider. Indeed, this is a bilateral preferential right to each data point, which may override the gatekeeper's general database right.

The gatekeeper still retains the prerogative to make all data available for all users [cf. Article 6(2) DMA]. Yet, in parallel, business users have been granted a data advantage vis-à-vis the platforms, should Article 6(10) be directly applicable for business users. Indeed, the combination of Article 6 paragraphs two and ten implicitly creates some form of compulsory access obligation that mirrors a right granted to the business user. The right to access can also be traded, or at least access should be given to third parties contracted by the business user, who are acting as processors of this data for the business user. The combination of the obligations stated in Article 6 of the DMA amounts to a right to access for the business user, yet the question is whether it is an overriding or countervailing right that prevents gatekeepers from using their intellectual property rights to prevent access.

Inferred data should also be accessible. However, drawing the line between data that originates from the business users and data that originates from the business (model) of the platform can be very difficult. Indeed, the preamble claims that data generated by business users and end users, as well as data inferred from that data, should be encompassed by the obligation, but in the case at hand, it can be difficult to identify the boundaries for that dataset.[27]

The preamble continues by stating:

> [i]n order to ensure that business users have access to the relevant data thus generated, the gatekeeper should, upon their request, provide effective access, free of charge, to such data. Such access should also be given to third parties contracted by the business user, who are acting as processors of this data for the business user. Data provided or generated by the same business users and the same end users of these business users in the context of other services provided by the same gatekeeper may be concerned where this is inextricably linked to the relevant request. To this end, a gatekeeper should not use any contractual or *other restrictions* to prevent business users from accessing relevant data and should enable business users to obtain consent of their end users for such data access and retrieval, where such consent is required under Regulation (EU) 2016/679 and Directive 2002/58/EC. Gatekeepers should also facilitate access to these data in real time by means

27 One possible means of addressing this is to require the use of blockchain, with rights for the business users to access the blocks reflecting the definition in Article 6(2), (9) and (10).

of appropriate technical measures, such as for example putting in place high quality application programming interfaces or integrated tools for small volume business users.[28]

The text above indicates that the model for data access imagined by the Commission is that the gatekeeper makes a data-access API available to business users. The gatekeeper is not allowed to use contractual or other restrictions to prevent such access. Is this an overriding right to all intellectual property rights held by the gatekeeper? The major issue is whether this gateway to access and portability of data is in fact such a revolutionary tool for creating interoperability, or whether, in the end, lack of a global technical API standard, intellectual property legal systems or the GDPR will *de facto* prevent data access and portability.

Recital 70 stipulates that the gatekeeper should not, with the aim to undermine interoperability, be allowed to use "unjustified technical protection measures", or "unlawfully claiming" a copyright on APIs. It is highly uncertain whether the breadth of copyright may be restricted by the text in a recital. Restriction fo copyright in a regulation may be in violation of teh right to property reflected in Article 17 of the EU Fundamental Rights Charter. Notwithstanding the text in recital 70, gatekeepers may try to prevent access to their platforms, and foremost their data by claiming that it is walled in by intellectual property rights. As mentioned above, copyright owners regularly resort to TPMs (cf. Article 6 InfoSoc) to prevent access to copyright-protected content. "Hacking", or breaching technical measures to gain access to data, can be a violation of Article 6 InfoSoc. Thus, Article 6 InfoSoc also protects the platforms from being "hacked" to gain access to unprotected data. APIs *can* be copyright protected. Platforms can also claim that the datasets they collect are trade secrets as defined under the new EU Directive,[29] or in the case of personal data, might be off-limits under the GDPR. For the data generated on the platforms, the gatekeepers would most likely acquire some intellectual property rights when storing the data in databases or in public centralised blockchains, such as *sui generis* database protection, which may also limit or even prevent the porting of whole datasets. On the other hand, do the obligations stipulated in Article 6(9) and (10) override these rights in order to uphold interoperability? It seems that Article 6(9) and (10) restrict the property rights held by the platforms.

Yet another major problem is that the DMA is unclear as to which data is in fact encompassed by the access and transfer right granted under the regulation; the DMA contains only an obligation for gatekeepers to give access. This could be a matter for litigation, and indeed data can originate from both the business users'

28 Preamble 60 DMA.

29 Cf. Article 3 of the Directive (EU) 2016/943 of the European Parliament and of the Council of 8 June 2016 on the protection of undisclosed know-how and business information (trade secrets) against their unlawful acquisition, use and disclosure [2016] OJ L157/1 (Trade Secret Directive) and preamble 16, stating that "Reverse engineering of a lawfully acquired product should be considered as a lawful means of acquiring information, except when otherwise contractually agreed. The freedom to enter into such contractual arrangements can, however, be limited by law".

activities and the platform providers' activities, especially in the case of inferred data.

In reference to the Data Act above, the DMA should be the preferred tool for business users to gain access not only to raw data, but also derived data, while a problem facing such users can be gatekeepers claiming *sui generis* database right to the relevant dataset. Moreover, it is not clear that users have a right to access data under Article 6 of the DMA, while the ECJ may still interpret Article 6 of the DMA to provide such a right. A difficult issue is the lengthy Articles in the Data Act concerning terms and conditions for the business user and third-party data recipients.

2.2.3 The Digital Service Act

The Digital Service Act provides rules for data access by the government of data collected by very large platforms. Indeed, the issue of accessing data from platforms may be needed for the government and researchers. According to Paddy Leerssen, the issue of research access is becoming ever more urgent. Over the past years, dominant platforms like Facebook have repeatedly interfered with independent research projects, prompting calls for reform. The matter went mainstream in October 2020, when – only weeks before the US elections – Facebook tried to shut down an independent audit of their political advertising by NYU. Facebook also suspended the researchers' Facebook accounts and stripped them of access to the Ad Library API and Crowdtangle research tools. Closer to home, Facebook also retaliated against data collection by the Berlin-based non-governmental organisation AlgorithmWatch, sending those involved "thinly veiled threats" of legal action on the grounds that independent data collection violated the platform's terms of service. Platforms are becoming gatekeepers not only of online content and commerce, but also of research into these phenomena.[30]

The DSA states in recital 63 of the preamble that very large online platforms should ensure public access to repositories of advertisements displayed on their online interfaces, to facilitate supervision and research into emerging risks brought about by the distribution of advertising online, for example in relation to illegal advertisements or manipulative techniques and disinformation with a real and foreseeable negative impact on public health, public security, civil discourse, political participation or equality. Repositories should include the contents of advertisements and related data on the advertiser and delivery of the advertisement, in particular where targeted advertising is concerned.

Moreover, to appropriately supervise the compliance of very large online platforms with the obligations in Article 26 regarding systemic risk and laid down by Member States or the Commission, these entities may require access to or reporting of specific data. Such requirements may include, for example, the data necessary

30 Paddy Leerseen, 'Platform Research Access in Article 31 of the Digital Services Act: Sword Without a Shield?' (*Verfassungsblog*, 7 September 2021) https://verfassungsblog.de/power-dsa-dma-14/ accessed 25 February 2025.

to assess the risks of illegal content of disinformation and possible harms brought about by a platform's systems; data on the accuracy; functioning and testing of algorithmic systems for content moderation; recommender systems or advertising systems; or data on processes and outputs of content moderation or of internal complaint-handling systems within the meaning of the DSA (cf. Article 26). According to the DSA, investigations by researchers on the evolution and severity of online systemic risks are particularly important for bridging information asymmetries and establishing resilient risk mitigation systems.

Thus, the DSA provides a framework for providing government and vetted researchers access to data from very large online platforms. All the requirements for access to data under that framework should be proportionate and appropriately protect the rights and legitimate interests, including trade secrets and other confidential information, of the platform and any other parties concerned, including service recipients.

The obligation that advertisement repositories are made available through application programming interfaces (APIs) is stipulated in Article 30. Under the Article 31 framework, regulators can order access for their own monitoring and enforcement purposes (paragraph one) or for use by third-party researchers (paragraph two).

In the Commission's proposal, data access was limited to academic ("vetted") researchers, subject to various conditions such as university affiliation, independence from commercial interests and compliance with confidentiality and security requirements (paragraph four). It should be underlined that the Council wanted to go further and create an independent right of access for researchers. Also, the European Parliament wanted to broaden the group that may access data to also include independent researchers working for or affiliated with non-profit organisations. The European Parliament proposal prevailed, while the researchers may only use the data for the purpose of research into "systemic risks" as defined in Article 26 DSA.[31]

Platforms may object to data access requests in cases where they do not have the data or where access would create "significant vulnerabilities" to security or prevent "protection of confidential information, in particular trade secrets". The same limitations apply to the obligation stipulated in Article 30 DSA. Indeed, as discussed above in the section on the DMA, platforms can claim that the datasets they have collected are trade secrets as defined under the EU Directive, or might be off-limits under the GDPR, in the case of personal data. Moreover, for data generated on their platforms, the gatekeepers would most likely acquire some intellectual property rights when storing the data in databases or in public centralised blockchains, such as *sui generis* database protection – which may also limit or even prevent access and porting of whole datasets. At the very least, this may serve as a ground for refusing access to repositories under Article 30 DSA. A claimant can thus try to use the Data Act to gain access, should the Data Act be applicable.

31 Ibid.

2.2.4 Open Data Directive

The Open Data Directive[32] stipulates routes for accessing government data.[33] It is not encompassed under the Data Act, and acts in its own universe. The focus of the Open Data Directive is very specific: to create a level playing field when making public-sector information (PSI) available as an input to a commercial activity, i.e. when the PSI is used as components in new products and services. This should release the full economic potential of a new emerging area of the ICT sector.[34] If public-sector bodies (PSBs) offer information products or services exclusively, chances are that they will not be able to provide these services as innovatively and efficiently as a structure governed by competition.[35] This could have a negative effect on competition in the European market. Therefore, the Open Data Directive aims to overcome these barriers, which limit the re-use of PSI in EU Member States. The Open Data Directive thereby stipulates that public-sector data collectors must grant access to data (cf. Article 3 of the Open Data Directive). The Open Data Directive tries to eliminate barriers, which could include attempts by PSBs to charge supracompetitive prices, unfair competition between the public and the private sectors, practical issues hindering re-use (such as the lack of information on available PSI) and the attitude of PSBs that are slow to realise the economic potential of PSI.[36]

Interestingly, the Open Data Directive includes non-discriminatory exclusion rules, similar to the ideas put forward in the French *GDF*[37] and *EDF* competition law cases.[38] Indeed, the Open Data Directive stipulates a prohibition preventing governments and government authorities from abusing the power inherent in the data collected, by not giving access, without the need to identify dominance in reference to the authority or the database. To some extent is the non-discrimination

32 Directive (EU) 2019/1024 of the European Parliament and of the Council of 20 June 2019 on open data and the re-use of public-sector information, [2019] OJ L172/56 56–83.

33 *See* also the Directive 2007/2/EC of the European Parliament and of the Council of 14 March 2007 establishing an Infrastructure for Spatial Information in the European Community (INSPIRE) regarding spatial data [2007] OJ L108/1, Articles 5 and 8. For the various legal tools making up the INSPIRE initiative *see* https://inspire.ec.europa.eu/inspire-directive/2.

34 European Commission, *Public Sector Information: A Key Resource for Europe Green Paper on Public Sector Information in the Information Society* COM(1998) 585 final, 20.1.1999, 5.

35 Björn Lundqvist, '"Turning Government Data into Gold": The Interface Between EU Competition Law and the Public Sector Information Directive – With Some Comments on the *Compass* Case' (2013) 44(1) IIC International Review of Intellectual Property and Competition Law 79.

36 Katleen Janssen and Jos Dumortier 'Towards a European Framework for the Re-Use of Public Sector Information: A Long and Winding Road' (2003) 11(2) International Journal of Law and Information Technology 195.

37 French Competition Authority Decision 14-MC-02 of 9 September 2014. The case is discussed in the German and French Competition Authorities, 'Competition Law and Data' (joint paper 10 May 2016) 20.

38 French Competition Authority Decision n°13-D-20 of 17 December 2013, confirmed on that point by the court of appeal on 21 May 2015.

rule in the Open Data Directive an analogy to the extensive FRAND requirements under the Data Act (cf. Articles 4–13 Data Act).

In several aspects, the Open Data Directive stipulates something akin to the compulsory licensing scheme for PSB-controlled databases holding reusable public data. From a Nordic law perspective, at least, the public authorities have historically been able to claim database rights (most likely *sui generis* protected database rights), and while admitting that the Open Data Directive creates an obligation to grant access to data, the database right is the platform for establishing licence arrangements with re-users.[39] The fact that the PSBs are funded by tax money does not prevent public authorities from being subject to database protection.[40] It should be noted that the new Open Data Directive from 2019 has somewhat reversed this situation, stating that PSBs shall not exercise their potential database rights to prevent the re-use of documents or to restrict re-use beyond the limits set by the new Open Data Directive. A similar rule has now been inserted in the Data Governance Act from 2022.

Indeed, the Open Data Directive could be considered to stipulate a compulsory licence scheme, or, more accurately, a general real-time access and portability right for business users to public "spin-off" data.[41] Such data is not the core activity of the public authority, but rather a by-product of their core activity. As noted elsewhere in this chapter, such access and portability rights could empower business users vis-à-vis system leaders and platforms because for many of these platforms, their investment is focused on their core activity, not on creation of databases. Platforms concentrate *inter alia* on acquisition, verification or presentation of the databases.[42]

It should be pointed out that the Open Data Directive is applicable only for public data that is not restricted by intellectual property rights held by the third party or the public authority or business confidentiality limitations, and under the GDPR, personal data is off-limits. Indeed, the right to access public-sector information

39 The previous PSI Directive stipulated in preamble 24 that "[t]his Directive is without prejudice to Directive 2001/29/EC of the European Parliament and of the Council of 22 May 2001 on the harmonisation of certain aspects of copyright and related rights in the information society (10) and Directive 96/9/EC of the European Parliament and of the Council of 11 March 1996 on the legal protection of databases". It spells out the conditions under which public-sector bodies can exercise their intellectual property rights in the internal information market when allowing re-use of documents.

40 Estelle Derclaye, *The Legal Protection of Databases: A Comparative Analysis* (Edward Elgar 2008) 72. Compare with Bernt Hugenholtz, 'Database Directive' in Thomas Dreier and Bernt Hugenholtz (eds), *Concise European Copyright Law* (2nd edn, Kluwer Law International 2016) 405.

41 The "spin-off" exemption under *sui generis* data protection has been discussed at length. The doctrine has been rejected by the ECJ. *See* Case C-203/02 *BHB v Hill* [2004] ECLI:EU:C:2004:695 paras 31–42; Case C-444/02 *Fixtures Marketing v Organismos prognostikon agonon podosfairou AE (OPAP)* [2004] ECLI:EU:C:2004:697 paras 40–53; Case C-46/02 *Fixtures Marketing v Oy Veikkaus Ab* [2004] ECLI:EU:C:2004:694 paras 34–49; Case C-338/02 *Fixtures Marketing v Svenska Spel AB* [2004] ECLI:EU:C:2004:696 paras 24–37.

42 Ibid.

concerns only public-good data.[43] However, this has been viewed as a clear limitation of the Open Data Directive and the Commission has therefore in the new Data Governance Act, that encompasses rules for public-sector data, made such data available for re-use in situations where such data is subject to rights of others.

Under the Data Governance Act, the public sector is invited to grant the right to re-use personal data, confidential data and data protected by IP rights to a natural or legal person (the re-user) for commercial or non-commercial purposes, provided that such re-use takes place in a manner that respects the rights and interests of businesses (non-personal data) and data subjects (personal data). Indeed, the rights are still protected, while the DGA does not provide a tool to override the rights held by third parties. However, the public-sector bodies should provide assistance for re-users to obtain necessary permission to access and use said information.

2.2.5 The Data Governance Act

2.2.5.1 Access to Data

The Data Governance Act aims to foster the availability of public data for re-use by increasing trust in data intermediaries and strengthening data-sharing mechanisms across the EU.

Article 5 in the Data Governance Act stipulates that public-sector bodies that are judged competent under national law to grant or refuse access for the re-use of data that is covered by commercial confidentiality, statistical confidentiality, protection of intellectual property rights of third parties or protection of personal data, shall make the conditions for allowing re-use of such data publicly available.[44] The conditions for re-use shall be non-discriminatory, proportionate and objectively justified with regard to categories of data, purposes of re-use and the nature of the

43 The preamble 54 of the Open Data Directive states "[t]he intellectual property rights of third parties are not affected by this Directive. For the avoidance of doubt, the term 'intellectual property rights' refers to copyright and related rights only, including *sui generis* forms of protection. This Directive does not apply to documents covered by industrial property rights, such as patents and registered designs and trade marks. The Directive neither affects the existence or ownership of intellectual property rights of public-sector bodies, nor does it limit the exercise of these rights in any way beyond the boundaries set by this Directive. The obligations imposed in accordance with this Directive should apply only insofar as they are compatible with international agreements on the protection of intellectual property rights, in particular the Berne Convention for the Protection of Literary and Artistic Works (Berne Convention), the Agreement on Trade-Related Aspects of Intellectual Property Rights (TRIPS Agreement) and the WIPO Copyright Treaty (WCT). Public-sector bodies should, however, exercise their copyright in a way that facilitates re-use".

44 The DGA does not create any obligation on public-sector bodies to allow re-use of data; nor would the Act release public-sector bodies from their confidentiality obligations. This chapter is without prejudice to Union and national law or international agreements to which the Union or Member States are parties on the protection of categories of data provided in paragraph one. This chapter is without prejudice to Union and national law on access to documents and to obligations of public-sector bodies under Union and national law to allow the re-use of data.

data for which re-use is allowed. These conditions, set out by the authority, shall not be used to restrict competition.

Interestingly, Article 5 further states that public-sector bodies can impose an obligation on the re-user to anonymise or pseudonymise personal data or delete commercially confidential information, including trade secrets, before the data may be re-used. Moreover, the public-sector body shall be able to verify any results of the re-user's processing of data and reserve the right to prohibit the use of results that contain information that jeopardises the rights and interests of third parties. When requested data is considered confidential, in accordance with Union or national law on commercial confidentiality, the public-sector bodies shall ensure that the confidential information is not disclosed as a result of the re-use.

Generally, under the Data Governance Act, the re-use of data is allowed only in compliance with intellectual property rights and the GDPR; if efforts by the public-sector body to comply – for example through anonymisation of personal data – are in vain, the re-use of data cannot be granted. However, the public-sector body shall support re-users in seeking consent from the data subjects and/or permission from the legal entities whose rights and interests may be affected by such re-use, where it is feasible and does not incur disproportionate cost for the public sector. However, there is one exemption: the right of a database maker as provided for in Article 7(1) of the Database Directive (96/9/EC) shall not be exercised by public-sector bodies to prevent the re-use of data or to restrict re-use beyond the limits set by the regulation.

2.2.5.2 Data-Sharing Service

It should further be noted that the Data Governance Act also contains rules for a new form of intermediates and platforms, in which an infrastructure is created for combining, pooling, providing notification for and using users' data. According to the Data Governance Act, business users of platforms that would like to combine their data would be able to pool their data, in situations where they can access and port the data held by gatekeepers.

The new Data Governance Act aims to foster the availability of public data for re-use by increasing trust in data intermediaries and by strengthening data-sharing mechanisms across the EU. The Data Governance Act therefore sets out to provide rules and a structure to set up data-sharing services, or data spaces, including means for notifying relevant authorities about such a sharing service (data space). The provider of a data-sharing service shall report service to relevant national authorities when the setup corresponds to the following (cf. Article 9):

(a) Intermediation services between data holders, which are legal persons and potential data users, including making available the technical or other means to enable such services; those services may include bilateral or multilateral exchanges of data or the creation of platforms or databases enabling the exchange or joint exploitation of data, as well as the establishment of a specific infrastructure for the interconnection of data holders and data users;

(b) Intermediation services between data subjects that seek to make their personal data available and potential data users, including making available the technical or other means to enable such services, in the exercise of the rights provided in Regulation (EU) 2016/679; vis-à-vis services of data cooperatives, that is to say services supporting data subjects or one-person companies or micro, small and medium-sized enterprises, who are members of the cooperative or who confer the power to the cooperative to negotiate terms and conditions for data processing before they consent, in making informed choices before consenting to data processing, and allowing for mechanisms to exchange views on data processing purposes and conditions that would best represent the interests of data subjects or legal persons.

The Data Governance Act also sets out rules for the collaboration. These rules originate from unfair competition legislation and practical IT law sources. Data-sharing services shall be subject to the following conditions:

(1) The provider may not use the data for which it provides services for other purposes than to put them at the disposal of data users and data-sharing services shall be placed in a separate legal entity;
(2) The metadata collected from the provision of the data-sharing service may be used only for the development of that service;
(3) The provider shall ensure that the procedure for access to its service is fair, transparent and non-discriminatory for both data holders and data users, including as regards prices;
(4) The provider shall facilitate the exchange of the data in the format in which it receives it from the data holder and shall convert the data into specific formats only to enhance interoperability within and across sectors or if requested by the data user or where mandated by Union law or to ensure harmonisation with international or European data standards;
(5) The provider shall have procedures in place to prevent fraudulent or abusive practices in relation to access to data from parties seeking access through their services;
(6) The provider shall ensure a reasonable continuity of provision of its services and, in the case of services which ensure storage of data, shall have sufficient guarantees in place that allow data holders and data users to obtain access to their data in case of insolvency;
(7) The provider shall put in place adequate technical, legal and organisational measures in order to prevent transfer or access to non-personal data that is unlawful under Union law;
(8) The provider shall take measures to ensure a high level of security for the storage and transmission of non-personal data;
(9) The provider shall have procedures in place to ensure compliance with the Union and national rules on competition.

According to the Data Governance Act, each Member State shall designate in its territory one or more authorities competent to carry out the tasks related to the notification framework. The designated competent authorities, data protection authorities, national competition authorities, authorities in charge of cybersecurity and other relevant sectoral authorities shall exchange the information necessary for the exercise of their tasks in relation to data-sharing providers. The competent authority shall monitor and supervise compliance with rules, including having the authority to render decisions. In this regard, the competent authorities shall be able, where appropriate:

(a) To impose dissuasive financial penalties which may include periodic penalties with retroactive effect;
(b) To require cessation or postponement of the provision of the data-sharing service.

In addition to these rules, the Data Governance Act also states that a special organ should be set up to provide best-practice guidelines – a formal expert group (the "European Data Innovation Board") which will "facilitate the emergence of best practices by Member States".

Business users under the Digital Markets Act or users under the Data Act that collect data may thus create a data-sharing facility and use a data-sharing service under the Data Governance Act. They can thereby create their own platform, even to the level of being a gatekeeper, under the Digital Markets Act.

Interestingly, the rules above somewhat mirror the competition rules for patent pools, or what academia has put forward as "data pools". These forms of collaboration are normally addressed under competition law and, interestingly, the rules set out above catering to regulation of the relationship between firms, including competitors. Indeed, the Regulation carves out a safe harbour for establishing intermediates for provided data-sharing services.

Still, the rules are somewhat fuzzy. It is not certain that all comers are welcome, and that the platform created to share data can deny access. Moreover, data-sharing services need to take several different legal systems into consideration: Data Act, Digital Markets Act, Data Governance Act and competition law. Indeed, an intermediate that establishes a data-sharing service through which business users can store their business user's data must take several access regimes into consideration, including competition law. What about data originating from an IoT device, can such data be shared under a data space when gatekeepers are also members of the data space? Or, will that violate the Data Act? Competition law?

Interestingly, under competition law, one could envision a safe harbour provision for data pools that requires dominant data pools to, for example, be open to all comers.

The Data Governance Act attempts to address the difficult issue of enabling access to public data with the aim to create a vibrant data industry. The hope is that by making public-sector data available for re-use, in situations where such data is subject to rights under an intellectual property legal system, rules and covenants in reference to confidentiality or under the General Data Protection Regulation

(GDPR), innovation will happen. The Act still does not provide any overriding rules under which access rights to data should trump rights held by others. Nonetheless, it puts in place a methodology, obligations and pressure on the public-sector bodies to resolve rights issues before granting access to data for re-use.

The Data Governance Act also provides the outlines to create new forms of intermediates – the providers of data-sharing facilities and data spaces. These entities could grow in importance. The question is whether firms defined and identified as gatekeepers under the Digital Markets Act should also be able to pool and access data under such an intermediate. Indeed, these facilities may cater more to large platforms with gatekeeping status that use each other's services than to small business users. However, the prohibition of making a gatekeeper a data recipient under the Data Act will possibly prevent the gatekeeper from being a member of such data space.

2.3 Special Sectoral Regulations of Data Sharing

2.3.1 Data Spaces

The Commission wishes to pursue a strategy of enacting data-access regimes on a sector-specific level. According to the strategy that has been in place since 2020, and was updated in 2024,[45] the EU will support so-called "data spaces", through investments and possibly sector-specific regulations. Under a data space both public and private entities should be encouraged and obligated to provide their data to the data spaces for the use of anyone that needs and wants access to develop new products and services, irrespective of whether the comer is a private or public entity.[46] The number of suggested data spaces have increased from nine in the first strategy 2020 to 14 in a 2024 working paper from the Commission.[47] It is difficult to do justice to all the data spaces in this paper, and some have developed further than others, however according to the Commission, the following areas are prone to hold common data spaces:

1) The European industrial (manufacturing) data space, allowing to capture the potential value of use of non-personal data in manufacturing. The aim to implement an industrial (manufacturing) data space will be initiated by the deployment of two operational manufacturing data spaces for asset management. To some extent the Data Act will help to facilitate such a large common data space;

45 European Commission, *Staff Working Document on Common European Data Spaces* SWD(2024) 21 final, 24.1.2024. Available at: https://digital-strategy.ec.europa.eu/en/library/second-staff-working-document-data-spaces.

46 European Commission, *A European Strategy for Data* COM(2020) 66 final, 19.2.2020, 21 *et seq*. *See* also the Appendix "Common European data spaces in strategic sectors and domains of public interest".

47 European Commission, *Staff Working Document on Common European Data Spaces* SWD(2024) 21 final, 24.1.2024. Available at: https://digital-strategy.ec.europa.eu/en/library/second-staff-working-document-data-spaces.

2) The European Green Deal data space, that would imply *inter alia* the implementation of EGD policies with relevant data (e.g. on air, water, soil quality with regard to the zero-pollution strategy) and contribute to a higher level of environmental transparency;
3) With the European mobility data space, the Commission aims to include connected cars as well as other modes of transport. Such data space will facilitate access, pooling and sharing of data from existing and future transport and mobility databases and help establish an efficient and interconnected multimodal transport system. From such a data space, mobility as a service may be developed on a large scale;[48]
4) The proposal for a European financial data space relates *inter alia* to business-to-business and business-to-consumer data sharing in the EU financial sector (open finance). The proposed framework on Financial Data Access (FIDA)[49] across various types of financial services and products complements the Payment Services Directive (PSD2) (discussed below), which introduced similar data-sharing requirements with respect to payment accounts. Under FIDA, both businesses and individual customers should retain control over their data held by financial service providers, whilst at the same time gaining access to innovative and more competitive services. This will enable a data space for financial data with access rights and obligations for customers and financial undertakings;[50]
5) With a European energy data space, the Commission aims to promote a stronger availability and cross-sector sharing of data in the energy sector and the proposal for a common European agriculture data space will enhance the sustainability performance and competitiveness of the agricultural sector through the processing and analysis of production and other data, allowing for precise and tailored application of production approaches at farm level. In the area of agriculture data, several public entities will be obliged to share relevant data that can be joined with data originating from private entities;
6) European data spaces for public administration, can be divided into different data spaces, *inter alia* (i) The legal data space aims to ensure easily accessible, reusable and interoperable data on legislation and case-law produced by both the EU and its Member States; (ii) Public procurement; (iii) The Once Only Technical System (OOTS) will enable eGovernment portals to automatically

48 Björn Lundqvist and Erion Murati, 'Collaborative Platforms and Data Pools for Smart Urban Societies and Mobility as a Service (MaaS) from a Competition Law Perspective' in Michele Finck, Mathias Lamping, Valentina Moscon and Heiko Richter (eds) *Smart Urban Mobility: law, regulation, and policy. MPI Studies on Intellectual Property and Competition Law* vol 29. (Berlin, Heidelberg, Springer 2020) 191–226.

49 European Commission, *Proposal for a Regulation of the European Parliament and of the council on a framework for Financial Data Access and amending Regulations (EU) No 1093/2010, (EU) No 1094/2010, (EU) No 1095/2010 and (EU) 2022/2554* (FIDA), COM(2023) 360 final, 28.6.23.

50 *See* European Commission framework for financial data access, https://finance.ec.europa.eu/digital-finance/framework-financial-data-access_en.

and securely gather evidence (in the form of documents or structured data) required in administrative procedures, directly from administrations in other Member States, upon the explicit request by citizens or businesses but without having to request this evidence from the applicant. The OOTS will form an EU-wide government-to-government data space, which will be seamlessly integrated into the common European data space for public administrations. With (iv) the security data space for innovation, the Commission continued to explore the feasibility of creating a security data space. It aims to improve access by law enforcement authorities to relevant data, allowing them to test, train and validate algorithms with the objective to develop and use Artificial Intelligence (AI);[51]

7) The ccommon European skills data space, to reduce the skills mismatches between the education and training system on the one hand and the labour market needs on the other. The aim is to offer a secure, trusted and human-centric infrastructure for the sharing, access and re-use of skills and education data for various purposes between various actors in the Member States.

Moreover, new initiatives in reference to data spaces as presented in 2024 are the common European data space for cultural heritage where the Commission wants to accelerate digital transformation of Europe's cultural sector and foster the creation and re-use of digital cultural heritage content. The European language data space started under the DIGITAL programme in January 2023. The primary objective is to deploy an ecosystem that enables the seamless collection, creation, sharing and re-use of multimodal language data and models across all sectors while navigating the complex terrain of legal regulations. As digital transition becomes a sheer necessity for media outlets in Europe, the media data space offers them a much greater scope for growth through trusted data sharing and exchange. For example, independent news creators who do not have their own platforms will gain visibility and increase their business opportunities. The Research and Innovation data space – EOSC (European Open Science Cloud) has been developing independently but is now included as a European data space. The common European tourism data space will serve the data needs of the public and private sector in a secure, transparent way. It will facilitate the sharing, processing and analysis of data within the sector.[52]

The most obvious and clear example of a data space is the common European health data space where both private and public actors are obliged to share data across the sector.

51 European Commission, *Staff Working Document on Common European Data Spaces* SWD(2024) 21 final, 24.1.2024. Available at: https://digital-strategy.ec.europa.eu/en/library/second-staff-working-document-data-spaces.

52 European Commission, *Staff Working Document on Common European Data Spaces* SWD(2024) 21 final, 24.1.2024. Available at: https://digital-strategy.ec.europa.eu/en/library/second-staff-working-document-data-spaces.

2.3.2 Health Data Space

As seen above, the European Strategy for Data foresaw initially the establishment of nine sectoral data spaces in different strategic fields. There are now 14 proposed data spaces, with the European Health Data Space (EHDS) being the first to be enacted.[53] As with the other legal systems presented in this chapter, the main aim of the EHDS is to make data accessible by "providing a consistent, trustworthy and efficient set-up for the use of health data for research, innovation, policy-making and regulatory activities".[54] The EHDS – being sector specific – is focused only on electronic health data, though the regulation covers data from both public and private entities, as well as rules directed at manufacturers and suppliers of electronic health records systems and wellness apps.[55] EHDS defines "secondary use of electronic health data" as the processing of electronic health data initially collected during the provision of healthcare with the purpose of supporting research, innovation, policy making and regulatory activities, among others.

Access may be granted for a number of reasons listed in the form of eight broad categories in Article 34 of the regulation.

Data should be available for conducting activities for reasons of public interest in the area of public and occupational health, such as protection against serious cross-border threats to health, public health surveillance or ensuring high levels of quality and safety of healthcare and of medicinal products or medical devices. Access should also be granted to support public-sector bodies or Union institutions, agencies and bodies including regulatory authorities, in the health or care sector to carry out their tasks defined in their mandates and to produce national, multi-national and Union level official statistics related to health or care sectors. Data access can also be granted for education or teaching activities in health or care sectors. The above mandates the public entities and the government to access data on a wide scale.

Data should be accessible for scientific research related to health or care sectors and for the development and innovation activities for products or services contributing to public health or social security, or ensuring high levels of quality and safety of healthcare, of medicinal products or of medical devices. Under these categories private undertakings conducting research to develop new drugs

53 The EHDS was adopted by the European Parliament on 24 April 2024. The final text is not published yet. For the European Commission proposal, *see Proposal for a Regulation of the European Parliament and of the Council on the European Health Data Space*, COM(2022) 197 final, 3.5.2022. For the latest version from the EU Parliament, *see* the Provisional agreement, https://www.europarl.europa.eu/meetdocs/2014_2019/plmrep/COMMITTEES/CJ43/AG/2024/04-09/1299790EN.pdf.

54 Preamble 1 EHDS.

55 Jane Reichel, 'The European Strategy for Data and Trust in EU Governance. The Case of Access to Publicly Held Data' (*CERIDAP*, 31 October 2023). Available at: https://ceridap.eu/the-european-strategy-for-data-and-trust-in-eu-governance-the-case-of-access-to-publicly-held-data/ accessed 25 February 2025. As Jane discusses, "the EHDS includes rules on both primary and secondary use of data, that is, not merely re-use of data, and on use of data for the benefit of the data subject or patient him- or herself. The rules on primary use of data are a continuation of the legislative initiatives in the Directive regarding the application of patients' rights in cross-border healthcare, where a voluntary eHealth Network was introduced – an EU-wide electronic platform for e-prescriptions and patient summaries".

and treatments may access data originating from the public, e.g. health records of patients (pseudonymised) or other private actors' data.

Data may also be accessed for training, testing and evaluating of algorithms, including in medical devices, AI systems and digital health applications, contributing to the public health or social security, or ensuring high levels of quality and safety of healthcare, of medicinal products or of medical devices; and for providing personalised healthcare consisting in assessing, maintaining or restoring the state of health of natural persons, based on the health data of other natural persons.

The EHDS thus identifies eight permissible purposes for which electronic health data can be processed for secondary use, while also listing five prohibited ones. The purposes shall be prohibited according to EHDS. Data cannot be accessed with the aim to make decisions detrimental to a natural person based on their electronic health data; in order to qualify as "decisions", they must produce legal effects or similarly significantly affect those natural persons. Or, for taking decisions in relation to a natural person or groups of natural persons to exclude them from the benefit of an insurance contract or to modify their contributions and insurance premiums.

Moreover, data should not be available for advertising or marketing activities towards health professionals, organisations in health or natural persons. Firms having granted access to data may not transfer such data to third parties, i.e. providing access to, or otherwise making available, the electronic health data to third parties not mentioned in the data permit is not allowed.

Generally, data should not be accessible for developing products or services that may harm individuals and societies at large, including, but not limited to illicit drugs, alcoholic beverages, tobacco products or goods or services which are designed or modified in such a way that they contravene public order or morality. This broad category could limit the development of new drugs in many areas, should it be implemented on a broad scale.

The EHDS provides for a compulsory scheme, ensuring legal, semantic and technical re-use of health data. The EHDS, however, requires that protected data are to be transferred in anonymised or pseudonymised forms only.

The EDHS sets up a scheme with defined roles and responsibilities for entities holding health data (data holders), actors requesting health data (data users), as well as a supervisory body (the health data access body) in each Member State. The definition of data holders in Article 2.1.y of the EHDS Regulation is wide. While micro-enterprises are excluded, all entities or bodies in the health and care sector, research institutes, EU institutions and bodies with the right or legal obligation to make data available are included. Indeed, health or care providers, organisations, professional associations and other institutions, as well as research institutions in the health sector are all data holders.[56]

56 Jane Reichel, 'The European Strategy for Data and Trust in EU Governance. The Case of Access to Publicly Held Data' (*CERIDAP*, 31 October 2023). Available at: https://ceridap.eu/the-european-strategy-for-data-and-trust-in-eu-governance-the-case-of-access-to-publicly-held-data/ accesed 25 February 2025. *See* also Veronique Cimina, 'The Proposal for a European Health Data Space: Between Pursued Objectives and Data Protection Challenges' (2023) 24(3) *ERA Forum* 343–359, https://link.springer.com/article/10.1007/s12027-023-00764-7, accessed 25 February 2025.

Interestingly, the duties and obligations of the health data access body, the data holders and the data users are also set out. In particular, data holders should cooperate with the health data access body to ensure availability of electronic health data for data users. Furthermore, responsibilities are defined for the health data access bodies and data users as joint controllers of the processed electronic health data under GDPR. According to Reichel, the health data access bodies must therefore continually monitor the processing conducted by the data users.[57]

The data holders are obligated to provide electronic health data in the fifteen categories listed in Article 33 of the EHDS Regulation to requesting data users. Article 33 lists the minimum categories of electronic health data to be processed for secondary use. Such a list includes a wide variety of health data such as EHRs, relevant pathogen genomic data impacting on human health, human genetic, genomic and proteomic data, electronic health data deriving from clinical trials, biobanks and dedicated databases, public health registries and medical registries for specific diseases.[58] The list also encompasses person-generated electronic health data, including medical devices, wellness applications or other digital health applications and electronic data related to insurance status, professional status, education, lifestyle, wellness and behaviour data relevant to health.[59]

Data that can be requested include thus electronic health records, health-related administrative data, including claims and reimbursement data, public health registries and electronic health data from medical devices, such as running apps and other health apps.[60]

The data user is identified as a natural or legal person who has lawful access to personal or non-personal electronic health data for secondary use. With reference to "data users", the EHDS provides that, in principle, any natural or legal person may

57 cf. fn 103 in Jane Reichel, 'The European Strategy for Data and Trust in EU Governance. The Case of Access to Publicly Held Data' (*CERIDAP*, 31 October 2023). Available at: https://ceridap.eu/the-european-strategy-for-data-and-trust-in-eu-governance-the-case-of-access-to-publicly-held-data/ accessed 25 February 2025. Article 51 proposed EHDS Regulation. The responsibilities of the controller are laid down in Article 24.1–2 GDPR: "*Taking into account the nature, scope, context and purposes of processing as well as the risks of varying likelihood and severity for the rights and freedoms of natural persons, the controller shall implement appropriate technical and organisational measures to ensure and to be able to demonstrate that processing is performed in accordance with this Regulation. Those measures shall be reviewed and updated where necessary. Where proportionate in relation to processing activities, the measures referred to in paragraph 1 shall include the implementation of appropriate data protection policies by the controller*". According to Article 66 proposed EHDS Regulation, the Commission is suggested to establish "*joint controllership groups*" for cross-border infrastructures of the type provided for in Articles 12 and 52.

58 Veronique Cimina, 'The Proposal for a European Health Data Space: Between Pursued Objectives and Data Protection Challenges' (2023) 24(30) *ERA Forum* 343–359.

59 In Jane Reichel, 'The European Strategy for Data and Trust in EU Governance. The Case of Access to Publicly Held Data' (*CERIDAP*, 31 October 2023). Available at: https://ceridap.eu/the-european-strategy-for-data-and-trust-in-eu-governance-the-case-of-access-to-publicly-held-data/ accessed 25 February 2025.

60 Ibid.

submit a data access application to an HDAB for allowed purposes under Article 34. Due to the special sensitivity of health data, the EHDS also states that data shall be always provided in an anonymised format. However, where the data user demonstrates that the purpose of the processing may not be achieved by accessing data in an anonymous format, the data may be provided in a pseudonymised format. The applicant will however be required to justify the reason for such data to be required in pseudonymised format.[61]

Electronic health data can be accessed in two ways, via a data access application or a data request – the latter being a simplified version containing only an anonymised statistical format, with no access to the underlying electronic health data. Both data applications and data requests can be submitted to a health data access body, but a data request, i.e. the simplified version of access, may also be submitted directly to a data holder, if the data sought are confined to a single data holder and a single Member State.[62]

Neither this common data space concept[63] nor the strategy as a whole takes into consideration the size or the market presence of the entities that should be allowed access to data. Indeed, they may become access tools and further fortify the dominance of already powerful platforms, even gatekeepers. Indeed, it is possible that the sector-specific regulations granting access to data from public and private entities should not be available to large platforms, so as to protect competition on future markets. However, the issue is whether from a constitutional perspective, large platforms can be excluded from gaining access to public data.

The sector-specific legal systems have a further major drawback. As with competition law, the EHDS stipulates liability rules in terms of access and portability of data. This is asking for trouble, and shows that a sector-specific regulation granting access rights to platform-held data is not a good idea. Access and claims for having the possibility to port data might not be refused by the large platforms, but the relevant data may be slow to access and difficult to obtain, and the set-up may become unsatisfactory owing to significant litigation regarding both access and remuneration. Indeed, dominant platforms will give preferred access to their own affiliated companies and ecosystems. Litigation regarding access will be long and cumbersome, and thus act as a tool to force firms several rungs down the ladder in the ecosystem run by a single platform or system leader.

61 Veronique Cimina, 'The Proposal for a European Health Data Space: Between Pursued Objectives and Data Protection Challenges' (2023) 24(3) *ERA Forum* 343–359.

62 Jane Reichel, 'The European Strategy for Data and Trust in EU Governance. The Case of Access to Publicly Held Data' (*CERIDAP*, 31 October 2023). Available at: https://ceridap.eu/the-european-strategy-for-data-and-trust-in-eu-governance-the-case-of-access-to-publicly-held-data/, accessed 25 February 2025.

63 Also including the Gaia-x initiative, *see* https://www.data-infrastructure.eu/GAIAX/Navigation/EN/Home/home.html. accessed 25 February 2025.

2.3.3 Directive on Payment Services

The updated Directive on Payment Services stipulates a right for third parties to access, under certain circumstances, the banking data of consumers. Consumers should be able to agree that third parties provide services, while accessing consumer bank accounts and internet bank sites. Under PSD2, banks must allow only third-party providers (TPPs) access to customers' payment account data, provided that the TPPs have the "explicit consent" of the customer (Articles 67 and 94, PSD2). The PSD2 may, as a way to promote competition, require banks to provide standardised API access to third parties under the auspices of the European Banking Authority (EBA).[64] This may enable third parties to tailor their banking service towards customers, while using data collected by a competitor. Thus, the PSD2 implements data portability requirements (but not full interoperability) for consumer data between certain financial institutions. However, full interoperability may soon be a reality where fintech companies will become business users of other financial institutions platforms, providing specific services on competitors' platforms or ecosystems.

Unlike the legal instruments discussed above, the PSD2 starts with the consent given from third parties under the GDPR and that triggers the right to access data for fintech companies. Interestingly, under the PSD2, the issue of whether the accessible data, i.e. customers' payment account data, could be considered protected by for example the trade secret rules, or whether the API as such could be copyright protected has not been addressed.[65]

Moreover, the Portuguese Competition Authority highlighted poor performance of APIs as one factor limiting the effectiveness of portability under PSD2 in promoting competition. Indeed, banks are not providing assistance to access the data under the PSD2, at least not to the extent public-sector bodies are obliged to give access to data and provide means for access under the Open Data legal system.

The Commission proposes to amend and modernise the current PSD2 which will become PSD3 and establish, in addition, a Payment Services Regulation (PSR).[66] The PSD3 updates PSD2 to incorporate new forms of payments systems, sets out stricter rules on access to payment systems and account information and

64 *See* Directive (EU) 2015/2366 of the European Parliament and of the Council of 25 November 2015 on payment services in the internal market, amending Directives 2002/65/EC, 2009/110/EC and 2013/36/EU and Regulation (EU) No 1093/2010, and repealing Directive 2007/64/EC (Text with EEA relevance) [2015] OJ L337/35 Cf. Commission (2015). *See* also Commission Delegated Regulation (EU) 2018/389 of 27 November 2017 supplementing Directive (EU) 2015/2366 of the European Parliament and of the Council with regard to regulatory technical standards for strong customer authentication and common and secure open standards of communication [2018] OJ L69/23.

65 OECD, *Data Portability, Interoperability and Digital Platform Competition*, (OECD Competition Committee Discussion Paper, 2021) 11 *et seq*. Available at: http://oe.cd/dpic accessed 25 February 2025.

66 Financial data access and payments package - European Commission (europa.eu) cf. https://finance.ec.europa.eu/publications/financial-data-access-and-payments-package_en accessed 25 February 2025.

on customer authentication. As mentioned above, the proposed framework on Financial Data Access (FIDA) from June 2023 complements PSD2 and introduces similar data-sharing requirements as PSD2 outside payment accounts. Under FIDA, both businesses and individual customers should retain control over their data held by financial service providers, the so-called Open Finance Framework. This will enable a data space for financial data such as mortgage credit agreements, loans and all other accounts which are not yet covered by PSD2 including balance, conditions and transaction details; creditworthiness assessments performed during a loan application process or a request for a credit rating; savings, investments in financial instruments, insurance-based investment products, crypto-assets, real estate and other related financial assets as well as the economic benefits derived from such assets. This will fall under rules regarding data access rights and obligations for customers and financial undertakings.[67]

2.3.4 Vehicle Data for Independent Repair Shops

Access to vehicle data has been regulated at EU level since 2007 for repair data and on-board diagnostics (OBD) to ensure fair competition on the repair and maintenance aftermarket. The rules regarding access to data are found in Article 61 of Regulation 2018/858[68] entitled "Manufacturers' obligations to provide vehicle OBD information and vehicle repair and maintenance information", and provides:

1. Manufacturers shall provide to independent operators unrestricted, standardised and non-discriminatory access to vehicle OBD information, diagnostic and other equipment, tools including the complete references, and available downloads, of the applicable software and vehicle repair and maintenance information. Information shall be presented in an easily accessible manner in the form of machine-readable and electronically processable datasets. [...]

The vehicle OBD information and the vehicle repair and maintenance information shall be made available on the websites of manufacturers using a standardised format or, if this is not feasible, due to the nature of the information, in another appropriate format. For independent operators other than repairers, the information shall also be given in a machine-readable format that is capable of being electronically processed with commonly available information technology tools and software and which allows independent operators to carry out the task associated with their business in the aftermarket supply chain.

67 Ibid. *See* Case C-238/05 *Asnef/Equifax v Ausbanc* [2006] ECLI:EU:C:2006:734.

68 Regulation (EU) 2018/858 of the European Parliament and of the Council of 30 May 2018 on the approval and market surveillance of motor vehicles and their trailers, and of systems, components and separate technical units intended for such vehicles, amending Regulations (EC) No 715/2007 and (EC) No 595/2009 and repealing Directive 2007/46/EC [2018] OJ L151/1 1.

2. Until the [European] Commission has adopted a relevant standard through the work of the European Committee for Standardisation (CEN) or a comparable standardisation body, the vehicle OBD information and vehicle repair and maintenance information shall be presented in an easily accessible manner that can be processed with reasonable effort by independent operators.

The specific technical details for accessing the data is provided in an annex to the regulation.

Interestingly, the ECJ has dissected Article 61 in the *Scania* case from November 2023 and held that the Article 61 does stipulate a right to access data for independent repair shops and also a legal obligation for the manufacturer to grant access even to potential personal data items.[69] The case was initiated in Germany by the GVA, the German industry association for the independent automotive parts trade. It complained on the behalf of its members that Scania violated Article 61 by only giving access through its website providing information on vehicle repair and maintenance via manual access. The national court made a reference to the ECJ, and the SCJ confirmed the obligation to provide data *inter alia* in an easily accessible manner in the form of machine-readable electronically processable datasets, while not being obliged to set up a specific database interface. The court moreover stated that Article 61 together with specific rule in the annex must be interpreted as meaning that it establishes a "legal obligation", within the meaning of the GDPR on car manufacturers, to make the vehicle identification number (VIN) of the vehicles available to independent operators, as "controllers", within the meaning of Article 4(7) of the GDPR. That is very revealing, indicating that sector-specific regulation may in fact work in conjunction with the GDPR, stipulating a hard obligation or right for undertaking to gain access also to personal data.

2.3.5 In-Vehicle Data Space Regulation?

It should be noted that since the first regulation regarding in-vehicle data was adopted, the market for connected vehicles has developed.[70] According to the Commission Call for evidence for an Impact Assessment for accessing in-vehicle data,[71] already in 2018, over 85% of all new cars were connected wirelessly; over 470 million connected vehicles are expected to be on the roads in Europe, the USA and China by 2025. Connected vehicles make it possible to remotely access vehicle data. They also give remote access to functions (e.g. remote door unlocking for car sharing, launching diagnostic routines) and resources (e.g. displaying information

69 Case C-319/22 *Gesamtverband Autoteile-Handel eV v Scania CV AB* [2023] ECLI:EU:C:2023:837.

70 Regulation (EU) 2018/858 of the European Parliament and of the Council of 30 May 2018 on the approval and market surveillance of motor vehicles and their trailers, and of systems, components and separate technical units intended for such vehicles, amending Regulations (EC) No 715/2007 and (EC) No 595/2009 and repealing Directive 2007/46/EC [2018] OJ L151/1.

71 European Commission, 'Call for Evidence for an Impact Assessment' (Ref. Ares(2022)2302201 - 29/03/2022, 2022).

on a vehicle's dashboard). This remote access enables remote diagnostics, but also new aftermarket services such as mobility as a service or pay-as-you-drive insurance.[72]

Given this background, the Commission has been investigating whether to regulate in-vehicle data sector specific. Exploring whether access rights granted in accordance with the Data Act should be complemented by an equvalent access rights to functions (e.g. the possibility of remotely unlocking the vehicle door for a shared mobility service) and access to resources (e.g. the possibility of displaying speed limit information on the vehicle dashboard for a navigation service, or to charging/discharging the battery for electric vehicle-related services) for all parties.

To ensure transparency, in addition to the Data Act transparency measures for users, the list of vehicle data, functions and resources accessible on a specific model or version of a vehicle would need to be published or otherwise made available by the vehicle's manufacturers. Rules would also address the interplay between the right to access data, functions and resources and the applicable cybersecurity rules. Finally, reporting obligations for manufacturers would be introduced, to inform competent authorities (e.g. type-approval authorities and the Commission) about the implementation of such access rights.

However, it is not clear that the Commission will pursue this effort and develop a draft regulation for in-vehicle data.

2.3.6 Other Sector Legal Systems Mandating Data Sharing

The above discussed sector-specific legal systems, which mandate data sharing in specific industries, can also be complemented with similar rules in reference to the chemical,[73] the electricity,[74] the telecom[75] and the postal sector.[76]

The REACH regulation catering to the exchange of data regarding testing of chemical substances on animals stipulates that the data holder and the potential user of the data "should make every effort" to reach a data-sharing agreement. Whether the rule implies that a data holder is required to share data is a matter of

72 Ibid.

73 Regulation (EC) No 1907/2006 of the European Parliament and of the Council of 18 December, 2006, concerning the Registration, Evaluation, Authorisation and Restriction of Chemicals (REACH), establishing a European Chemicals Agency, amending Directive 1999/45/EC and repealing Council Regulation (EEC) No 793/93 and Commission Regulation (EC) No 1488/94, as well as Council Directive 76/769/EEC and Commission Directives 91/155/EEC, 93/67/EEC, 93/105/EC and 2000/21/EC [2006] OJ L396/1.

74 Directive (EU) 2019/944 of the European Parliament and of the Council of 5 June 2019, on common rules for the internal market for electricity and amending Directive 2012/27/EU [2019] OJ L158/125 Art 23.

75 Directive (EU) 2018/1972 of the European Parliament and of the Council of 11 December 2018, establishing the European Electronic Communications Code (EECC) [2018] OJ L321/36 Art 112.

76 Directive 2008/6/EC of the European Parliament and of the Council of 20 February 2008, amending Directive 97/67/EC with regard to the full accomplishment of the internal market of Community postal services [2008] OJ L52/3 Art 11a.

interpretation. The REACH regulation aims to achieve a public interest goal of limiting chemical tests on animals, data-sharing obligations in other sector legislation aim to solve market failures such as information asymmetry and excessive data concentrations.

Article 23 of the 2019 electricity directive is an example of this requiring the sharing of final user data to be understood as to include metering and consumption data as well as data required for customer switching, demand response and other services to eligible parties. Eligible parties should be understood as also including competitors, while the sharing of personal data should comply with GDPR.[77] The 2008 Postal Service Directive[78] requires postal operators to share certain limited datasets. Incumbent actors should share in a non-discriminatory fashion *inter alia* address databases, postcodes etc.

Finally the European Electronic Communications Code (EECC)[79] requires telecoms operators to provide data concerning telephone numbers and users with the providers of telephone directory enquiry services.[80] The European Court of Justice (ECJ) has confirmed that the operators are required to share such data in *KPN Telecom*.[81]

2.4 Conclusions

As stated above, the Data Act, the DMA and the PSD2 share similar structural or constitutional points of departure in reference to establishing a legal system of access and transfer of data, while the Open Data Directive and the Data Governance Act and the Digital Service Act use a different constitutional structure. On top of this, each sector or industry has its rule for accessing data.

In reference to G2P (government to platform) all government data should in principle be available for any comer for free or at marginal cost under the Open Data paradigm, while for P2G (platform to government), for data transfer to be required certain requirements in reference to systemic risk need to be fulfilled. However, there are also users for several of the services provided by the government platforms. The large data holders within the public system are often organised with platforms in the centre of digital ecosystems. Indeed, real estate data, corporate information, weather data etc. are organised with users and business users providing and generating data for the platforms. That could imply that they could be regulated in a similar fashion as the Data Act, the DMA and the PSD2 and legally obliged to share access to their data with their users. Indeed, in principle, the

77 *See* the French *GDF* and *EDF* competition law cases dealing with somewhat similar issues. French Competition Authority Decision n°13-D-20 of 17 December 2013, confirmed on that point by the court of appeal on 21 May 2015.

78 *See* Art 11a Directive 2008/6/EC.

79 *Supra,* Directive (EU) 2018/1972.

80 *Supra,* Art 112(1) Directive (EU) 2018/1972.

81 Case C-109/03, *KPN Telecom BV v Onafhankelijke Post en Telecommunicatie Autoriteit* [2004] ECLI:EU:C:2004:749.

regulation of access to data G2P could be built around the principle of empowering the users to have a right to access and transfer of the data they generate. Moreover, it should be acknowledged that at the centre of several of the large public-sector databases are cloud services provided often by large platforms, even gatekeepers, where the gatekeepers have contractual access to the public data available in the clouds. There are thus several overlaps between private and public data holders, making use of each other's services.

From a competition law perspective, the non-compete rules in the Data Act stand out. According to Articles 5, 6 and 7 of the Data Act, the user and data recipient is severely restricted to be able to compete vis-à-vis the data holder, and to innovate. Indeed, the Data Act stipulates a broad non-compete obligation, intricate rules regarding adherence to trade secret restrictions and data processing restrictions in reference to personal data. Moreover, the Data Act also restricts the data holder to use data in competition with third parties.[82] Thus, as a general rule, the Data Act does not oblige the data holder, user nor a third-party data recipient to create a levelled playing field vis-à-vis each other. The Data Act creates a legal basis for dividing the market in segments between the data holder, user and the third-party data recipient. The Data Act allows for non-compete clauses, i.e. enables them to prevent competition and divide the markets. That might be in violation of Article 101 TFEU or Article 4(3) TEU, the loyalty clause read together with Article 101 TFEU.

The Data Act fails also to integrate the regulation of public-sector information (Data Governance Act) and the Open Data PSI Directive, while not providing rules for when data holders may not harvest data from IoT products that have been purchased by public bodies. The public can possibly address this under public procurement procedures, while it should still have been addressed under the Data Act.

Nonetheless, the public data holder can refuse access, claiming that the data is covered by third-party rights or is personal data, not covered by an applicable ground for sharing under Article 6 of GDPR. These restrictions have been viewed as a clear limitation of the Open Data Directive and the Commission has therefore in the new Data Governance Act encouraged public data holders to make such data available for re-use.

Article 5 DGA therefore states that public-sector bodies can impose an obligation on the re-user to anonymise or pseudonymise personal data or delete commercially confidential information, including trade secrets, before the data may be re-used. This may make it possible to re-use the data previously covered by third-party rights or GDPR restrictions. Moreover, the shall be able to verify any results

82 Article 5(6) reads "A data holder shall not use any readily available data to derive insights about the economic situation, assets and production methods of, or the use by, the third party in any other manner that could undermine the commercial position of the third party on the markets in which the third party is active, unless the third party has given permission to such use and has the technical possibility to easily withdraw that permission at any time".

of the re-user's processing of data and reserve the right to prohibit the use of results that contain information that jeopardises the rights and interests of third parties.

Generally, under the Data Governance Act, the re-use of data is allowed only in compliance with intellectual property rights and the GDPR; if efforts by the public-sector body to comply – for example through anonymisation of personal data – are in vain, the re-use of data cannot be granted. However, the public-sector body shall support re-users in seeking consent from the data subjects and/or permission from the legal entities whose rights and interests may be affected by such re-use, where it is feasible and does not incur disproportionate cost for the public sector.

In reference to the Data Act, the DMA should be the preferred tool – if applicable – for business users to gain access not only to raw data, but also derived data, while a problem facing such users can be gatekeepers claiming *sui generis* database right to the relevant dataset. Moreover, it is not clear that users have a right to access data under Article 6 of the DMA. However, can a business user cherry pick between the rules in the different Acts? For example, can a business user make use of the restriction for data holders not to apply *sui generis* database protection under the Data Act, while accessing derived data under the DMA? This issue has not been addressed by the Commission. Moreover, the difficult issue is the lengthy Articles in the Data Act concerning terms and conditions for the user and third-party data recipients to abide by, for example the FRAND fees commitment.

Interestingly, the problem posed by intellectual property rights or GDPR, is universal. Users under the DMA and even the Data Act face similar barriers to access data compared to re-users under the Open Data paradigm. Indeed, data holders control legal access barriers to data that enable them to control data flows and to exclude competitors. The health data space regulation however addresses this problem and stipulates that the data holders are obligated to provide electronic health data in several categories listed in the EHDS Regulation to requesting data users. Indeed, Article 33 states:

> [e]lectronic health data entailing protected intellectual property and trade secrets from private enterprises shall be made available for secondary use. Where such data is made available for secondary use, all measures necessary to preserve the confidentiality of IP rights and trade secrets shall be taken.

Also, Articles 34 and 37 make clear that the designated health data authority should have access to such data. In point 40 of the preamble, the Commission makes clear that the EHDS regulation actually is a tool for public authorities to access for example copyright protected data originating from medical device companies or pharmaceutical companies. This is quite a bold step, however the EHDS deals only with bilateral exchanges of anonymised or pseudonymised data transferred via a health data authority, which indeed helps in reference to complying with both GDPR and the intellectual property regime.

The Data Governance Act also sets out rules for the data collaborations. These rules originate from unfair competition legislation and practical IT law sources. Data-sharing services shall be subject to conditions discussed above. The conditions are focused on procedural fairness.

The metadata collected from the provision of the data-sharing service may be used only for the development of that service. The provider shall ensure that the procedure for access to its service is fair, transparent and non-discriminatory for both data holders and data users, including as regards prices.

The provider shall facilitate the exchange of the data in the format in which it receives it from the data holder and shall convert the data into specific formats only to enhance interoperability within and across sectors or if requested by the data user or where mandated by Union law or to ensure harmonisation with international or European data standards. In addition, the provider should have the technical facility to provide access in a timely and secure manner.

Generally the providers shall accordingly have procedures in place to prevent fraudulent or abusive practices in relation to access to data from parties seeking access through their services. Indeed, the requirements above mirror to some extent the guidelines set out in the Horizontal Guidelines for information exchanges (data pools) and even patent pools.[83] Indeed, the DSA carves out a safe harbour under Competition law for establishing intermediates for provided data-sharing services, based on procedural rules, without taking into consideration market power and barriers to entry.

Still, the rules are somewhat fuzzy. Can access for a newcomer be denied? What if the data space or pool becomes dominant? What if a member becomes a gatekeeper that provides a core platform service according to the Digital Markets Act? Will access then need to be granted to any comers? What about data originating from an IoT device, can such data be shared under the DGA when gatekeepers are also members of the data space? Difficult issues to address in the interface between the different sector-specific legal systems.

Indeed, the above scheme implies that any and all data can be shared. According to the Competition Law Horizontal Guidelines, participants in a reciprocal data-sharing arrangement such as a data pool should in principle only have access to their own information and the final, aggregated, information of other participants. According to the Commission, technical and practical measures can ensure that a participant is unable to obtain commercially sensitive information from other participants. The management of a data pool can be assigned to a trustee that is subject to strict confidentiality rules as regards the information received from participants in the data pool. Undertakings that manage a data pool should also ensure that only information that is necessary for the implementation of the legitimate purpose of the data pool is collected. That is a limited safe harbour for hub-and-spokes provided by the Horizontal Guidelines, which is silent with respect to the difference between aggregated data and anonymised and pseudoanonymised data.[84] Do these terms cover the same data? How does that difference play with the set-up in the

83 European Commission, *Guidelines on the applicability of Article 101 of the Treaty on the Functioning of the European Union to horizontal co-operation agreements* C(2023) 4752 final (New Horizontal Guidelines), 17.7.2023, paras 89 and 108.

84 Cf. Ibid. paras 89 and 108.

DGA? The above safe harbour is focused on the data pool scenario rather than the data space scenario in the DGA.[85]

Taking the above into consideration, one thing that is clear is that the interfaces between the different legal systems of data access are developing into a complicated system. Legal certainty is at risk. The guiding principle for the data-driven economy should instead reflect an equal access and transfer right to data for users as well as data holders. The right should also address the general intrinsic limitation and restriction reflected by the intellectual property rights held by data holders, while also addressing the restriction of competition created by the GDPR.

It can be argued that the Data Act, the DMA, the DPS2 and the Open Data/DGA could be amended with a "countervailing" right for accessing and transferring the data that is collected and stored on the data holders' server interface, i.e. most likely a database. Such an access right including data mining or reverse-engineering right would allow users to circumvent or trump the data holders' right to protection under TPMs, database rights and trade-secret legislation to gain access to the data generated by themselves. Such a limited access and transfer right (ATR) could be included in the Data Act as a *lex generalis* applicable within the whole field of the data-driven economy or perhaps in an updated version of the database directive.

Moreover, users should have equal access also under GDPR when providing the same level of protection. This would solve the general problems faced by all the sector-specific access and transfer of data legal systems now being implemented. The right to access and transfer for users should also be aligned with the GDPR, giving a user the right to also access personal data when the user can provide equal protection under the GDPR as the original data holder. Indeed, the ECJ in the *Scania* case from November 2023 indicates that an data access obligation stipulated in a sector-specific regulation may create a legal obligation for the manufacturer to grant access even to personal data covered by GDPR.[86] GDPR must also be included in the general legal system for data-driven economy and should be judged and analysed in reference to the countervailing rights or principles held by the party wanting access to the data.

The right could be supplemented in an updated version of the database directive, for the benefit of users generating data. The database directive could moreover go further and grant a more elaborated right when users have invested time and/or effort to create useful data to the level that it would become a database in its own right, i.e. with a limited exclusive right to prevent certain large data dumps. That would normally apply to business users of platforms.

Finally, the Competition Law Horizontal Guidelines need to align with the DGA, so that legal certainty regarding how data pools can be constructed is provided.

85 European Commission, *Proposal for a Regulation of the European Parliament and of the Council on the European Health Data Space* COM(2022) 197 final, 3.5.2022. Available at: https://eur-lex.europa.eu/legal-content/EN/TXT/?uri=CELEX%3A52022PC0197.

86 Case C-319/22 *Gesamtverband Autoteile-Handel eV v Scania CV AB* [2023] ECLI:EU:C:2023:837.

3 Protection of Personal Data in the European Union and Its Role in Setting the Regulatory Framework for Data Sharing

Joanna Mazur

3.1 Introduction

While it is trivial in 2025 to argue for the importance of data for the economy, it remains crucial to argue for the importance of data protection. Even though the experiences of the last decade linked to the use of personal data for economic benefits with little regard to other values,[1] strengthened the power of voices that attempted to raise awareness of these issues,[2] it did not result in any significant changes to the way in which big-tech operates. Thus, establishing what are the boundaries that data protection law sets for data sharing remains an important topic and deserves closer scrutiny in the light of the ongoing developments in this area of regulation.

The chapter focuses on European Union (EU) data protection law, and, to be more specific, on the analysis of the relevant provisions of the General Data Protection Regulation (GDPR)[3] and decisions issued by the national data protection authorities (DPA) on its basis. Other legal acts are mentioned only when they are important for explaining the specific character of certain data-sharing models or data sharing in particular sectors. When it is necessary, the chapter refers to other legal orders, mostly, international law. Firstly, references to the Convention for the Protection of Human Rights and Fundamental Freedoms (European Convention on Human Rights – ECHR)[4] and Convention for the Protection of Individuals with regard to Automatic Processing of Personal Data (Convention 108+)[5] are sometimes

1 With the Cambridge Analytica scandal being the most famous example.

2 Which can be illustrated with the popularity of a book by Shoshana Zuboff, *The Age of Surveillance Capitalism: The Fight for a Human Future at the New Frontier of Power* (New York, PublicAffairs 2019).

3 Regulation (EU) 2016/679 of the European Parliament and of the Council of 27 April 2016 on the protection of natural persons with regard to the processing of personal data and on the free movement of such data, and repealing Directive 95/46/EC (General Data Protection Regulation) [2016] OJ L119/1.

4 Council of Europe, *Convention for the Protection of Human Rights and Fundamental Freedoms* (CETS no 005).

5 Council of Europe, *Convention for the Protection of Individuals with regard to Automatic Processing of Personal Data* (CETS no 108); Council of Europe, *Protocol amending the Convention for the Protection of Individuals with regard to Automatic Processing of Personal Data* (CETS no 223). The modernized convention in the article is referred to as Convention 108+.

DOI: 10.4324/9781003248255-5

relevant for the discussed issues. Secondly, as some of the regional trade agreements (RTAs) signed by the EU also include provisions on data protection, they are also included in the analysis. The chapter also provides the references to the relevant case law and decisions, as well as the guidelines of the European Data Protection Board (EDPB) and relevant scholarly literature.

In order to complete the task of providing the overview of the boundaries that data protection law sets for data sharing, the chapter addresses the following issues. Firstly, the question of what kind of datasets are subjected to the data protection regulation is addressed by discussing terms such as personal data, pseudonymisation and anonymisation. Additionally, the explanation on special categories of data and personal data concerning children is provided, as the inclusion of these types of data in a dataset changes the rules to which its processing is subjected. Next, the chapter discusses the category of purpose of processing and its significance for the processing's lawfulness. This section is followed by the analysis of the principles relating to processing of personal data, as they also set limits in regard to what is allowed under GDPR's provisions in terms of data sharing. Fourthly, the issue of data sharing is approached from the perspective of the data subject's rights. Next, this chapter discusses data transfers as a form of data sharing.

Last but not least, the chapter discusses the attempts to balance between the protection of personal data on the one hand, and allowing for data flows to take place, on the other hand. Next to personal data protection, the purpose of the GDPR is to establish the rules for the free movement of such data. The adoption of the regulation, which replaced the directive, was crucial for unifying the rules for processing data across the Member States. Some of the rights of data subjects (e.g., right to data portability) shows that facilitating the free movement of data is supported by the GDPR's provisions. The chapter's conclusions include a proposal of the way to assess which of the GDPR's provisions should be considered when planning to conduct data-sharing operations and an assessment of their significance for, on the one hand, data protection, and, on the other hand, free movement of personal data.

3.2 Personal Data and Their Specific Character: Identifiability, Anonymisation and Pseudonymisation

Protection of personal data is one of the fundamental rights guaranteed by the Charter of Fundamental Rights of European Union (Charter),[6] in which Article 8 contains basic characteristics of the model of personal data protection developed by the EU, and Article 7 refers to the protection of private and family life.[7]

6 Charter of Fundamental Rights of the European Union [2012] OJ C326/391. On the topic of the emergence of personal data protection as a fundamental right, *see* Gloria González Fuster, *The Emergence of Personal Data Protection as a Fundamental Right of the EU* (vol 16, Law, Governance and Technology Series, Cham, Springer International Publishing 2014). Available at: https://link.springer.com/book/10.1007/978-3-319-05023-2–1 .

7 Thus, Article 7 is equivalent of Article 8 of the ECHR.

Following the approaches that advocate for distinction between these two,[8] the chapter focuses solely on the issues related to data protection law. Thus, what needs to be established first, is the definition of the term 'personal data', which scope determines whether data protection law is applicable to the given situation.

The definition of personal data is included in Article 4(1) of the GDPR, and it 'means any information relating to an identified or identifiable natural person ("data subject")'. The predecessor of EDPB, the Working Party on the Protection of Individuals with regard to the Processing of Personal Data (Article 29 Working Party), issued an opinion on the interpretation of this term,[9] that breaks it down into four elements, namely: (1) 'Any information'; (2) 'Relating to'; (3) 'Identified or identifiable'; (4) 'Natural person'.[10] Even though the document was published under the Directive 95/46/EC of the European Parliament and of the Council of 24 October 1995 on the protection of individuals with regard to the processing of personal data and on the free movement of such data (Data Protection Directive – DPD),[11] as the content of these elements of the definition of personal data remained the same under the GDPR, the guidelines are still to a great extent valid for its interpretation.

Due to the character of data protection as a fundamental right, 'European data protection law, including the GDPR, tends to adopt a broad conception of personal data in order to provide a high level of data protection that does justice to the fundamental rights at stake'.[12] Thus, the scope of the term covers broad category of 'any information', which can include, e.g., images of individuals captured by a video surveillance system, when these individuals are recognisable,[13] or exam scripts and the comments of examiners on those scripts.[14] If information – be it, e.g., text, visual material, numbers, fingerprints, voice – relates to an individual, meaning that 'the information, by reason of its content, purpose or effect, is linked

8 *See* Orla Lynskey, 'Deconstructing Data Protection: The "Added-Value" of a Right to Data Protection in the EU Legal Order' (2014) 63(3) International & Comparative Law Quarterly 569–97, https://doi.org/10.1017/S0020589314000244. accessed 21 February 2025; Juliane Kokott and Christoph Sobotta, 'The Distinction between Privacy and Data Protection in the Jurisprudence of the CJEU and the ECtHR' (2013) 3(4) International Data Privacy Law 222–28 https://doi.org/10.1093/idpl/ipt017, accessed 21 February 2025.

9 Article 29 Working Party, 'Opinion 4/2007 on the Concept of Personal Data' (01248/07/EN,WP136, 2007). Available at: https://ec.europa.eu/justice/article-29/documentation/opinion-recommendation/files/2007/wp136_en.pdf.

10 *See* Lee A Bygrave and Luca Tosoni, 'Article 4(1). Personal Data', in Christopher Kuner et al. (eds), *The EU General Data Protection Regulation (GDPR): A Commentary* (Oxford University Press 2020) 106, 109. Available at: https://doi.org/10.1093/oso/9780198826491.003.0007.

11 Directive 95/46/EC of the European Parliament and of the Council of 24 October 1995 on the protection of individuals with regard to the processing of personal data and on the free movement of such data [1995] OJ L281/31.

12 Lee A Bygrave and Luca Tosoni, 'Article 4(1). Personal Data' 109.

13 Example presented in Article 29 Working Party, 'Opinion 4/2007 on the Concept of Personal Data' (01248/07/EN,WP136, 2007) 8.

14 *See* Judgment of the Court of 20 December 2017 in Case C-434/16, *Peter Nowak v Data Protection Commissioner* [2017] ECLI:EU:C:2017:994, para 62 (for the reasoning, *see* paras 34–61).

to a particular person',[15] it can constitute personal data. The third condition refers to the identifiability of a natural person. Article 4(1) specifies, that

> an identifiable natural person is one who can be identified, directly or indirectly, in particular by reference to an identifier such as a name, an identification number, location data, an online identifier or to one or more factors specific to the physical, physiological, genetic, mental, economic, cultural or social identity of that natural person.

Accordingly to the case law of the Court of Justice of the European Union (CJEU) and the recitals of the GDPR, information which enables the identification of a natural person does not need to be known to the controller.[16] If it is possible by 'all the means reasonably likely to be used, such as singling out, either by the controller or by another person to identify the natural person directly or indirectly',[17] information can be considered as leading to the identifiability of a natural person. Finally, information must concern a natural person, thus, e.g., legal persons are not protected by data protection law.

Due to the broad scope of what constitutes personal data, the question appears: what types of data should not be considered as personal data and, therefore, not be covered by data protection law? The broad term used to define this type of data in Regulation (EU) 2018/1807 of the European Parliament and of the Council of 14 November 2018 on a framework for the free flow of non-personal data in the European Union (regulation on the free flow of non-personal data)[18] is 'data'. Article 3(1) of the regulation on the free flow of non-personal data refers to data as 'data other than personal data [...]', however, for clarity, non-personal data will be referred to as non-personal data. The category of non-personal data includes, on the one hand, data which were not personal from the start (e.g., industrial data), but, on the other hand, also anonymised data, so data that used to be personal data, but, e.g., due to their aggregation or selection of certain elements of the initial dataset, cannot lead to identification of particular natural persons – and, therefore, cannot be considered as personal data anymore.

The category which shows the broad scope of the term personal data in EU law, is pseudonymised data. Article 4(2) of the GDPR defines pseudonymisation as 'the processing of personal data in such a manner that the personal data can no longer be attributed to a specific data subject without the use of additional information'. Additional information needs to be kept separately, and be subject to technical and organisational measures to ensure that the personal data are not attributed to an identified or identifiable natural person. However, as it remains possible to link

15 Judgment of the Court of 20 December 2017 in Case C-434/16, *Peter Nowak v Data Protection Commissioner* [2017] ECLI:EU:C:2017:994, para 34.

16 *See* Judgment of the Court of 19 October 2016 in Case C-582/14, *Patrick Breyer v Bundesrepublik Deutschland* [2016] ECLI:EU:C:2016:779, para 43.

17 Recital 26, GDPR.

18 Regulation (EU) 2018/1807 of the European Parliament and of the Council of 14 November 2018 on a framework for the free flow of non-personal data in the European Union [2018] OJ L303/59.

(back) pseudonymised data with identifiable natural person, this technique cannot be perceived as a method of anonymisation. Therefore, pseudonymised data are still considered as subjected to data protection law,[19] and:

> Accordingly, applying pseudonymization technique should not be seen by businesses sharing personal data as a way to avoid application of data protection rules. On the contrary, it should be seen as a measure to strengthen the individuals' data protection rights.[20]

However, the General Court of the European Union (GC) in a recent judgement *SRB versus European Data Protection Supervisor* (EDPS) noted that if the recipient of data is not in possession of data allowing for de-pseudonymisation of the given dataset, such data should not be considered to be personal data.[21] Thus, if the case will not be successfully appealed by the EDPS, each of the situations in which pseudonymised data are used needs to be considered separately, depending on the possibilities of data re-identification that occur in the particular context.

To sum up, in the context of data sharing data protection law is applicable always when shared data are personal data. In the context of mixed datasets, which include non-personal and personal data, GDPR is applicable to personal data in such datasets and the flows of non-personal data are governed by the regulation on the free flow of non-personal data. However, according to Article 2(2) of the regulation on the free flow of non-personal data, '[w]here personal and non-personal data in a data set are inextricably linked, this Regulation shall not prejudice the application of [GDPR]'. Thus, similar to the need to apply data protection law to pseudonymised data where it is possible to re-identify (or de-pseudonymise), the provisions of the GDPR should be applied when there is a link between personal and non-personal data.[22]

3.2.1 Limitations Concerning the Processing of Special Categories of Data

Within the scope of applicability of the GDPR the EU's data protection law distinguishes also special categories of data – often referred to in the literature as sensitive data – which require a higher level of protection. Article 9 of the GDPR includes an exhaustive catalogue of types of data that should be considered as

19 *See* Luca Tosoni, 'Article 4(5). Pseudonymisation', in Christopher Kuner et al. (eds), *The EU General Data Protection Regulation (GDPR): A Commentary* (Oxford University Press 2020) 135. Available at: https://doi.org/10.1093/oso/9780198826491.003.0011.

20 Francesca Mauro and Debora Stella, 'Brief Overview of the Legal Instruments and Restrictions for Sharing Data While Complying with the EU Data Protection Law' in Sven Casteleyn, Peter Dolog, and Cesare Pautasso (eds), *Current Trends in Web Engineering* (Cham, Springer International Publishing 2016) 66.

21 *See* judgment of the General Court of 26 April 2023 in Case T-557/20, *Single Resolution Board v European Data Protection Supervisor* [2023] ECLI:EU:T:2023:219, para 99.

22 'if the non- personal data part and the personal data parts are "inextricably linked", the data protection rights and obligations stemming from the GDPR fully apply to the whole mixed dataset, also when personal data represent only a small part of the dataset'. – Lee A Bygrave and Luca Tosoni, 'Article 4(1). Personal Data' 113.

special categories of data, namely: personal data revealing racial or ethnic origin, political opinions, religious or philosophical beliefs, or trade union membership, genetic data,[23] biometric data, data concerning health or data concerning a natural person's sex life or sexual orientation.[24]

The importance of the rules concerning special categories of data for data sharing stems from the differences between the approach to their processing. Special categories of data can be processed only if there is at least one of the legal bases for processing of personal data (the catalogue included in Article 6 of the GDPR), and at least one of the exceptions from the prohibition of the processing of special categories of data (the catalogue included in Article 9 of the GDPR).[25] Unless one of ten legal exceptions enumerated in Article (9)(2) is taking place, the processing of these types of personal data is prohibited. This shows that the approach to processing of special categories of data is stricter than to the processing of personal data in general.

3.2.2 Limitations Concerning the Processing of Personal Data of Children

Another unique category of data whose treatment in some cases is differentiated from personal data in general in the GDPR, is personal data of children. Article 8 of the GDPR refers to very specific cases of processing based on consent and in the context of offering of information society services directly to a child. Such processing should be lawful where the child is at least 16 years old.[26] In the case of younger children, the consent must be given or authorised by the holder of parental responsibility over the child. Obtaining such a consent may be an important element of ensuring the lawfulness of data processing, and, subsequently, of data sharing.

3.3 Legal Basis for Processing and Data Sharing

European data protection law does not use terms such as data sharing, data use or data reuse as foundational concepts.[27] Instead, it is focused on the term 'processing', defined in Article 4(2) of the GDPR as:

23 Genetic data, biometric data and data concerning health are three types of special categories of data which are defined in the GDPR, in, respectively, Article 4(13), 4(14) and 4(15).

24 For the analysis of these specific categories, *see* Ludmila Georgieva and Christopher Kuner, 'Article 9 Processing of Special Categories of Personal Data' in Christopher Kuner et al. (eds), *The EU General Data Protection Regulation (GDPR): A Commentary* (Oxford University Press 2020) 373–375. Available at: https://doi.org/10.1093/oso/9780198826491.003.0038

25 For such interpretation, *see* Ludmila Georgieva and Christopher Kuner, 'Article 9 Processing of Special Categories of Personal Data' 376–377; European Data Protection Board, 'Guidelines 3/2019 on Processing of Personal Data through Video Devices', (Version 2.0, 29 January 2020) 17, para 68. Available at: https://edpb.europa.eu/sites/default/files/files/file1/edpb_guidelines_201903_video_devices.pdf.

26 The article allows for the Member States to 'provide by law for a lower age for those purposes provided that such lower age is not below 13 years'. – Article 8(1), GDPR.

27 *See* Bart Custers and Helena Uršič, 'Big Data and Data Reuse: A Taxonomy of Data Reuse for Balancing Big Data Benefits and Personal Data Protection' (2016) 6(1) International Data Privacy Law 8 https://doi.org/10.1093/idpl/ipv028, accessed 21 February 2025.

> any operation or set of operations which is performed on personal data or on sets of personal data, whether or not by automated means, such as collection, recording, organisation, structuring, storage, adaptation or alteration, retrieval, consultation, use, disclosure by transmission, dissemination or otherwise making available, alignment or combination, restriction, erasure or destruction.

This broad formulation covers – as the catalogue is not exhaustive – all the operations that are performed on personal data, including its use and disclosure by transmission and dissemination – which can be understood as data sharing.

It is the lawfulness of processing, understood as the processing being based on at least one of the legal bases, which constitutes one of the fundamental rules of the European data protection law. It is enshrined in the Charter, in which Article 8(2) mentions the necessity of the processing to take place 'on the basis of the consent of the person concerned or some other legitimate basis laid down by law', next to the condition of data to be processed fairly for specified purposes.

Article 6 of the GDPR specifies the exhaustive catalogue of the grounds for lawful processing. As it provides legal bases that are necessary for the processing to be lawful, it embodies the principle of data processing included in Article 5(1)(a) of the GDPR, which states that data must processed lawfully, fairly and in a transparent manner in relation to the data subject. Simultaneously, every lawful processing needs to follow other principles enumerated in Article 5 (*see* the next section of this text). The manner in which these two provisions are intertwined was summarised by Waltraut Kotschy:

> The principle of 'lawful processing', which is one of several data protection principles under Article 5 GDPR, requires that every processing operation involving personal data has a legal basis. Article 6(1) exhaustively stipulates what may constitute such a legal basis. At the same time, it must be kept in mind that legally sound processing of personal data will necessitate fulfilling also all other of the core principles for processing personal data set out by Article 5(1).[28]

From the perspective of data sharing the most important question is how the provisions on the legal basis for processing shape the possibility of collecting and using data: to what extent do they allow for any kind of data sharing to take place? This section starts with the explanation on the interplay between the legal grounds enumerated in Article 6 of the GDPR and the possibilities of data sharing (section 3.1). Next, the issue of using personal data for other purposes than the initial one – compatible further processing, as regulated by Article 6(4) of the GDPR – is addressed (section 3.2).

28 Waltraut Kotschy, 'Article 6 Lawfulness of Processing' in Christopher Kuner et al. (eds), *The EU General Data Protection Regulation (GDPR): A Commentary* (Oxford University Press 2020) 325. Available at: https://doi.org/10.1093/oso/9780198826491.003.0035.

The importance of legal basis for processing stems also from the fact that if data is shared, the data recipient 'also needs his own specific lawful basis for the processing of the data that will be done once he has received the data covered by the data sharing remedy'.[29] Thus, every processing needs to be based on one of the legal grounds foreseen in the GDPR.

3.3.1 Legal Basis for Processing and the Possibilities for Data Sharing

The catalogue of the legal basis for processing opens with consent: processing shall be considered lawful, if, e.g., 'the data subject has given consent to the processing of his or her personal data for one or more specific purposes'.[30] The definition of consent is included in Article 4(11) and, additionally, conditions for consent to be considered lawful are described in Article 7 of the GDPR. On the basis of these provisions consent should be defined as 'freely given, specific, informed and unambiguous indication of the data subject's wishes by which he or she, by a statement or by a clear affirmative action, signifies agreement to the processing of personal data relating to him or her'.[31] The data subject must be able to withdraw his or her consent any time, however, the processing based on consent that already took place remains lawful.[32] Such a withdrawal should be as easy, as giving the consent. Moreover, the assessment of whether consent is freely given takes into account, among others, if 'the performance of a contract, including the provision of a service, is conditional on consent to the processing of personal data that is not necessary for the performance of that contract'.[33]

The elements of this definition and conditions that are important for shaping the regulatory framework governing data sharing include the definition of purposes for which the consent can be given. On the one hand, the provision of Article 6(1)(a) refers to 'one or more specific purposes', which suggest the possibility of asking for consent for data sharing. The use of this interpretation can be illustrated with the boxes that ask for the data subject's permission to share his or her data with third-parties.[34] On the other hand, the consent which does not fulfil the conditions

29 *See* Thomas Tombal, 'GDPR As Shield to a Data Sharing Remedy' (Accepted paper for the CPDP 2020 and ASCOLA 2020 Conferences, 2020) 10. Available at: https://ssrn.com/abstract=3516718.

30 Article 6(1)(a), GDPR. For a complex, though published in 2013, monograph on the concept of consent, *see* Eleni Kosta, *Consent in European Data Protection Law* (vol 3, Nijhoff Studies in EU Law, Leiden, Martinus Nijhoff Publishers 2013).

31 Article 4(11), GDPR.

32 Article 7(3), GDPR.

33 Article 7(4), GDPR.

34 Which can be perceived as a sign of over-using the notice-and-consent model by the providers of services in digital environment. For a criticism of the dominance of this approach, *see* Alessandro Mantelero, 'The Future of Consumer Data Protection in the E.U. Re-Thinking the "Notice and Consent" Paradigm in the New Era of Predictive Analytics' (2014) 30(6) Computer Law & Security Review 643–60 https://doi.org/10.1016/j.clsr.2014.09.004, accessed 21 February 2025; Fred H Cate and Viktor Mayer-Schönberger, 'Notice and Consent in a World of Big Data' (2013) 3(2) International Data Privacy Law 67–73 https://doi.org/10.1093/idpl/ipt005, accessed 21 February 2025.

of being, among others, freely given, specific and informed, cannot be considered lawful. Thus, the question appears, whether the general consent for sharing data with third-parties is specific and informed enough, to fulfil these conditions.

Firstly, the granularity of consent leads to the requirement of allowing the data subject to consent separately to various purposes of processing, and sharing data with other parties should be enumerated as such a separate purpose for which the consent is necessary. Moreover, in order for the consent to be informed, 'if the data is to be transferred to or processed by other controllers who wish to rely on the original consent, these organisations should all be named'.[35]

Secondly, the EDPB's guidelines in this regard refer to the above-mentioned provision on conditionality of consent. The document presents an example of a bank asking customers to consent for the third-parties' use of their payment details for marketing purposes. According to the guidelines, '[i]f the customer's refusal to consent to this processing purpose would lead to the denial of banking services, closure of the bank account, or, depending on the case, an increase of the fee, consent cannot be freely given',[36] and, therefore, it cannot be considered as lawful.

Thirdly, there are situations in which some characteristics of processing lead to consent not being an appropriate legal basis for this type of processing. The examples include an imbalance of power between data subject and controller (public authorities, employer) that results in the consent not being freely given.[37] In such cases other legal bases for processing should be considered as more adequate.

Fourthly, the important question is whether the possibility of withdrawing the consent for processing is maintained despite the fact that data has been shared with a third-party. The controller needs to ensure that there is no processing of personal data after the withdrawal of consent: both by the controller, and by the third parties that data were shared with. This shows that while it is possible to use consent as a legal basis for data sharing, there are multiply conditions that need to be fulfilled in such a case.[38]

35 European Data Protection Board, 'Guidelines 05/2020 on Consent under Regulation 2016/679' (Version 1.1, 4 May 2020) 16, para 65. Available at: https://edpb.europa.eu/sites/default/files/files/file1/edpb_guidelines_202005_consent_en.pdf.

36 European Data Protection Board, 'Guidelines 05/2020 on Consent under Regulation 2016/679' 11, para 33.

37 European Data Protection Board, 'Guidelines 05/2020 on Consent under Regulation 2016/679' 8–9, paras 16–24.

38 It must be noted that consent as the key mechanism on which data protection law is based is criticised as a facilitator of widespread use of personal data. For such a critical approach to consent, *see*, e.g., Eoin Carolan, 'The Continuing Problems with Online Consent under the EU's Emerging Data Protection Principles' (2016) 32(3) Computer Law & Security Review 462–73 https://doi.org/10.1016/j.clsr.2016.02.004, accessed 21 February 2025.

The example of the decision which concerned the use of consent as a legal basis for data sharing is the decision issued by the Norwegian DPA in the case of dating app Grindr.[39] Grindr's privacy policy did not allow data subjects to consent to various purposes of processing separately. As a result, it was not possible for the users not to agree to data sharing which took place between Grindr and various companies operating in the area of advertisement and marketing, if they wanted to be able to use the app. Moreover, Grindr did not fulfil the conditions to invoke any of the exceptions under which it is legal to process special categories of data (*see* section 3.4 below) in regard to the fact that such data was shared with its advertising partners.

Other legal grounds for processing are defined in relation to the purpose of processing ('processing is necessary for...', 'processing is necessary in order to...'). This limits the scope of types of processing allowed on their basis. However, it is possible that data sharing would result from, e.g., a contract between data controller and data subject [Article 6(1)(b)], legal obligations of the controller [Article 6(1)(c)], necessity to protect vital interests of the data subject or another natural person [Article 6(1)(d)] or performance of a task carried out in the public interest or in the exercise of official authority vested in the controller [Article 6(1)(e)] or for the purposes the legitimate interests pursued by the controller or by a third party [Article 6(1)(f)].

Each of these legal bases for processing has its own specificity,[40] and, therefore, may be perceived as a legal basis for particular types of data sharing. For example, the legal obligation of the controller can lead to the necessity of providing public authorities with certain types of data which constitutes a type of business-to-government data transfer. Contractual basis for data processing may involve the necessity to share data with another company, which constitutes business-to-business data sharing. The main advantage of the legal grounds for processing other than consent is that they cannot be revoked by the data subject.[41] Thus, the data controller is not dependent on the data subject's decision in this regard. On the other hand, the main principle of data processing to be considered lawful is its necessity. The criterion that is vital in this regard is the purpose of the processing: the processing should be limited to what is necessary to achieve its purpose. Such an approach

39 Datatilsynet, *Administrative fine – Grindr LLC* (20/02136-18, 13 December 2021) https://www.datatilsynet.no/contentassets/8ad827efefcb489ab1c7ba129609edb5/administrative-fine---grindr-llc.pdf.

40 *See* Waltraut Kotschy, 'Article 6 Lawfulness of Processing' 330–339.

41 However, if the processing is based on the performance of a task carried out in the public interest or in the exercise of official authority vested in the controller or for the purposes of the legitimate interests pursued by the controller or by a third party, the data subject may object to the processing and the effect of such objection may be similar to the withdrawal of the consent – *see* Waltraut Kotschy, 'Article 6 Lawfulness of Processing' 339.

goes against what can be understood as a basic rationale for data sharing, meaning, allowing the use of datasets by another entity for the purposes different to the ones that data were initially collected for.

> The example of an attempt of data collection and sharing operation which was supposed to be based on legal obligations of the controller was the project of the Polish Chief Country's Surveyor (CCS). The CCS made available information from various local land registers. Registers included vast amounts of personal data. In the decision issued by the Polish DPA,[42] the sharing was deemed as infringing the GDPR's Article 6 and 5 (principle of lawfulness), as such a project must be prescribed by law.

3.3.2 Legal Basis for Compatible Further Processing and Data Sharing

What the GDPR's provisions address, is the possibility of compatible further processing, regulated in Article 6(4). This type of processing concerns situations in which even though a new purpose of processing is different than the initial one, it remains compatible with the initial one and, therefore, it can be based on the initial legal basis. Article 6(4) excludes from its scope processing based on consent or on the law of the EU or Member States which constitutes restrictions of the data subject rights or other provisions on data protection which aim to safeguard the objectives enumerated in Article 23(1), e.g., national and public security, defence. Recital 50 states that in such cases 'the controller should be allowed to further process the personal data irrespective of the compatibility of the purposes', however, the application of the principles concerning the processing and the compliance with the rights of the data subject need to be ensured.

In reference to other legal grounds for processing, recital 50 specifies that if the processing is necessary for the performance of a task carried out in the public interest or in the exercise of official authority vested in the controller, EU or domestic law may determine and specify the tasks and purposes for which the further processing should be regarded as compatible and lawful, and that the legal basis provided by EU or domestic law for the processing of personal data may also provide a legal basis for further processing. The recital also refers to further processing for archiving purposes in the public interest, scientific or historical research purposes and statistical purposes.[43] All of them, according to the interpretation suggested by recital 50, should be 'considered to be compatible lawful processing operations'.

42 Polish DPA, 'Decision' (DKN.5112.13.2020, 24 August 2020). Available at: https://uodo.gov.pl/decyzje/DKN.5112.13.2020.

43 For more on this type of processing, *see* section 3.3 in this chapter.

This way of presenting these purposes as 'compatible' is intriguing, as it diverges from what is presented as compatible in the light of Article 6(4), which includes an open catalogue of factors that need to be taken into account when assessing the compatibility of further processing with the initial one. Among them, is the necessity to analyse the link between the purposes and the context of data collection and its further processing, the nature of the processed data (e.g., whether the processing concerns special categories of personal data), as well as the existence of appropriate safeguards. As noted by Kotschy:

> Compatibility of purposes exists also where the new purpose is different but correlates to the initial purpose in the sense that these purposes usually are pursued 'together' in close vicinity in a timely as well as a contextual sense, or that the further purpose is the logical consequence of the initial purpose.[44]

The assessment of this compatibility, as stated in recital 50, includes reference to the 'reasonable expectation of data subject' regarding the context in which data were collected and the relationship between the controller and data subject.

3.3.3 Legal Basis for Processing by Businesses and by Government

The issue of the 'reasonable expectations of data subject' brings us to the question of diversifying between the legal bases and purposes of processing which concern sharing data by businesses and by government. This sub-section is an attempt to link the regulatory framework of the GDPR with the terminology used in the context of data sharing: on the one hand, the catalogue of legal bases for processing included in Article 6 of the GDPR, and, on the other hand, the categorisation of data sharing into business-to-business (B2B), business-to-government (B2G), government-to-business (G2B) and government-to-government (G2G).

The main criterion for assessing the possibility of sharing data in these various configurations should be the specific characteristics of each of the legal bases enumerated in Article 6. Thus, for B2B sharing the most suitable manner of fulfilling the obligations concerning lawful processing seems to be getting the consent of the data subject for the purpose of sharing his or her data. However, it has the disadvantage of the possibility that data subjects will withdraw their consent. Another possibility is – technically – referring to the legal basis foreseen for the processing necessary for the purposes of the legitimate interests pursued by the controller or by a third party. In this case, however, the interests of the controller may be overridden by the interests of data subjects and the protection of their fundamental rights.

The example of the national DPA concerning this problem is the decision of Agencia Española de Protección de Datos (AEPD) that found an infringement in

44 Waltraut Kotschy, 'Article 6 Lawfulness of Processing' 341.

using Article 6(1)(f) as a basis for using shared personal data by a company for the purpose of direct marketing.[45]

Next, B2B data sharing may result from the contract. Also in this case it is necessary to follow the principles of data protection law which require, among others, to limit the processing of personal data to what is necessary to achieve the given purpose.[46] The example of such misuse, is using personal data obtained on the basis of a consumer benefit program for the purpose of direct marketing.[47] On the other hand, the example of a situation in which sharing data with a third-party was considered lawful under Article 6(1)(b) and 6(1)(f), was the veterinarian providing details about his patients to the company collecting fees from the customers that did not pay for his services.[48]

It is also possible to base data sharing on the legal grounds necessary for compliance with a legal obligation to which the controller is subject. Law can oblige companies to share their data with other companies, however, personal data are rather treated with care in this regard. The examples include the provision of the Digital Markets Act (DMA) which specifies the conditions upon which personal data of the end users engaging with the products or services provided by business users could be shared with these business users or third-parties authorised by business users.[49] While DMA obliges gatekeepers to share certain types of data with business users, in the case of personal data there is a need for the data subject to consent to such data-sharing practice.

In terms of data sharing involving the government; grounds foreseen in the form of legal obligations of data controllers; processing which is necessary in order to protect the vital interests of the data subject or of another natural person; and data sharing resulting from the necessity to perform a task carried out in the public interest or in the exercise of official authority vested in the controller seems to be typically the most appropriate for these types of data sharing. On the level of the GDPR's provisions, the inclusion of the possibility of using data for archiving in public interest, scientific or historical research purposes, as well as statistical purposes shows that a certain level of data sharing is allowed by data protection

45 AEPD, *Decision in case AEPD PS-00508-2022*, https://www.aepd.es/es/documento/ps-00508-2022.pdf. For the note about the case, *see* Teresa López, *AEPD (Spain) - EXP202102778*. Available at: (gdprhub.eu), https://gdprhub.eu/index.php?title=AEPD_(Spain)_-_EXP202102778.

46 On principle of data protection law, *see* the next section.

47 *See* Datatilsynet, *Final Decision – Compliance Order and Reprimand* (20/02319-8, 11 November 2021) https://edpb.europa.eu/system/files/2022-02/no_2021-11_decisionpublic.pdf. For the note about the case, *see* Tore Anderson, *Datatilsynet (Norway) - 20/02319*. Available at:(gdprhub.eu), https://gdprhub.eu/index.php?title=Datatilsynet_(Norway)_-_20/02319

48 *See* VG Mainz on 20 February 2020 in Case 1K 467/19.MZ, ECLI:DE:VGMAINZ:2020:0220.1K467.19.00, https://www.landesrecht.rlp.de/bsrp/document/NJRE001418857. For the note about the case, *see*, n/a, *VG Mainz - 1 K 467/19.MZ*. Available at: (gdprhub.eu), https://gdprhub.eu/index.php?title=VG_Mainz_-_1_K_467/19.MZ.

49 Article 6(10), Regulation (EU) 2022/1925 of the European Parliament and of the Council of 14 September 2022 on contestable and fair markets in the digital sector and amending Directives (EU) 2019/1937 and (EU) 2020/1828 (Digital Markets Act) [2022] OJ L265/1.

law itself.[50] This example concerns practices that involve data repurposing, which means using it for another purpose than it was initially collected for, and recontextualisation, which describes using it in another context than it was initially collected for.[51] This shows that – from the perspective of data protection law – processing which is motivated by public interest can be more easily justified than processing which is strictly profit-driven. However, even in this case the preferred manner of processing personal data would be to use them in pseudonymised form.

3.3.4 Legal Basis for Processing of Special Categories of Data

One more nuance that needs to be considered regarding the legal basis for processing is the additional set of conditions that needs to be fulfilled when the processed data belong to the category of special categories of data. As mentioned above, for the processing of the special categories of data to be legal, it must belong to one of the exceptions foreseen in Article 9(2).[52]

One of the important differences regarding data sharing is the fact that – in relation to the processing of the special categories of data – the EU or the national laws of Member States can foresee the prohibition of giving the consent to the processing of this type of data [Article 9(2)(1)]. Another important issue is the fact that Article 9(2)(e) allows for processing that relates to personal data which are manifestly made public by the data subject. However, such a processing still needs to take place on one of the legal bases enumerated in Article 6. Thus, it is not legal in the light of the EU data protection law to, e.g., without any other legal basis, use for a purpose different than the initial one, information published by the data subject on the internet. Last but not least, in regard to the exceptions foreseen in Article 9(2) which refer to the processing regulated in EU or Member States' law, all the restrictions concerning the processing need to be followed.

3.4 Principles of the EU's Data Protection Law as Boundaries for Data Sharing

For the processing to be legal, not only does it have to be carried out in accordance with the legal bases enumerated in the GDPR's provisions, but it must also be in compliance with all the principles enshrined in the GDPR,[53] and guarantee all the

50 Article 89 and recitals 156–161, GDPR.

51 For the division of data use into the categories of data recycling, repurposing and recontextualisation, *see* Bart Custers and Helena Uršič, 'Big Data and Data Reuse: A Taxonomy of Data Reuse for Balancing Big Data Benefits and Personal Data Protection' (2016) 6(1) International Data Privacy Law 13 https://doi.org/10.1093/idpl/ipv028, accessed 21 February 2025.

52 As this section only sketches the selected elements of Article 9, which are of importance for the subject of data sharing, for a more detailed overview of the regulatory framework governing this issue, *see* Ludmila Georgieva and Christopher Kuner, 'Article 9 Processing of Special Categories of Personal Data' 9.

53 *See* Inge Graef, Thomas Tombal, and Alexandre de Streel, 'Limits and Enablers of Data Sharing. An Analytical Framework for EU Competition, Data Protection and Consumer Law' (TILEC Dis-

rights that are foreseen for data subjects. For this reason, this section of the chapter briefly characterises the impact that each of the data protection principles has on the possibilities of data sharing.

3.4.1 Lawfulness, Fairness and Transparency

The requirement that personal data must be processed lawfully, fairly and in a transparent manner in relation to the data subject is linked with the above-described necessity to base the processing on one of the legal grounds enumerated in Article 6 and the need to comply with all the obligations foreseen in the GDPR. For the processing to be fair,[54] data cannot be 'obtained nor otherwise processed through unfair means, by deception or without the data subject's knowledge'.[55] This could be interpreted as an indirect requirement of informing the data subject on any processing which is taking place as a result of data sharing (to ensure the data subject's knowledge on this processing). Moreover, the transparency of processing requires providing the data subject with information on data collection and processing, which strengthens the information obligation of the data controller. In the context of data sharing, the importance of informing the data subject about the purposes of processing and the recipients of data which is to be shared constitute types of information that need to be provided on the basis of provisions on information obligations (*see* section 5.2).

3.4.2 Purpose Limitation

According to purpose limitation it is not legal to process personal data without specific, explicit and legitimate purpose: 'Purpose limitation, in the sense of purpose specification, reflects the idea that data processing should be foreseeable for the data subject and should not go beyond the reasonable expectations of the person concerned'.[56] Article 5(1)(b) highlights that personal data cannot be further

---

cussion Paper no DP 2019-024, 2019) 30. Available at: https://doi.org/10.2139/ssrn.3494212. It is important to note that the history of the development of the catalogue of the principles of data protection involves the work of the Organisation of Economic Cooperation and Development (OECD), *see* OECD, *OECD Guidelines on the Protection of Privacy and Transborder Flows of Personal Data* (23 September 1980). Available at: https://www.refworld.org/docid/3dde56854.html; and the catalogue adopted in Article 5 of Convention 108.

54 For the analysis of fairness as data protection law principle, *see* Damian Clifford and Jef Ausloos, 'Data Protection and the Role of Fairness' (2018) 37 Yearbook of European Law 130–87 https://doi.org/10.1093/yel/yey004, accessed 21 February 2025.

55 Cécile de Terwangne, 'Article 5 Principles Relating to Processing of Personal Data', in Christopher Kuner et al. (eds), *The EU General Data Protection Regulation (GDPR): A Commentary* (Oxford University Press 2020) 314. Available at: https://doi.org/10.1093/oso/9780198826491.003.0034, accessed 21 February 2025.

56 Evelien Brouwer, 'Legality and Data Protection Law: The Forgotten Purpose of Purpose Limitation' in Leonard Besselink, Frans Pennings and Sacha Prechal (eds), *The Eclipse of the Legality Principle in the European Union* (Kluwer Law International 2011) 279.

processed in a way incompatible with the initial purpose with the exception of the above-mentioned list of purposes which are not considered as incompatible with the initial purposes.

Purpose limitation is one of the most important principles of data protection law, however, its meaning is still in the making, and, therefore, the character of its significance for data sharing. Nevertheless, it is one of the principles which is most often indicated as crucial for establishing the scope of data sharing allowed under GDPR's regulatory framework. For example, Tal Zarsky focuses on purpose limitation as one of the principles that create obstacles for the development of big data-driven solutions,[57] similarly to Inge Graef, Thomas Tombal and Alexandre de Streel, who note that purpose limitation – next to data minimisation – are data protection law principles limiting the potential of data sharing.[58] However, as shows Evelien Brouwer, the EU's policies and legislation allow for 'function creep' understood as undermining 'the meaning of purpose limitation, by providing vague definitions on the intended use of personal information, the establishment of multifunctional databases, and by extending the use of existing databases for other purposes'.[59] This 'function creep' is contrary to the interpretation of the purpose limitation principle by the CJEU and the European Court of Human Rights (ECtHR), which emphasises its 'functions of legitimacy, attribution, and regulation'.[60]

3.4.3 Data Minimisation

Data minimisation, understood as the processing being 'adequate, relevant and limited to what is necessary in relation to the purposes for which they are processed',[61] is yet another principle that is often presented as an obstacle for data sharing and its use for the purposes related to big data analysis.[62] The principle compliments the principle of purpose limitation: 'even if the act of data sharing complies with the purpose limitation principle, the categories and amount of data that can be shared

57 *See* Tal Z Zarsky, 'Incompatible: The GDPR in the Age of Big Data' (2017) 47(4(2)) Seton Hall Law Review 1005–1009, https://scholarship.shu.edu/shlr/vol47/iss4/2/, accessed 21 February 2025. For another analysis on this topic, *see* Nikolaus Forgó, Stefanie Hänold, and Benjamin Schütze, 'The Principle of Purpose Limitation and Big Data' in Marcelo Corrales, Mark Fenwick, and Nikolaus Forgó (eds), *New Technology, Big Data and the Law* (Singapore, Springer Singapore 2017) 17–42. Available at: https://doi.org/10.1007/978-981-10-5038-1_2.

58 Inge Graef, Thomas Tombal, and Alexandre de Streel, 'Limits and Enablers of Data Sharing. An Analytical Framework for EU Competition, Data Protection and Consumer Law' 11–12.

59 Evelien Brouwer, 'Legality and Data Protection Law: The Forgotten Purpose of Purpose Limitation' in Leonard Besselink, Frans Pennings and Sacha Prechal (eds) 293.

60 Evelien Brouwer, 'Legality and Data Protection Law: The Forgotten Purpose of Purpose Limitation' in Leonard Besselink, Frans Pennings and Sacha Prechal (eds) 293.

61 Article 5(1)(c), GDPR.

62 *See* Inge Graef, Thomas Tombal, and Alexandre de Streel, 'Limits and Enablers of Data Sharing. An Analytical Framework for EU Competition, Data Protection and Consumer Law' 11–12; and Tal Z Zarsky, 'Incompatible: The GDPR in the Age of Big Data' (2017) 47(4(2)) Seton Hall Law Review 1009–1011.

should nevertheless be limited to what is necessary to meet this purpose'.[63] Thus, even if data sharing is taking place in accordance with the GDPR's provisions, it is necessary to ensure that it concerns only these types of data and these types of operations performed on them, which are necessary from the perspective of the purposes which they serve.

> An example of the decision which concerns the compliance of data sharing with the data minimisation principle is the decision issued by the Hellenic DPA in the case concerning processing and sharing of health data.[64] Inter-municipal Water Supply – Sewerage Company X (DEYA X) shared health data of its employee both within the company and with other entities. Such a behaviour was assessed as exceeding what is allowed under the data minimisation principle.

3.4.4 Accuracy

The principle of accuracy concerns the quality of data that may be used for processing. By itself, it does not limit the possibilities of sharing data. However, it should be interpreted as a requirement – also on the side of data recipient – to ensure that data are kept up to date and in the case of their inaccuracy, they are 'erased or rectified without delay'.[65]

3.4.5 Storage Limitation

The principle of storage limitation sets certain standards concerning the manner in which personal data can be processed: they are supposed to be kept in a form that allows for identification of an individual for the shortest possible time in the light of the purpose of the processing. This means that if pseudonymised or anonymised data allow for achieving the purpose of processing, they should be chosen over the format which includes identifiable data. An exception directly mentioned in Article 5(1)(e), is the processing for aims linked to public interest, research and statistical purposes, which permit for longer storage of personal data. However, the safeguard foreseen in and implemented on the basis of Article 89(1) must be used.

63 Inge Graef, Thomas Tombal, and Alexandre de Streel, 'Limits and Enablers of Data Sharing. An Analytical Framework for EU Competition, Data Protection and Consumer Law' 11.

64 Hellenic DPA, 'Penalty for Violation of the Minimization Principle' (Decision no 31, 11 October 2023). Available at: https://www.dpa.gr/el/enimerwtiko/prakseisArxis/prostimo-gia-parabiasi-tis-arhis-tis-elahistopoiisis

65 Article 5(1)(d), GDPR.

3.4.6 Integrity and Confidentiality

Similarly to the principle of data accuracy, the principle of integrity and confidentiality concerns the conditions on which personal data should be processed. It requires using appropriate security measures, which protect data against unauthorised or unlawful processing or its loss, destruction or damage.

3.4.7 Data Protection by Design and by Default

Even though data protection by design and data protection by default are included in the chapter of the GDPR entitled 'Controller and processor', they can be approached as yet two more general rules which should be taken into account 'at the time of the determination of the means for processing and at the time of the processing itself'.[66] As the content of Article 25 refers to the principles of data protection, such as data minimisation and the content of purpose limitation, data protection by design and by default may be perceived as rules that specify measures that should be taken in order to follow the general principles of the GDPR.

What is helpful in this regard are the measures provided as the examples of means that could be used to ensure data protection by design and by default, enumerated in recital 78:

> minimising the processing of personal data, pseudonymising personal data as soon as possible, transparency with regard to the functions and processing of personal data, enabling the data subject to monitor the data processing, enabling the controller to create and improve security features.

These measures should cover both the technical and organisational aspects of processing.

3.4.8 Accountability

The last principle included in Article 5(2) is the principle of accountability. It states that the controller shall be responsible for, and be able to demonstrate compliance with the principles enshrined in Article 5(1). This brings us to more general and highly important issue of the necessity to translate data-sharing scenarios into the nomenclature of data protection law concerning the actors responsible for ensuring compliance with data protection law.

3.4.8.1 *Who Is Responsible for the Compliance with Data Protection Principles in the Context of Data Sharing?*

According to Article 4(7) of the GDPR, controller means 'the natural or legal person, public authority, agency or other body which, alone or jointly with others,

66 Article 25(1), GDPR.

determines the purposes and means of the processing of personal data'. Among the criteria present in this provision, the reasons for processing (why the processing is taking place), and the measures used for the processing (how it is taking place), 'the decisive element for attaining controller status is determination of purposes',[67] are of huge importance for establishing the responsibility for following data protection rules in the context of data sharing. GDPR stipulates that the controllership may be joint, when two or more parties decide upon the aims and measures used for the processing.

Next to the controller, the GDPR also defines the processor, who is 'a natural or legal person, public authority, agency or other body which processes personal data on behalf of the controller' [Article 4(8)]. The main characteristic of the role of the processor is dependency on the purposes of the processing as defined by the controller:

> When a processor undertakes processing of personal data outside the controller's dictates, and in so doing determines the purposes and means of that processing, it ceases to be a processor and assumes the role of controller in respect of that processing.[68]

Moreover, the GDPR also refers to the recipient, who is 'a natural or legal person, public authority, agency or another body, to which the personal data are disclosed, whether a third party or not' [Article 4(9)] and the third party, understood as 'a natural or legal person, public authority, agency or body other than the data subject, controller, processor and persons who, under the direct authority of the controller or processor, are authorized to process personal data' [Article 4(10)].

The criteria used for defining these categories, when linked to the situations of data sharing, show that the main factor that should be taken into consideration when establishing the responsibility of the entities taking part in data processing is who decides upon the purposes and means of processing. When such a decision is made by a given enterprise, this enterprise should be perceived as the controller, and it is responsible for complying with all the obligations foreseen for the controllers. When such a decision is made by another enterprise, the relevant categories would be a processor or a third-party, as enterprises that performs the processing do so 'on behalf of' the controller. When perceived from such a perspective, the recipient can be assigned either to the category of controllers, if – after receiving

67 Lee A Bygrave and Luca Tosoni, 'Article 4(7). Controller' in Christopher Kuner et al. (eds), *The EU General Data Protection Regulation (GDPR): A Commentary* (Oxford University Press 2020) 145. Available at: https://doi.org/10.1093/oso/9780198826491.003.0013. *See* also European Data Protection Supervisor, 'EDPS Guidelines on the Concepts of Controller, Processor and Joint Controllership under Regulation (EU) 2018/1725' (7 November 2019) 9–10. Available at: https://edps.europa.eu/sites/default/files/publication/19-11-07_edps_guidelines_on_controller_processor_and_jc_reg_2018_1725_en.pdf

68 Lee A Bygrave and Luca Tosoni, 'Article 4(8). Processor' in Christopher Kuner et al. (eds), *The EU General Data Protection Regulation (GDPR): A Commentary* (Oxford University Press 2020) 160. Available at: https://doi.org/10.1093/oso/9780198826491.003.0014

personal data – it determines the purposes and means of processing,[69] or a processor or a third-party, when the purposes and means of processing are defined by another body.

3.4.8.2 Regulatory Measures Supporting Accountability: Data Protection Impact Assessments in the Context of Data Sharing

One of the tools which can be perceived as supporting accountability of data controllers, is data protection impact assessment (DPIA).[70] It constitutes a novelty in comparison to DPD[71] and its goal is to ensure that in case of processing that is likely to result in a high risk to the rights and freedoms of natural persons, *ex ante* analysis of these risks and measures that should be taken to mitigate them will be performed.

Despite the fact that the catalogue of three salutations directly indicated in Article 35(3) as requiring carrying out DPIA does not include data sharing, it is still possible that such assessment would be necessary. This may result from the fact that the operations involve, e.g., processing special categories of data on a large scale [Article 35(3)(b)]. Another example of a situation in which DPIA would be necessary, is, e.g., when the context or purposes of the processing indicate the existence of high risk to the rights and freedoms of natural persons.

3.5 Data Subjects' Rights and Data Sharing

Next to all the conditions for data sharing that result from the regulatory framework described above, it is also necessary to ensure that the relevant rights of data subjects will be respected. In the context of the potential of data protection law for data sharing often the right to data portability is mentioned.[72] However, for providing an overview of the conditions that determine the possibilities to share data which are established by data protection regulatory framework, it is necessary to take a broader perspective and include the analysis of more of data subjects' rights.

The importance of data subject rights for establishing the limits of data sharing grows from the concepts which lay foundations for data protection law: informational self-determination (or autonomy) of the data subject. Information self-determination, understood as 'every individual's right and opportunity to

69 Or as a joint controller.

70 For DPIA as a tool supporting accountability, *see* Katerina Demetzou, 'Data Protection Impact Assessment: A Tool for Accountability and the Unclarified Concept of "High Risk" in the General Data Protection Regulation' (2019) 35(6) Computer Law & Security Review 105342 https://doi.org/10.1016/j.clsr.2019.105342, accessed 21 February 2025.

71 Although, not in data protection law in general, *see* Eleni Kosta, 'Article 35 Data Protection Impact Assessment' in Christopher Kuner et al. (eds), *The EU General Data Protection Regulation (GDPR): A Commentary* (Oxford University Press 2020), 668. Available at: https://doi.org/10.1093/oso/9780198826491.003.0072

72 *See*, e.g., Bertin Martens, Alexandre de Streel, Inge Graef, Thomas Tombal and Néstor Duch-Brown, 'Business to Business Data Sharing: An Economic and Legal Analysis' (European Commission, JRC121366, Seville, 2020).

determine which information about him- or herself is disclosed to others and for what purposes such information may be used',[73] translates into a number of rights concerning the information that the data subject should be provided with before or when the processing is taking place. While such an approach – based on notices and consents to processing – is criticised in the literature as not adequate for addressing the challenges related to the use of personal data in a digital environment,[74] it nonetheless establishes requirements concerning data sharing, e.g., concerning information that should be provided to the data subject, the rights to rectification or erasure of personal data, as well as the right to data portability, that enables the data subject – to a certain extent – to control the way in which their data is shared.

3.5.1 Information on Recipients of Personal Data and on Further Processing

The first group of provisions in the GDPR's chapter concerning the data subject's rights that influences the way that data can be shared are the provisions on information which has to be provided to data subjects (Article 13 and 14) and the right to access (Article 15). These provisions may be linked to the principle of transparency, as well as fairness, which belong to the principles governing the EU's data protection law (*see* above):

> Informing the data subject of the details of the processing activity can be construed as one of the conditions of fair processing, and is certainly a *sine qua non* for transparency. While transparency can be achieved in several ways, its most important building block is the information given to the data subject at the beginning of the processing activity, or before the processing takes place (the 'data protection notice' or the 'privacy notice'), which should then be made easily accessible throughout the processing operation.[75]

To achieve this prerequisite of transparency, GDPR foresees a number of information obligations on the side of the controller: Article 13 refers to the situation in which personal data relating to a data subject are collected from the data subject; Article 14 to the situation where personal data have not been obtained from the data

73 Florent Thouvenin, 'Informational Self-Determination: A Convincing Rationale for Data Protection Law?' (2021) 12(4) JIPITEC 248 https://www.jipitec.eu/jipitec/article/view/323, accessed 21 February 2025, and the literature cited there.

74 *See*, e.g., Florent Thouvenin, 'Informational Self-Determination: A Convincing Rationale for Data Protection Law?'; Brendan Van Alsenoy, Eleni Kosta, and Jos Dumortier, 'Privacy Notices versus Informational Self-Determination: Minding the Gap' (2014) 28(2) International Review of Law, Computers & Technology 185–203 https://doi.org/10.1080/13600869.2013.812594, accessed 21 February 2025; Alessandro Mantelero, 'The Future of Consumer Data Protection in the E.U. Re-Thinking the "Notice and Consent" Paradigm in the New Era of Predictive Analytics'; Fred H Cate and Viktor Mayer-Schönberger, 'Notice and Consent in a World of Big Data'.

75 Gabriela Zanfir-Fortuna, 'Article 13 Information to Be Provided Where Personal Data Are Collected from the Data Subject' in Christopher Kuner et al. (eds), *The EU General Data Protection Regulation (GDPR): A Commentary* (Oxford University Press 2020) 415. Available at: https://doi.org/10.1093/oso/9780198826491.003.0044

subject. Article 15 approaches this issue from a different perspective, at it foresees the right of the data subject to obtain from the controller confirmation as to whether or not personal data concerning him or her are being processed, and, if the processing is taking place, to access the personal data and the information which include information important from the point of view of data sharing.[76]

All of these articles, in the catalogue of information that needs to be provided to the data subject, include the purposes of data processing.[77] Additionally, Article 13(1)(d) and Article 14(2)(b) refer also to the necessity of providing the data subject with an information on the legitimate interests pursued by the controller or by a third party if the processing is based on Article 6(1)(f). Thus, if the controller attempts to use this legal basis for processing for the purposes of data sharing, such an information needs to be provided to the data subject. Moreover, Article 13 in paragraph three and Article 14 in paragraph four oblige the controller, if they intend to further process the personal data for a purpose other than that for which the personal data were collected, to 'provide the data subject prior to that further processing with information on that other purpose and with any relevant further information as referred to in paragraph 2'. In the case of Article 14, the catalogue of these types of information includes information on 'from which source the personal data originate, and if applicable, whether it came from publicly accessible sources' [Article 14(2)(f)].

This shows that the data subject should be informed about data-sharing operations which the controller plans to pursue. Moreover, all three provisions include the recipients or categories of recipients of the personal data among the types of information that need to be provided to the data subject.[78] In this regard Article 15 is phrased differently than Article 12 and 13, as it refers to information on 'the recipients or categories of recipient to whom the personal data have been or will be disclosed, in particular recipients in third countries or international organisations'. This provision was interpreted by the CJEU, as including:

> an obligation on the part of the controller to provide the data subject with the actual identity of those recipients, unless it is impossible to identify those recipients or the controller demonstrates that the data subject's requests for access are manifestly unfounded or excessive within the meaning of Article 12(5) of Regulation 2016/679, in which cases the controller may indicate to the data subject only the categories of recipient in question.[79]

This shows that information provided to the data subject should be very detailed and the recipients of data should be indicated with a high level of precision. Moreover,

76 It is worth noticing that right of access by the data subject is included in Article 7 of the Charter, which states that: 'Everyone has the right of access to data which has been collected concerning him or her, and the right to have it rectified'.

77 Articles 13(1)(c), 14(1)(c) and 15(1)(a), GDPR.

78 Articles 13(1)(e), 14(1)(e) and 15(1)(c), GDPR.

79 Judgment of the Court of 12 January 2023 in Case C-154/21, *RW v Österreichische Post AG* [2023] ECLI:EU:C:2023:3, thesis.

the CJEU in this case underscores the link of the right to access to the principle of transparency as well as its importance for the enforcement of other rights foreseen in the GDPR.[80]

The exemption, which is important in the context of data sharing, is foreseen in Article 14(5)(b), and concerns the situations in which providing the data subject with information enumerated in this article 'proves impossible or would involve a disproportionate effort'. As the examples of such a scenario, the archiving purposes in the public interest, scientific or historical research purposes or statistical purposes are named. However, even in such a case, it is necessary to take appropriate measures to protect data subjects' rights.

3.5.2 Rights to Rectification, Erasure, Restriction and Objection to Processing

While next to data portability only the right to be forgotten, as the right to erasure is usually called, is sometimes mentioned in the context of data sharing,[81] I argue that the catalogue of the data subject's rights that may have an impact on the possible scope and character of data sharing is broader. Right to rectification (Article 16), right to restriction (Article 18) and right to object to processing (Article 21) concern the possibility of the data subject to control the quality of data used for the processing, as well as the fact that the processing is taking place. Thus, if enforced, they also may result in the necessity to implement changes to data that were shared by the controller.

Right to rectification foresees the possibility to amend inaccurate personal data and the possibility to complete personal data which are used in the processing operations. Right to restriction of processing covers three types of situations concerning data subjects:

> when they have exercised the right to rectification and the right to object, to ensure that the processing of the personal data at stake is limited while the applicability of such rights is being confirmed; when the data processing is unlawful, but the data subject nevertheless prefers to prevent the erasure of the data; and when the data are no longer of use for the data controller (which means they could be deleted), but the data subject needs them for the establishment, exercise or defence of legal claims.[82]

80 *See* Judgment of the Court of 12 January 2023 in Case C-154/21, *RW v Österreichische Post AG* [2023] ECLI:EU:C:2023:3, para 42.

81 *See*, e.g., Bart Custers and Helena Uršič, 'Big Data and Data Reuse: A Taxonomy of Data Reuse for Balancing Big Data Benefits and Personal Data Protection' (2016) 6(1) International Data Privacy Law 14 https://doi.org/10.1093/idpl/ipv028, accessed 21 February 2025. The authors distinguish three major types of data reuse from a data subject's perspective, namely, data sharing or data disclosure, understood as allowing for use or reuse of personal data, data portability and the right to be forgotten.

82 Gloria González Fuster, 'Article 18 Right to Restriction of Processing' in Christopher Kuner et al. (eds), *The EU General Data Protection Regulation (GDPR): A Commentary* (Oxford University Press 2020) 486–87. Available at: https://doi.org/10.1093/oso/9780198826491.003.0050

Right to object to processing refers to the processing which is based either on the necessity for the performance of a task carried out in the public interest or in the exercise of official authority vested in the controller [Article 6(1)(e)] or on necessity for the purposes of the legitimate interests pursued by the controller or by a third party [Article 6(1)(f)]. The right to object should cover also profiling based on these legal grounds. Separately, Article 21(2) enumerates processing for direct marketing purposes as a situation in which the data subject should be able to object at any time to processing of their personal data. Additionally, right to object must be also guaranteed to data subjects when their personal data are processed for scientific or historical research purposes or statistical purposes [Article 6(5)]. These objections have to be based on grounds related to their particular situation. However, the necessity of the processing for the performance of a task carried out for reasons of public interest can overweigh the right to object.

In comparison, the catalogue of grounds on which is the request to erase personal data foreseen in Article 17 – which concerns right to erasure – is possible, is broader. The right to be forgotten is strongly linked with other rights of data subjects, as the obligation to erase data can result from, among others, objection to the processing[83] or withdrawal of the consent for the processing.[84] The request for the erasure also affects the processing which resulted from making personal data public, as the controller is obliged to inform controllers which are processing personal data that result from such disclosure.[85] However, the broad scope of the right to erasure is narrowed by the catalogue of exemptions included in Article 17(3). It includes processing for archiving purposes in the public interest, scientific or historical research purposes or statistical purposes in so far as the erasure 'is likely to render impossible or seriously impair the achievement of the objectives of that processing' [Article 17(3)(d)].

For the purposes of processing which includes data sharing, it must be noted that the controller is obliged to communicate any rectification or erasure of personal data or restriction of processing based on above-mentioned provisions to each recipient to whom the personal data have been disclosed.[86] This obligation includes an exemption concerning the situation in which such communication proves impossible or involves disproportionate effort. Thus, Article 19 strengthens the right that the data subject has regarding receiving information on the recipients of personal data by including a provision that obliged the controller to inform the data subject about the recipients involved in the processing upon the data subject's request.

The need to ensure the possibility of enforcement of these rights shows the limits that data protection law imposes on the possibilities of data sharing. There are some purposes that may be perceived as allowing for a greater level of flexibility

83 *See* Article 17(1)(c), GDPR.
84 *See* Article 17(1)(b), GDPR.
85 *See* Article 17(2), GDPR.
86 *See* Article 19, GDPR.

regarding the reuse of personal data – e.g., archiving purposes in the public interest, scientific or historical research purposes or statistical purposes. However, in strictly commercial context, the need to comply with data subjects' rights creates another layer of conditions that needs to be fulfilled in order to be able to lawfully share data.

3.5.3 Data Portability

Data portability is the most adequate tool for achieving the purposes related to data sharing among the provisions included in the GDPR. However, it approaches this issue from the perspective of the rights of data subjects. Thus, it should be perceived as a bottom-up approach, which focuses on ensuring the possibility for the data subject to, as it is defined in Article 20(1) of the GDPR:

> receive the personal data concerning him or her, which he or she has provided to a controller, in a structured, commonly used and machine-readable format and have the right to transmit those data to another controller without hindrance from the controller to which the personal data have been provided.

Right of data portability can be perceived as a more specialised form of the right to access one's data, complemented with foreseeing the purpose of transmitting data to another controller. This being a form of the right to access data is illustrated by the fact that it is only possible to invoke in relation to the data which concern the data subject requesting the access to them. Its specialised character is envisaged by the characteristics of the format in which data is to be received, namely, structured, commonly used and machine-readable.

The possibility to use this right is limited to situations in which the processing is based either on consent, or on contract, and which is carried out by automated means. Another limitation is imposed by Article 20(3), which states that the right to data portability does not apply to processing necessary for the performance of a task carried out in the public interest or in the exercise of official authority vested in the controller.

Even though the right to data portability is included in the catalogue of data subjects' rights, it can be approached as a solution which 'opens the door for a roundabout B2C2B way to achieve B2B data sharing in the case of personal data'.[87] In practice such a 'roundabout way' requires the user of the service to request their data from one controller either – if technically feasible – to share this data with another controller [on the basis of Article 20(2)], or to upload their data by themselves to another service provider. However, as noticed by, e.g., Inge Graef and Jens Prüfer,[88] such a solution is not enough if one considers the perspective which

87 Bertin Martens, Alexandre de Streel, Inge Graef, Thomas Tombal and Néstor Duch-Brown, 'Business to Business Data Sharing: An Economic and Legal Analysis' 66.

88 *See* Inge Graef and Jens Prüfer, 'Governance of Data Sharing: A Law & Economics Proposal' (2021) 50(9) Research Policy 104330, https://doi.org/10.1016/j.respol.2021.104330, accessed 21 February 2025.

is focused on data sharing and its potential, not on the informational autonomy of the data subject, which is in focus of the right to data portability guaranteed by the GDPR.[89]

3.6 Data Transfers and Their Role for Data Sharing

The last group of provisions which needs to be presented when analysing the regulatory framework governing data sharing in EU data protection law, are the provisions concerning international data transfers. Their importance for data sharing stems from the fact that in the case of sharing which involves processing data in the third country or by an international organisation, these specific conditions upon which such transfers are possible must be followed.[90]

3.6.1 International Data Transfers

GDPR foresees three mechanisms that can be used to ensure that data transfers would take place accordingly to data protection rules, as summarised by Laura Drechsler and Irene Kamara:

> The first tier of the regime has the concept of 'adequate level of protection' at heart, according to which the Commission adopts decisions on the level of adequacy of a third-non-EU-country ('adequacy decisions'). The second tier provides legal bases for data transfers subject to 'appropriate safeguards', whereby controllers and processors exporting personal provide guarantees for the processing conducted by controllers or processors in the third countries. Third, a list of 'derogations' is provided, which qualify transfers as lawful, when certain conditions prescribed in the relevant GDPR articles are met.[91]

89 This difference in perspectives that can be taken when analysing data portability is also visible in the negative reaction of the American scholars to such an idea as the right to data portability, *see* Laura Drechsler 'Practical challenges to the right to data portability in the collaborative economy' in *Collaborative Economy: Challenges and Opportunities* (Actas del 14º Congreso Internacional Internet, Derecho y Política. Universitat Oberta de Catalunya, Barcelona, 21–22 de junio de 2018, Huygens Editorial 2018) 219–235, at 227–228, 232.

90 For the example of the significance of international data transfers for digital environment, *see* the table which shows to which countries and for what purposes personal data is transferred by Netflix: https://help.netflix.com/legal/uk-eea-disclosure-and-international-transfers. Such transfers are necessary for ensuring the availability of certain indispensable elements of service (e.g., payment services), and for the purposes of which necessary character is much more debatable (e.g., digital advertising).

91 Laura Drechsler and Irene Kamara, 'Chapter 13: Essential Equivalence as a Benchmark for International Data Transfers after Schrems II' in Eleni Kosta, Ronald Leenes, and Irene Kamara (eds), *Research Handbook on EU Data Protection Law* (Cheltenham, UK, Edward Elgar Publishing 2022) 321. Available at: https://doi.org/10.4337/9781800371682.00022.

The three categories of measures which can be used for data transfers should be perceived as having a hierarchical order: the appropriate safeguards can be used in the absence of adequacy decisions, while derogations in the absence of appropriate safeguards. What needs to be highlighted is that each of these solutions needs to be used in the compliance with the general principles for transfers, thus, 'in order to ensure that the level of protection of natural persons guaranteed by this Regulation is not undermined'.[92]

3.6.1.1 Adequacy Decisions

Adequacy decisions, regulated in Article 45 of the GDPR, are based on the assessment of the adequacy of protection guaranteed by the third country.[93] The Commission conducts an analysis of the selected aspects of the third country's legal system, e.g., the rule of law and respect for human rights and fundamental freedoms. In particular, the legislation relevant for data protection is scrutinised, including the presence of 'effective and enforceable data subject rights and effective administrative and judicial redress for the data subjects whose personal data are being transferred'.[94] In the presence of adequacy decisions, data transfers between the EU and the third country are considered in accordance with the GDPR.

An example of an adequacy decision was Safe Harbour:[95] a decision which established the rules allowing the American companies to self-certificate as complying with the adequate standards of data protection. The decision was annulled by the CJEU in a processing initiated by Max Schrems, an Austrian privacy activist (Schrems I[96]). In Schrems I the CJEU stated, among others, that the decision did not foresee the judicial remedy for the individuals whose data protection rights would be infringed. Thus, it was not compliant with the EU's approach to the fundamental rights. The Commission adopted the second adequacy decision, called Privacy Shield,[97] which was also annulled by the CJEU in another case initiated

92 Article 44, GDPR.

93 To be precise, Article 45 mentions 'the third country, a territory or one or more specified sectors within that third country, or the international organisation', however, so far the decisions have been issued in the case of Andorra, Argentina, Canada (commercial organisations), Faroe Islands, Guernsey, Israel, Isle of Man, Japan, Jersey, New Zealand, Republic of Korea, Switzerland, the United Kingdom under the GDPR and the LED and Uruguay (*see*, European Commission, 'Adequacy Decisions' https://commission.europa.eu/law/law-topic/data-protection/international-dimension-data-protection/adequacy-decisions_en).

94 Article 45(2)(a), GDPR.

95 2000/520/EC: Commission Decision of 26 July 2000 pursuant to Directive 95/46/EC of the European Parliament and of the Council on the adequacy of the protection provided by the safe harbour privacy principles and related frequently asked questions issued by the US Department of Commerce (notified under document number C(2000) 2441) [2000] OJ L215/7.

96 Judgment of the Court of 6 October 2015 in Case C-362/14, *Maximillian Schrems v Data Protection Commissioner* [2015] ECLI:EU:C:2015:650.

97 Commission Implementing Decision (EU) 2016/1250 of 12 July 2016 pursuant to Directive 95/46/EC of the European Parliament and of the Council on the adequacy of the protection provided by the EU-U.S. Privacy Shield (notified under document C(2016) 4176) [2016] OJ L207/1.

by Schrems (Schrems II[98]) on a very similar basis. In 2023, the new decision was adopted, EU-US Data Privacy Framework.[99]

One of the changes implemented due to the adoption of the decision is the establishment of the Data Protection Review Court which has the right to order the deletion of data if they were processed in the manner infringing the EU-US Data Privacy Framework. The decision also includes solutions concerning data sharing. As the decision states:

> The level of protection afforded to personal data transferred from the Union to organisations in the United States must not be undermined by the further transfer of such data to a recipient in the United States or another third country.[100]

This translates into an obligation of informing data subjects about the onward transfer and allowing them to opt out, and, in the case of sensitive data, providing consent for such a transfer (opt-in mechanism). Moreover, the decision also refers to the rules on the further use of data collected by federal criminal law enforcement authorities (in section 3.1.1.2) and the further use of the information collected by the intelligence services (in section 3.2.1.3).

3.6.1.2 Appropriate Safeguards

Under the term appropriate safeguards, the GDPR's Article 46(2) enumerates several measures that can be used as legal basis for data transfers.[101] They can be used for ensuring data transfers' lawfulness, however, under the condition that 'enforceable data subject rights and effective legal remedies for data subjects are available'.[102]

The most commonly used[103] among appropriate safeguards are standard data protection clauses (standard contractual clauses – SCC). Adopted by the Commission,

98 Judgment of the Court of 16 July 2020 in Case C-311/18, *Data Protection Commissioner v Facebook Ireland Limited and Maximillian Schrems* [2020] ECLI:EU:C:2020:559.

99 Commission Implementing Decision EU 2023/1795 of 10 July 2023 pursuant to Regulation (EU) 2016/679 of the European Parliament and of the Council on the adequate level of protection of personal data under the EU-US Data Privacy Framework (notified under document C(2023)4745) [2023] OJ L231/118.

100 Commission Implementing Decision EU 2023/1795 of 10 July 2023 pursuant to Regulation (EU) 2016/679 of the European Parliament and of the Council on the adequate level of protection of personal data under the EU-US Data Privacy Framework (notified under document C(2023)4745) [2023] OJ L231/118 para 37.

101 For the commentary on Article 46, *see* Christopher Kuner, 'Article 46 Transfers Subject to Appropriate Safeguards' in Christopher Kuner et al. (eds), *The EU General Data Protection Regulation (GDPR): A Commentary* (Oxford University Press 2020). Available at: https://doi.org/10.1093/oso/9780198826491.003.0086

102 Article 46(1), GDPR.

103 'In practice, the most widely used appropriate safeguards mechanisms are SCCs, which are model contracts, drafted by the Commission, concluded between the EU exporter and importer'. – Laura

they are a template for the contract that the data importer and exporter can conclude in order to establish the conditions upon which the transfers would take place.[104] The possibility of using SCC seems to be open for all types of entities, as they are defined in the Commission's decision as 'the natural or legal person(s), public authority/ies, agency/ies or other body/ies (hereinafter "entity/ies") transferring the personal data'.[105] Thus, e.g., public institutions and companies can use SCC as legal basis for data transfers.

However, in the context of G2G data transfers more adequate solutions could be the adoption of a legally binding and enforceable instrument between public authorities or bodies, as such a measure is foreseen in Article 46(2)(a) of the GDPR. On the other hand, data sharing which takes place among the members of the group of undertakings, or group of enterprises engaged in a joint economic activity can be based on binding corporate rules (BCR), thus, SCC may also not be the most effective mechanisms to be used for data transfer. Moreover, Article 46(2)(e) and 46(2)(f) foresee the possibility to use approved codes of conduct and certification mechanisms, together with binding and enforceable commitments of the controller or processor in the third country to apply the appropriate safeguards, including as regards data subjects' rights. This shows that the catalogue of appropriate safeguards guarantees a certain level of flexibility to data controllers, who can select the mechanisms they use for data transfers.

3.6.1.3 Derogations

Finally, the GDPR allows for data transfers to take place in the absence of adequacy decisions or appropriate safeguards, if one of the foreseen derogations is taking place. The catalogue of derogations to a certain extent resembles the catalogue of the legal basis for lawful processing, however, they are completed with certain requirements. For example, it is possible to conduct data transfer on the basis of explicit consent of the data subject, if they are informed of the possible risks of such transfers for the data subject due to the absence of an adequacy decision and appropriate safeguards.[106] For data sharing, important elements of this catalogue are also transfers necessary for the performance of a contract between the data subject and the controller or the implementation of pre-contractual measures taken at the data subject's request[107] and transfers necessary for the conclusion or performance of a contract concluded in the interest of the data subject between the

Drechsler and Irene Kamara, 'Chapter 13: Essential Equivalence as a Benchmark for International Data Transfers after Schrems II' 323.

104 Commission Implementing Decision (EU) 2021/914 of 4 June 2021 on standard contractual clauses for the transfer of personal data to third countries pursuant to Regulation (EU) 2016/679 of the European Parliament and of the Council [2021] OJ L199/31.

105 Annex, Section 1, Clause 1(b)(i), Commission Implementing Decision (EU) 2021/914 of 4 June 2021 on standard contractual clauses for the transfer of personal data to third countries pursuant to Regulation (EU) 2016/679 of the European Parliament and of the Council [2021] OJ L199/31.

106 *See* Article 49(1)(a), GDPR.

107 *See* Article 49(1)(b), GDPR.

controller and another natural or legal person.[108] These three derogations cannot be used by public authorities in the exercise of their public powers,[109] however, they may serve as legal basis for the processing carried out, e.g., by the companies.

3.6.2 Data Protection and Data Flow in the Regional Trade Agreements of the EU

In recent years an interesting tension has arisen in regard to the EU's rules governing international data transfers and the way in which they interplay with the new type of provisions concerning data flow that started to appear in RTAs. This new type of provisions, present mostly in the agreements signed by the United States (US) and by Australia, liberalises data flows by establishing that: 'No Party shall prohibit or restrict the cross-border transfer of information, including personal information, by electronic means if this activity is for the conduct of the business of a covered person'.[110] Such a way of regulating data transfers may be interpreted as limiting the possibilities of states in regard to the adoption of rules which govern what kind of basis transfers are allowed.[111]

However, the provisions foresee the exception to this rule. The adopted provisions refer to the possibility of implementing certain regulatory requirements by parties, as long as they are implemented for the purpose of achieving a legitimate public policy objective, are not discriminatory and are proportionate. Moreover, in the agreements signed by Australia, this possibility is underscored by the paragraph which notes that the parties recognise that each party may have its own regulatory requirements concerning the transfer of information by electronic means.[112]

This manner of addressing the issue of data flows is further complicated by the presence of provisions on data protection in said agreements. It is not clear how in practice the balancing between ensuring data protection while also not implementing rules restricting data transfers will be shaped. As this type of provision is present in the agreements which were adopted only recently, it is impossible to unequivocally assess how it will be interpreted and to what an extent the EU's rules governing data transfers could be perceived as justified under this type of approach. What is however certain, is that the presence of this model of regulating data flows

108 *See* Article 49(1)(c), GDPR.

109 *See* Article 49(3), GDPR.

110 *See*, e.g., Article 19.11, ch 19 Digital Trade, *United States-Mexico-Canada Agreement* (USMCA). Available at: https://ustr.gov/sites/default/files/files/agreements/FTA/USMCA/Text/19-Digital-Trade.pdf.

111 On this topic, *see* Andrew D Mitchell and Neha Mishra, 'Regulating Cross-Border Data Flows in a Data-Driven World: How WTO Law Can Contribute' (2019) 22(3) Journal of International Economic Law 389; Andrew D Mitchell and Neha Mishra, 'WTO Law and Cross-Border Data Flows: An Unfinished Agenda' in Mira Burri (ed), *Big Data and Global Trade Law* (Cambridge University Press 2021) 83.

112 *See*, e.g., Article 23(1), *Australia-Singapore Digital Economy Agreement* (SADEA). Available at: https://www.dfat.gov.au/sites/default/files/australia-singapore-digital-economy-agreement.pdf

in international economic law influences the process of negotiation of the plurilateral agreement on digital trade under the World Trade Organization.[113]

The leaked version of the negotiated agreements shows the discrepancy between the position represented, among others, by the US, and the approach to data flow preferred by the EU. The EU's position is based on the enumeration of specific obstacles to data flows which should not be adopted by the states (e.g., concerning localisation requirements). Such a proposal is impossible to align with the type of provision on cross-border information transfers promoted by, e.g., the US, presented above. Thus, the question which appears is to what extent the EU will give in to the dominating model of regulating data flows in international economic law. Especially, the lack of certainty concerning the way in which these new types of provisions would be interpreted by bodies adjudicating cases concerning measures implemented by the states on the basis of the exceptions granted in the text of these agreements should indicate the need to remain cautious in agreeing to the provisions seemingly favouring data flow over data protection.

3.7 Interplay between the GDPR and Other Legal Acts Concerning Data Flows

The EU's regulatory framework governing flow of data includes a number of legal acts, whose aim is to facilitate data flow. Below, I briefly present selected regulations which are particularly important for establishing the way the application of these various approaches should be managed, namely, the regulation on the free flow of non-personal data and Digital Markets Act (DMA).[114]

3.7.1 Coordination between the GDPR and the Regulation on the Free Flow of Non-Personal Data

The coordination between the GDPR and the regulation on the free flow of non-personal data is based on the manner in which the scope of the latter legal acts was defined. Its Article 1 states that this regulation concerns free flow of data other than personal data. The interplay between datasets which include personal data and non-personal data is clarified in Article 2(2):

> In the case of a data set composed of both personal and non-personal data, this Regulation applies to the non-personal data part of the data set. Where personal and non-personal data in a data set are inextricably linked, this Regulation shall not prejudice the application of Regulation (EU) 2016/679.

113 The leaked file of the text of the e-commerce plurilateral agreement negotiated under the WTO, *see* World Trade Organisation, 'Electronic Commerce Negotiations: Consolidated Negotiating Text' (leaked), www.bilaterals.org/IMG/pdf/wto_plurilateral_ecommerce_draft_consolidated_text.pdf

114 Regulation (EU) 2022/1925 of the European Parliament and of the Council of 14 September 2022 on contestable and fair markets in the digital sector and amending Directives (EU) 2019/1937 and (EU) 2020/1828 (Digital Markets Act) [2022] OJ L265/1.

Such a solution indicates that in any situation in which processed data would allow for the possibility of identifying a given individual, and therefore should be considered as personal data, GDPR should be applicable.

Thus, the coordination between the GDPR and the regulation on the free flow of non-personal data takes place on the basis of the way of defining personal data, and the measures foreseen in the regulation on the free flow of non-personal data should be applicable to data which are clearly non-personal. Thus, the prohibition of localisation requirements (Article 4) and the requirements concerning data availability for competent authorities (Article 5) refer to this type of data. Facilitation of free flow of data should be, therefore, perceived as a set of tools which can be used for, e.g., data which are processed in an industrial setting, but – also – anonymised data, as they are not treated as personal data under the GDPR (*see* section 2).

3.7.2 Coordination between the GDPR and Digital Markets Act

As DMA includes provisions which aim to facilitate the possibility of acquiring data from the gatekeepers by other parties, there is a need to coordinate between these newly adopted solutions and the provisions of the GDPR.

Firstly, Article 5(2) of the DMA makes the lawfulness of certain types of activities pursued by the gatekeepers conditional upon obtaining consent of the data subject or, alternatively, basing these types of operations on another legal bases for the processing. The catalogue of the operations enumerated in Article 5(2) includes types of activities which are based on combining personal data from various services by the gatekeepers, which constitutes a type of data sharing within one enterprise. This shows that in regard to combating the dominance of the gatekeepers one of the possible solutions is limiting this type of data sharing.

On the other hand, the attempts to tackle the position of the gatekeepers are based on facilitation of the process of acquiring data from the gatekeepers by the users of their services. For example, Article 6(9) of the DMA contains a version of the right to data portability, which appears also in the GDPR. It refers to the obligation of the gatekeeper to:

> provide end users and third parties authorised by an end user, at their request and free of charge, with effective portability of data provided by the end user or generated through the activity of the end user in the context of the use of the relevant core platform service.

The provisions add that the gatekeepers should provide continuous and real-time access to such data.

Additionally, Article 6(10) provides the business users and third parties authorised by business users with the possibility to receive from the gatekeepers data, including personal data, which were provided for, or generated due to, the use of the core platform services or services provided in support of, or together with, them by those business users and end users engaging with the services provided by those business users. Such an access should be allowed for free of charge, in an effective, high-quality, continuous and real-time manner, and cover both aggregated and non-aggregated data. The provision specifies that in regard to personal data such access should be allowed if, among others, end users opt-in to such sharing by giving their consent.[115]

Finally, Article 7(8) sets the conditions for a particular type of data sharing. It concerns situations in which the gatekeeper exchanges data with the provider of number-independent interpersonal communication services which makes a request for interoperability. In such a case only personal data of end users which are necessary to provide effective interoperability can be shared between these two entities, and only if such sharing is compliant with the provisions of, among others, the GDPR.

Next to these substantive provisions concerning obligations of gatekeepers, the DMA also underscores that when ensuring compliance with these obligations, the gatekeepers must ensure that the measures adopted will be complaint with, among others, the GDPR.[116] However, Article 13(5) of the DMA implements a certain shift in the way that the possibility of obtaining data is addressed by the GDPR. The provision states that in the cases in which the consent of the data subject is required to ensure compliance with DMA, a gatekeeper should enable business users to directly obtain such a consent in a manner no more burdensome than it is for the services provided by the gatekeeper, or comply with data protection rules in another way, e.g., by providing these business users with anonymised data.

While it is still too soon to assess the effects of the adoption of the DMA, the way these provisions are shaped suggests that the need to comply with data protection law may be used by the gatekeepers to avoid sharing some datasets with business users. As the business model of at least some of the enterprises identified as the gatekeepers is based on the so called 'walled garden' approach – in which the processing of data and provision of services on its bases is performed by the gatekeeper – sharing data is to be perceived as a threat to such type of activities.[117] Thus, it is possible that the same enterprises that are the main protagonists of the most (in)famous proceedings concerning the infringements of data protection law will also use the arguments based on the necessity to ensure high levels of data protection to avoid the obligations concerning data sharing.

3.8 Conclusions

In this summarising section, an attempt to provide a simplified overview of the questions that need to be answered in order to ensure the lawfulness of data sharing is developed.

115 Moreover, Article 6(11) of the DMA refers to access concerning 'ranking, query, click and view data in relation to free and paid search generated by end users on its online search engines'. However, it specifies that this data should be anonymised, thus, it would not constitute personal data.

116 *See* Article 8, DMA.

117 *See* Björn Lundqvist, *Regulating Access and Transfer of Data* (Global Competition Law and Economics Policy, Cambridge, Cambridge University Press 2023) 8. Available at: https://doi.org/10.1017/9781009335195

Firstly, it is necessary to check whether datasets that are subjected to data sharing include personal data. If they do not, data protection rules are not applicable. This is the case when data sharing concerns anonymised data. However, when datasets include personal data, even in the pseudonymised form, data protection rules are applicable to these elements of datasets. The broad definition of personal data leads to the situation in which many types of the processing taking place in the digital economy are subjected to data protection rules.

Secondly, it is necessary to analyse if special categories of data are to be subjected to data sharing. If they are, the grounds which allow for the legal processing must cover both the elements of the catalogue of the legal grounds for the processing included in Article 6 of the GDPR, and one of the exceptions to the prohibition of processing special categories of data foreseen in Article 9 of the GDPR. If there are no special categories of data included in the given dataset, the processing must be based on one of the legal bases from Article 6 of the GDPR. Such a solution can be perceived as facilitation of processing in cases in which it does not involve the special categories of data.

Thirdly, any type of processing needs to comply with the principles of processing included in Article 5 of the GDPR. This element of the assessment is vital, as the principles form the foundations of data protection law, and their content is often interpreted broadly. The broad interpretation of the principles such as, for example, data minimisation, can lead to the limitation for data sharing.

Fourthly, throughout the whole processing it is necessary to ensure that the rights of data subjects are respected. From the catalogue of information that needs to be provided to the data subject on the recipients of their data, to right of data rectification or erasure – depending on the legal bases on which the processing is taking place, the relevant rights need to be respected. This aspect of data protection regulatory framework constitutes yet another dimension of obligations for the companies which would like to use data sharing in their economic activities.

Last but not least, if the processing involves international data transfers, it is necessary to ensure that the relevant legal bases for them are covered. The possibilities concerning the types of legal bases on which it is possible to base such transfers depend on, among others, which third-country is involved (e.g., whether it is covered by an adequacy decision), and on whether transfers are taking place within an enterprise or between various entities.

Even this brief and simplified overview shows that it is understandable that data protection law is perceived as an obstacle to data sharing. However, it must be underscored that there are certain types of data sharing of which facilitation is also in the heart of EU's data protection law, namely, the processing that takes place in public interest and for research purposes.[118] What seems to create more doubts is

118 For the analysis of the GDPR indicating these two dimensions (next to one which is data subject-centered), *see* Giovanni Comandè and Giulia Schneider, 'Differential Data Protection Regimes in Data-Driven Research: Why the GDPR Is More Research-Friendly Than You Think' (2022) 23(4) German Law Journal 559–96 https://doi.org/10.1017/glj.2022.30

the role that data protection law plays in regard to strictly commercial, profit-driven data-sharing initiatives.

Data sharing in the business context is limited by a number of legal requirements. These limitations are, however, not evenly distributed. It is the smaller enterprises, that are burdened with the conditions concerning data sharing present in data protection law, while:

> [l]arge players using broad consent covenants and data-driven business models over a multitude of services and markets, such as Google with Google search, Google Maps, and the other Google services within the Google ecosystem, are better equipped to manage GDPR requirements than smaller players. [...] Large, well-known platforms easily obtain broad and detailed consent from individuals.[119]

This shows that the side of the GDPR which is focused on ensuring free movement of data currently brings more benefits to the huge companies. This is indicative of the potential directions of the data protection law framework's adjustments: allowing for the development of the solutions tailored to the needs of small enterprises which would, on the one hand, ensure the adequate level of data protection, and, on the other hand, provide conditions for the development of innovative solutions. What needs to be, however, stressed is that there is a number of other regulatory acts which constitute the regulatory framework governing data sharing, and it is the interplay between them which must be taken into consideration when proposing potential new solutions.

119 Björn Lundqvist, *Regulating Access and Transfer of Data* (Global Competition Law and Economics Policy, Cambridge, Cambridge University Press 2023) 142. Available at: https://doi.org/10.1017/9781009335195.

4 Data-Sharing Compensation

Analysis of the Emerging EU Data Sharing *Acquis*

Marco Botta

4.1 Introduction

Data is generally defined as the 'oil' of the 21st century economy:[1] companies that successfully collect and process a large amount of data (i.e., the, so-called, 'Big Data') manage to provide more personalized services to their customers and to reduce their production costs, thus becoming more competitive. During the past decade, online platforms have been proven to be successful in this regard, by collecting, combining and extracting useful information from the personal data provided by their users. The advent of the Internet of Things (IoT) is expected to lead to an exponential growth in the number of 'data harvesting': sensors that are installed in different electronic devices and that collect an increasing amount of data, including non-personal data concerning the environment in which devices operate, as well as real-time diagnostic information about a device's functioning.[2] The larger amount of collected data is expected to improve the functioning of Artificial Intelligence (AI): data, in fact, is essential in order to train algorithms and thus to improve the quality of AI decision-making.[3]

The value of the EU data economy has steadily increased over the past decade.[4] However, the latter remains far less developed if compared to the US data

1 Shannon Tellis, 'Data is the 21st Century's Oil, says Siemens CEO Joe Kaeser' (*The Economic Times*, 24 May 2018). The article is available at: https://economictimes.indiatimes.com/magazines/panache/data-is-the-21st-centurys-oil-says-siemens-ceo-joe-kaeser/articleshow/64298125.cms?from=mdr (last accessed 25 January 2024).

2 For an overview of the impact of IoT on business models and market dynamics, *see* McKinsey, 'Unlocking the Potential of the Internet of Things' (*McKinsey Digital*, 1 June 2015). https://www.mckinsey.com/business-functions/mckinsey-digital/our-insights/the-internet-of-things-the-value-of-digitizing-the-physical-world (last accessed 25 January 2024).

3 For an analysis of the impact of Big Data on firms' business models that rely on AI, *see* Ajay Agrawal, Joshua Gans and Avi Goldfarb, *Prediction Machines: The Simple Economics of Artificial Intelligence* (Harvard Business Review, 2018).

4 In a study published in 2022, the EU Commission estimated that, in 2014, the value of the EU data economy corresponded to 1.85% of the EU27's GDP. This value had increased to 2.4% in 2018, and it is expected to more than double by 2025. European Commission, *Study on Model Contract Terms and Fairness Control in Data Sharing and in Cloud Contracts and on Data Access Rights* (Publications Office, 2022) 18. The text of the study is available at:
https://op.europa.eu/en/publication-detail/-/publication/dfb3a486-e6d4-11ec-a534-01aa75ed71a1 (last accessed 25 January 2024).

DOI: 10.4324/9781003248255-6

market.[5] Countless studies have pointed out that improving access to data can foster a firm's competitiveness, and thus its economic growth.[6] The OECD, for instance, estimates that data sharing may lead to a GDP increase of between 0.1% and 1.5%, in the case of public sector data, and of between 1% and 2.5% when also including private sector data.[7] However, the same reports have also pointed out that only a limited number of firms currently 'share' their data with other companies. As President Von der Leyen noted, '…80% of the industrial data is collected and never used'.[8] A similar conclusion was reached by the EU Commission in its 2020 Data Strategy.[9] In particular, data sharing is rather common among high tech firms, utilities and providers of financial services, while public agencies, pharmaceutical companies and health care providers rarely grant third parties' access to their datasets.[10]

The lack of interoperability among datasets, regulatory barriers, as well as security and data protection concerns, are the main obstacles to data sharing.[11] In addition, an incentive problem undermines data sharing: with the lack of a functioning market, firms cannot effectively assess the value of their dataset.[12] As a consequence, either firms decide to opt for an open-access approach (i.e., requesting no compensation) or, more often, decide not to share their dataset.[13] As pointed out by the EU Commission, data sharing should be compensated: without compensation, in fact, the party collecting the data would not have any incentive to share its

5 According to the 2020 EU Commission study, in 2019 the value of the EU data market was 'approximately 2.5% smaller than that produced in the US'. European Commission, *The European Data Market Monitoring Tool* (Publications Office, 2020) 9. The report is available at: https://ec.europa.eu/newsroom/dae/redirection/document/68015 (last accessed 25 January 2024).

6 *Ibid.*, p 7.

7 OECD, *Enhancing Access to and Sharing of Data: Reconciling Risks and Benefits for Data Re-Use across Societies* (2019) 59–64. The text of the report is available at: https://www.oecd.org/en/publications/enhancing-access-to-and-sharing-of-data_276aaca8-en.html (last accessed 25 January 2024).

8 Ursula Von der Leyen, *Building the World We Want to Live in: A Union of Vitality in a World of Fragility* (State of the Union speech, delivered in Brussels on 16 September 2020). The speech is available at: https://ec.europa.eu/commission/presscorner/detail/en/SPEECH_20_1655 (last accessed 25 January 2024).

9 in its 2020 Data Strategy, the EU Commission noticed that '…there is not enough data available for innovative re-use, including for the development of artificial intelligence'. European Commission Communication, *A European Strategy for Data* 19.2.2020 (COM/2020/66 final) 6.

10 AIG, 'The Data Sharing Economy: Quantifying Tradeoffs that Power New Business Models' (2016). The report is available at: https://www.familyoffice.com/knowledge-center/data-sharing-economy-quantifying-tradeoffs-power-new-business-models-part-3-series (last accessed 25 January 2024).

11 Richard Feasey and Alexandre de Streel, 'Data Sharing for Digital Markets' Contestability: Towards a Governance Framework' (CERRE Report, 2020) 15. The report is available at: https://cerre.eu/publications/data-sharing-digital-markets-competition-governance (last accessed 25 January 2024).

12 Deloitte, *Study on Emerging Issues of Data Ownership, Interoperability, (Re-)Usability and Access to Data and Liability* (European Commission, 2018) 56. The study is available at: https://op.europa.eu/en/publication-detail/-/publication/74cca30c-4833-11e8-be1d-01aa75ed71a1/language-en (last accessed 25 January 2024).

13 According to the 2018 Deloitte study, only 15% of the firms that joined the study actively engaged in data sharing, and they usually opt for the open data regime. *Ibid.*, 57.

dataset with third parties.[14] In a nutshell, we are witnessing a sort of 'data-sharing paradox': on the one hand, data is acquiring an increasing value in the 21st century economy; access to data becomes essential for every firm operating in the digital economy. On the other hand, due to several obstacles, firms are reluctant to share the collected data; they prefer to 'seal' the data, rather than concluding a sharing agreement with a third party.[15]

The lack of economic incentives mostly affects business2business (B2B) data sharing. However, it can also undermine government2business (G2B) data sharing, when transactions that take place via a data platform, marketplace or technical enabler – i.e., G2B data sharing based on an economic rationale, as B2B data sharing. By contrast, other typologies of G2B and business2government (B2G) data sharing, such as open data, civic data sharing, data prizes/awards and data philanthropy, may not be affected by the lack of economic incentives, since the data holder allows the data's re-use to achieve an objective that is of general interest, rather than looking for compensation.

In order to tackle the data-sharing paradox, during the recent years, the European Union has developed a new legal framework. As demonstrated in Chapter 2, the new regulatory framework includes two 'layers': on the one hand, the EU is supporting the creation of Common European Data Spaces in strategic sectors, in order to overcome the technical, privacy and security barriers that currently undermine data sharing in specific industries.[16] Secondly, the EU Commission has put forward a number of cross-sector legislative proposals to establish a common EU

14 According to the EU Commission, 'the term "sharing" should not be understood as meaning "for free"'. European Commission, *Study on Data Sharing between Companies in Europe* (Publications Office, 2018) viii. The text of the study is available at: https://op.europa.eu/en/publication-detail/-/publication/8b8776ff-4834-11e8-be1d-01aa75ed71a1/language-en (last accessed 25 January 2024).

15 Alberto Alemanno, 'Big Data for Good: Unlocking Privately-Held Data to the Benefit of the Many' (2018) 9(2) European Journal of Risk Regulation 185. https://www.cambridge.org/core/journals/european-journal-of-risk-regulation/article/big-data-for-good-unlocking-privatelyheld-data-to-the-benefit-of-the-many/C739E1DE223088FD3D761466DCDA2EFE (last accessed 25 January 2024).

16 After having been announced in the 2020 Data Strategy, the European Commission provided further details about the Common European Data Spaces in the Staff Working Document published in February 2022. The European Commission plans to establish, in the coming years, Common Data Spaces in relation to health care, industrial manufacturing, agriculture, finance, mobility, the Green Deal, energy, public administration and skills. The objective of each Data Space is to establish a single market for data, thus favoring data sharing among the firms operating in a specific industry. For each Data Space, the European Commission will put forward common interoperability standards, sectoral data governance rules (i.e., model contracts, licenses, access rights), while the EU budget will finance the development of a common IT infrastructure for each Data Space.

At the moment of writing the EU Commission has proposed the establishment of a common data space in the health care sector (*see* more in Chapter 2 of this volume).

European Commission, *Staff Working Document on Common European Data Spaces* 23.2.2022 (SWD/2022/45 final). The document is available at: https://digital-strategy.ec.europa.eu/en/library/staff-working-document-data-spaces (last accessed 25 January 2024).

For further information concerning the development of the Common European Data Spaces initiative *see* http://dataspaces.info/common-european-data-spaces/ (last accessed 25 January 2024).

regulatory framework on data sharing. First, 2019 Open Data Directive (ODD),[17] which replaces the previous Public Sector Information (PSI) Directive, has introduced new rules to stimulate the sharing of data held by public authorities with the private sector (i.e., G2B data sharing). Secondly, the Data Governance Act (DGA) has introduced a governance framework to stimulate both G2B and B2B data sharing.[18] Thirdly, the Data Act, recently adopted by the Council and by the European Parliament, has introduced rules to stimulate B2B data sharing, as well as to mandate data sharing from the private to the public sector in case of a public emergency (i.e., B2G data sharing).[19] Fourthly, the Digital Markets Act (DMA)[20] includes a number of specific data-sharing obligations, mandating digital gatekeepers to share their data with competitors under certain circumstances. The DMA complements sector-specific rules, which mandate data sharing in specific industries, such as in the chemical,[21] banking,[22] automotive,[23] electricity,[24] telecom[25] and postal sector.[26] Finally, the right to data portability may also be considered part of the EU data sharing legal framework: Art. 20 of the General Data Protection

17 Directive 2019/1024 of the European Parliament and of the Council of 20 June 2019 on open data and the re-use of public sector information (ODD) [2019] OJ L172/56.

18 Regulation (EU) 2022/868 of the European Parliament and of the Council of 30 May 2022 on European data governance and amending Regulation (EU) 2018/1724 (Data Governance Act) [2022] OJ L152/1.

19 Regulation (EU) 2023/2854 of the European Parliament and of the Council of 13 December 2023 on harmonized rules on fair access to and use of data and amending Regulation (EU) 2017/2394 and Directive (EU) 2020/1828 (Data Act) [2023] OJ L, 2023/2854.

20 Regulation (EU) 2022/1925 of the European Parliament and of the Council of 14 September 2022 on contestable and fair markets in the digital sector, amending Directives (EU) 2019/1937 and (EU) 2020/1828 (Digital Markets Act) [2022] OJ L265/1.

21 Regulation (EC) No 1907/2006 of the European Parliament and of the Council of 18 December 2006 concerning the Registration, Evaluation, Authorization and Restriction of Chemicals (REACH), establishing a European Chemicals Agency, amending Directive 1999/45/EC and repealing Council Regulation (EEC) No 793/93 and Commission Regulation (EC) No 1488/94, as well as Council Directive 76/769/EEC and Commission Directives 91/155/EEC, 93/67/EEC, 93/105/EC and 2000/21/EC [2006] OJ L396/1.

22 Directive (EU) 2015/2366 of the European Parliament and of the Council of 25 November 2015 on payment services in the internal market, amending Directives 2002/65/EC, 2009/110/EC and 2013/36/EU and Regulation (EU) No 1093/2010, and repealing Directive 2007/64/EC (PSD2) [2015] OJ L337/35 Art 36.

23 Regulation (EU) 2018/858 of the European Parliament and of the Council of 30 May 2018 on the approval and market surveillance of motor vehicles and their trailers, and of systems, components and separate technical units intended for such vehicles, amending Regulations (EC) No 715/2007 and (EC) No 595/2009 and repealing Directive 2007/46/EC [2018] OJ L151/1 Art 61.

24 Directive (EU) 2019/944 of the European Parliament and of the Council of 5 June 2019 on common rules for the internal market for electricity and amending Directive 2012/27/EU [2019] OJ L158/125 Art 23.

25 Directive (EU) 2018/1972 of the European Parliament and of the Council of 11 December 2018 establishing the European Electronic Communications Code (EECC) [2018] OJ L321/36 Art 112.

26 Directive 2008/6/EC of the European Parliament and of the Council of 20 February 2008 amending Directive 97/67/EC with regard to the full accomplishment of the internal market of Community postal services [2008] OJ L52/3 Art 11a.

Regulation (GDPR), in fact, empowers the data subject to request the data controller to transfer his/her personal data to a third party, which results in a B2B data sharing transaction.[27]

The new EU legal framework, therefore, covers both B2B, G2B and B2G data sharing. The framework aims to stimulate data sharing by introducing a common EU regulatory framework (i.e., increasing legal certainty), rather than imposing a sharing obligation.[28] Mandated data sharing is introduced only in specific circumstances, in which the EU legislator identifies either a specific market failure or a reason that is of public interest (e.g., the B2G data-sharing obligation in the case of a public emergency), which justify a direct intervention in market dynamics. In other words, mandated data sharing is thus the exception, rather than the general rule, within the new EU regulatory framework. Finally, it is worth mentioning that the new EU regulatory framework has introduced general rules on compensation to solve the incentive problem discussed above. Since the degree of compensation varies, depending on the data's quality, their value in both the supply chain and industry practices, the EU legislator has provided only 'general' rules on compensation. In other words, it is up to the parties to define the precise value of compensation in each transaction.

The present chapter aims at analyzing the emerging EU data sharing *acquis* with a particular emphasis on the rules on data access compensation. The chapter first provides an overview of the main business models emerging in the contest of B2B, G2B and B2G data sharing. Secondly, the chapter discusses the benefits and barriers to data sharing. Finally, the chapter analyzes the EU data sharing *acquis* with a particular emphasis on the rules of data access compensation. In particular, the chapter investigates whether and to what extent the EU legislator has introduced a consistent legal framework in relation to data-sharing compensation. The chapter thus complements the other contributions in the present volume, especially Chapter 2.

4.2 Data-Sharing Business Models

Data sharing may take place in accordance with different 'models', which are influenced by a number of factors, such as the type of data to be shared (i.e., personal v. non-personal data), the actors involved (i.e., B2B, G2B, B2G data sharing), the industry specificities, as well as by the business model that has been selected by the data holder. There are thus a multitude of data-sharing models, which are difficult

27 Regulation 2016/679 of the European Parliament and of the Council of 27 April 2016 on the protection of natural persons with regard to the processing of personal data and on the free movement of such data, and repealing Directive 95/46/EC (General Data Protection Regulation, GDPR) [2016] OJ L119/1 Art 20.

28 'The European Commission's general strategic focus has been on encouraging and facilitating voluntary data sharing, rather than on introducing any obligation to share data'. *Supra*, European Commission, *Study on Model Contract Terms and Fairness Control in Data Sharing and in Cloud Contracts and on Data Access Rights* (2022) 7.

to categorize, and the number of business models is increasing with the development of data sharing.

4.2.1 B2B Data-Sharing Models

In the context of B2B data sharing, a bilateral agreement between companies to grant data access/re-use in exchange for monetary compensation is quite rare, in practice.[29] When companies want to share non-personal data, they often establish 'data platforms', which allow participants to exchange their industrial data within a secure environment.[30] Participants, in fact, can agree on common Application Programming Interfaces (APIs), which facilitate data sharing from a technical point of view. In other words, data platforms remove some of the barriers to data sharing, and this is further discussed in the pages that follow, e.g., security and interoperability considerations. In terms of compensation, platform participants are remunerated by having access to a common/larger data pool, rather than by receiving monetary compensation for every transaction.[31] Skywise is an example of a data platform. It was established among Airbus and the airlines which have purchased Airbus airplanes for their commercial fleets.[32] The airlines participating in the Skywise programme freely provides to Airbus real-time diagnostic data about their airplanes. This data allows Airbus to test the functioning of its airplanes in different scenarios, thus allowing Airbus to improve the technical qualities of its airplanes in the long term. In the short term, however, Airbus monitors the 'health' of the vehicles and can thus provide information about the predictive maintenance of the airplanes; via real-time diagnostics, the airlines can reduce the risk of accidents, as well as the airplanes' maintenance costs. Finally, it is worth noting that when data platforms are concluded between competitors, they represent a horizontal cooperation agreement, which may be subject to competition law scrutiny.[33]

An alternative model of B2B data sharing is the so-called 'marketplace'. Unlike a data platform, a marketplace is open to a potentially unlimited number of data

29 *Supra*, European Commission, *Study on Model Contract Terms and Fairness Control in Data Sharing and in Cloud Contracts and on Data Access Rights* (2022) 56.

30 European Commission Staff Working Document, Guidance on Sharing Private Sector Data in the European Data Economy. Brussels, 25.4.2018, SWD(2018) 125 final. Section 3.3. https://eur-lex.europa.eu/legal-content/EN/TXT/?uri=celex:52018SC0125 (last accessed 21 February 2025).

31 Thomas Tombal, *Imposing Data Sharing among Private Actors: A Tale of Evolving Balances* (Kluwer Law International, Wolters Kluwer 2022) 110.

32 https://aircraft.airbus.com/en/services/enhance/skywise (last accessed 25 January 2024).

33 The revised Horizontal Cooperation Guidelines, published by the EU Commission in March 2022, point out that participants in a data pool may only have access to the data provided, as well as to the aggregated data generated by the pool. In other words, the data pool should not become a mechanism with which to allow the exchange of sensitive business information among competitors. European Commission Communication, *Guidelines on the applicability of Article 101 of the Treaty on the Functioning of the European Union to horizontal co-operation agreements*. Brussels, 1.3.2022, C(2022) 1159 final. Para 440. https://eur-lex.europa.eu/legal-content/EN/TXT/PDF/?uri=CELEX:52023XC0721(01)

holders and recipients. The marketplace works as an intermediary between the parties, acting as the matchmaker between the potential data suppliers and the buyers, thus providing a framework in which to allow the transaction to take place and, *ex-post,* certifying that a data sharing transaction has taken place.[34] Snowflake is an example of a data marketplace: it provides access to several types of datasets that are offered by different providers. Snowflake categorizes the datasets under different typologies (e.g., financial, government, health care, travel, weather…).[35] The buyer selects which dataset to download; after the first downloading, the dataset is automatically updated by the provider. In terms of remuneration, Snowflake follows a standard subscription fee, while other marketplaces may opt for an *ad hoc* fee for the downloading of each dataset, a fee which has previously been defined by the data holder.[36]

Marketplaces simply facilitate the data-sharing process, but they do not always guarantee the interoperability of the acquired data with the buyer's dataset. An alternative solution is represented by the 'technical enablers' – i.e., the intermediaries, which provide a number of services to both the data supplier and the recipient, in addition to facilitating the transaction.[37] Unlike a simple marketplace, the technical enabler will also design APIs to facilitate the data-sharing process and to provide anonymization services for the personal data, in order to solve in advance any data protection concerns. Nallian is a good example of a technical enabler.[38] This company has developed a cloud-based platform that enables real-time data sharing in the context of air cargo transportation. Nallian allows air cargo firms, ground handlers, freight forwarders, trucking companies, carriers, shippers and the airport administration, to have access to the real-time data relating to specific cargo. By facilitating the exchange of data between different logistics firms, placed on different levels of the supply chain, Nallian reduces the delivery time of air cargo. Nallian, and other technical enablers, mostly work based on a subscription fee, which is paid by the firms that would like to have access to the data-sharing platform provided by Nallian.

Data platforms, marketplaces and technical enablers are the three main business models in B2B data sharing. However, these models are not exhaustive; as mentioned above, the data-sharing models are constantly evolving. Overall, it is worth noting that bilateral B2B data sharing rarely takes place in practice. Similarly, monetary compensation that is based on a fee paid for each transaction is also quite

34 *Supra,* 2018 European Commission, *Staff Working Paper on Common European Data Space*, Section 3.3.

35 Snowflake, 'What is a Data Marketplace?' https://www.snowflake.com/guides/what-data-marketplace (last accessed 25 January 2024).

36 Forbes, 'The Ins and Outs of a Data Marketplace' https://www.forbes.com/sites/forbestechcouncil/2021/05/12/the-ins-and-outs-of-a-data-marketplace/?sh=4d8ed6da19ea (last accessed 25 January 2024).

37 *Supra,* 2018 European Commission, *Staff Working Paper on Common European Data Space*, Section 3.3.

38 Nallian, 'About us' https://nallian.com/about-us (last accessed 25 January 2024).

uncommon; firms would rather provide their data in exchange for other data, or by paying a standard subscription fee. Even when data is shared 'for free', the data supplier is expected to receive a service from the data recipient (*see*, for example, the diagnostic data provided by Airbus to the airline companies who are members of the Skywise programme). The different models of compensation are an important aspect of assessing the EU legal framework on data sharing, as is further discussed in Section 5.

4.2.2 G2B and B2G Data-Sharing Models

Government2business (G2B) and business2government (B2G) data sharing often follow the same B2B sharing modalities. Public institutions, in fact, often establish platforms, marketplaces and technical enablers to provide data to private operators. In 2013, for instance, Hitachi, a leading Japanese IT firm, won the public tender organized by the municipality of Copenhagen, which aimed to establish a platform on which to facilitate G2B data sharing.[39] Via this project, Copenhagen's city administration aimed to establish a common platform on which to share local mobility data with apps' developers and the providers of mobility and advertising services.[40] Amongst others, the data sharing aimed to reduce traffic congestion in the city. Similarly, in 2018, the French government established a *Centre d'Accès Sécurisé aux Données* (CASD, Centre for Secure Data Access) – i.e., a common data platform on which to share the datasets generated by different public authorities in France.[41] Via a centralized sharing platform, CASD ensures compliance with safety and data protection rules. In order to access CASD datasets, the potential receiver has to pay a monthly fee, which is influenced by the number of users that will have access to the data platform and the number of datasets to which the users will gain access.[42]

While Copenhagen and CASD established centralized platforms to share public data with a plurality of business actors, several public institutions have established cooperation platforms, on which they actively transfer data to business operators in exchange for other data. Waze Connected Citizens program is a good example of this sharing modality.[43] Waze is a well-known navigation app; unlike Google and Apple maps, Waze users can share real-time information about traffic jams and road closures; the algorithm collects and processes the data, and it shares

39 https://cphsolutionslab.dk/media/site/1837671186-1717797306/city-data-exchange-cde-lessons-learned-from-a-public-private-data-collaboration.pdf (last accessed 25 January 2024).

40 City Data Exchange, 'Lessons Learned from a Public/Private Data Collaboration' https://cphsolutionslab.dk/media/site/1837671186-1601734920/city-data-exchange-cde-lessons-learned-from-a-public-private-data-collaboration.pdf (last accessed 25 January 2024).

41 CASD, 'Governance and Missions' https://www.casd.eu/en/le-centre-dacces-securise-aux-donnees-casd/gouvernance-et-missions/ (last accessed 25 January 2024).

42 CASD, 'Price List' https://www.casd.eu/en/tarifs-2/ (last accessed 25 January 2024).

43 Wazeopedia, 'Connected Citizens Program' https://wazeopedia.waze.com/wiki/UAE/Connected_Citizens_Program/ (last accessed 25 January 2024).

up-to-date road information with Waze users. In the context of the Connected Citizens program, Waze has concluded data-sharing agreements with the municipal administrations of several cities around the world. The cities share with Waze real-time information about traffic congestion and road closures, and, at the same time, Waze also shares the data collected by its users with the local police and municipal authorities. Waze Connected Citizen program is a case of B2G and G2B data sharing, in which both parties exchange similar types of data in order to solve traffic congestion issues.

Finally, a number of public authorities have facilitated G2B data sharing by opting for a technical enabler, rather than a data platform or a marketplace. By establishing Findata, for instance, the government of Finland introduced a system to facilitate the data sharing of the health care data of Finnish citizens, to foster medical research.[44] Findata not only shares the data, but it checks that these data have been aggregated and anonymized before being shared, so as to comply with data protection rules.

In addition to platforms, marketplaces and technical enablers, G2B and B2G are characterized by specific data-sharing typologies, which are not present in the B2B scenario. Contrary to the B2B scenario, in fact, data sharing between public and private institutions does not necessarily take place for a 'remuneration'; there may be non-economic goals at the origin of the sharing process, such as fostering research, or reducing traffic and energy consumption.[45] In addition, the data may be shared for 're-use', rather than being specifically collected and processed to be shared. A few public institutions have opted for an 'open data model' to foster data re-use. Data.Gov, is an initiative of the US government to share, via an integrated open platform, different datasets that are generated by US federal agencies.[46] In Europe, statistical offices and weather forecasting agencies have engaged in open data sharing in relation to the different datasets. However, only a few of the EU Member States have so far followed the example of Data.Gov and established centralized agencies that oversee administering an open data policy.

An alternative model that is emerging in the context of G2B data sharing is the so-called 'civic data sharing/data altruism'.[47] Individuals are increasingly aware of the relevance of their personal data in achieving different objectives that are of public interest; individuals are increasingly aware that they can pull their personal

44 Findata, 'Finnish Social and Health Data Permit Authority Findata' https://findata.fi/en/ (last accessed 25 January 2024).

45 For an overview of the benefits of an open data approach, *see*: European Commission, Directorate-General for the Information Society and Media, Wendy Carrara, Wae San Chan, Sander Fischer, Eva van Steenbergen, *Creating Value Through Open Data: Study on the Impact of Re-Use of Public Data Resources* (Publications Office, 2015). The study is available at: https://data.europa.eu/sites/default/files/edp_creating_value_through_open_data_0.pdf (last accessed 25 January 2024).

46 Data.gov, 'The Home of the U.S. Government's Open Data' https://data.gov/ (last accessed 25 January 2024).

47 *Supra*, 2018 European Commission, *Staff Working Paper on Common European Data Space*, Section 4.

data together, and that they can share the aggregated data with third parties in order to achieve objectives that are of general interest.[48] Midata is a data cooperative that is funded by ETH Zurich and a group of public universities in Switzerland.[49] The Midata project aims to collect health care data via an app that can be installed on smart watches and mobile phones. Individuals who download the app agree to provide a number of items of personal information to Midata, together with real-time health data (e.g., blood pressure, body temperature, heart rate). The platform shares the aggregated data that is provided by individuals with pharmaceutical companies and other actors who are involved in research on new medicines and medical therapies. Individuals who join the project always have full control of their data which, in any case, are shared in an anonymous manner with third parties. Midata applies an open data policy – i.e., the data are shared, free of charge, with third parties. Midata acts as a 'trusted intermediary' between individuals and data recipients; a similar model may exist in B2G data sharing, whenever a third-party acts as an intermediary between the business data provider and the public data recipient.

Data may also represent the 'prize'/'award', which is shared by public and private data holders with qualified recipients.[50] The prize/award model is common in the research area, and it can take place in the context of both G2B and B2G data sharing: a private firm, for instance, can share a dataset with a public university, in order to carry out specific research. Alternatively, a public institution can share its dataset with a firm that is committed to using it for specific research. In both cases, we are talking about the re-use of an existing dataset, shared via an open-access approach, in order to achieve an objective of general interest. An example of B2G data prize/award is represented by the Mastercard Center for Inclusive Growth.[51] During the past decade, Mastercard has shared a large amount of data concerning financial transactions, which has been collected from around the world, with government agencies and non-profit organizations, to foster access to credit, and thus to fostering economic growth in under-developed regions of the world.

Similarly to the data prize/award model, firms may also share their data with public entities in the context of public emergencies. The latter practice is generally known as 'data philanthropy'.[52] Between 2008 and 2015, for instance, Google shared data concerning potential 'flu' outbreaks in the USA with public health

48 Marina Micheli, Marisa Ponti, Max Craglia and Anna Berti Suman, 'Emerging Models of Data Governance in the Age of Datafication' (2020) 7(2) Big Data and Society 1–15. https://journals.sagepub.com/doi/full/10.1177/2053951720948087(last accessed 21 February 2025)

49 Midata, 'My Data – Our Health' https://www.midata.coop/it/homepage/ (last accessed 25 January 2024).

50 *Supra,* 2018 European Commission, *Staff Working Paper on Common European Data Space*, Section 4.

51 Data.org, 'Mastercard Center for Inclusive Growth' https://data.org/organizations/mastercard/ (last accessed 25 January 2024).

52 Brice McKeever, Solomon Greene, Graham MacDonald, Peter A Tatian and Deondre' Jones, 'Data Philanthropy: Unlocking the Power of Private Data for Public Good' (Urban Institute, 2018). The text of the study is available at: https://www.urban.org/research/publication/data-philanthropy-unlocking-power-private-data-public-good (last accessed 25 January 2024).

institutions, to anticipate new 'flu' outbreaks in specific geographical areas.[53] Google could elaborate such data on the basis of the search queries typed in by its users in specific geographical areas. Before a 'flu' outbreak, Internet users were usually searching on Google information for information relating to 'flu' symptoms and possible remedies. During the COVID-19 pandemic, several digital platforms have followed a similar pattern, sharing their datasets with public institutions. Similarly to the models described above, data philanthropy takes place via an open-access regime, mostly via data re-use; it is the model that most characterizes B2G data sharing.

Open data, civic data sharing, data prizes/awards and data philanthropy are emerging models in B2G and G2B data sharing, in addition to the traditional models that are based on compensation, such as data platforms, marketplace and technical enabler. As mentioned in relation to B2B, it is difficult to categorize these models, which are continuously evolving, following technological development and the spreading of data-sharing practices.

4.3 Benefits of Data Sharing

As mentioned in the introduction, data represents an essential input in the context of the digital economy. First, data sharing improves the efficiency of the recipient undertaking: by improving its understanding of the consumers' demands, the recipient firm can develop more personalized products, and market them via targeted advertising.[54] Data sharing therefore improves the ability of the recipient firm to innovate, in terms of new products released on the market and/or the improvement of existing ones so that they are available in a more personalized way. Secondly, by analyzing customers' data, a firm can also reduce its production costs: instead of cutting costs on a random basis, data analytics provide insight that allows companies to make strategic adjustments in terms of their production costs.[55] Finally, by releasing a new product on the market, the data-sharing recipient undertaking may enter into a new market; in other words, data sharing stimulates the entry of innovative and efficient firms into the market, thus stimulating the overall market competition.[56]

Fostering innovation, efficiency and market competition are the main economic benefits of data sharing; they arise both in B2B and G2B data-sharing scenarios. However, economic benefits are not the only justification for the current EU effort to stimulate data sharing. Increased data sharing, in fact, not only benefits private

53 Govlab, 'Google Flu Trends' https://datacollaboratives.org/cases/google-flu-trends.html (last accessed 25 January 2024).

54 *Supra,* European Commission, *Study on Model Contract Terms and Fairness Control in Data Sharing and in Cloud Contracts and on Data Access Rights* (2022) 16.

55 *Supra,* European Commission, *Study on Model Contract Terms and Fairness Control in Data Sharing and in Cloud Contracts and on Data Access Rights* (2022) 16.

56 *Supra,* European Commission, *Study on Model Contract Terms and Fairness Control in Data Sharing and in Cloud Contracts and on Data Access Rights* (2022) 16.

firms, but society as a whole. As was noted by the European Commission in its 2020 Data Strategy,

> making more data available and improving the way in which data is used is essential for tackling societal, climate and environment-related challenges, contributing to healthier, more prosperous and more sustainable societies.[57]

Firstly, increased data sharing may stimulate research, and this is the case between private firms in a B2B scenario, but also when public authorities allow private actors to access their datasets (G2B), as well as when private data holders share their datasets with public research institutions, like universities (B2G).[58] According to the EU Data Strategy, increased data sharing may also improve mobility, reduce CO2 consumption and, ultimately, allow the EU to achieve its goal of becoming carbon-neutral by 2050.[59] For instance, by sharing real-time traffic data with car drivers, local authorities may reduce traffic in our cities, as well as pollution. B2B and G2B data sharing may also improve manufacturing and production processes, limiting the use of energy and natural resources. For example, in the agricultural sector, public authorities may help farmers to reduce water and fertilizer waste by sharing meteorological data and observations. Finally, increased data sharing may also contribute to the prevention, diagnosis and treatment of diseases.[60] From this point of view, COVID-19 has resulted in a 'fundamental overhaul', stimulating both B2B data sharing between pharmaceutical companies, and G2B and B2G data sharing. The increased data sharing has helped pharmaceutical companies to develop and test new vaccines and medical treatments thus contributing to reducing the duration of the pandemic.[61]

Research, climate, mobility, agriculture and health care are a few examples of areas in which increased B2B, G2B and B2G data sharing allows the achievement of certain public interest goals. As mentioned in the introduction, the EU Commission has identified ten Common European Data Spaces, where an increased degree of data sharing between public and private actors might allow the achievement of certain public policy objectives.[62]

57 *Supra*, European Commission Communication, *A European Strategy for Data*, 3.

58 *Supra*, Tombal, *Imposing Data Sharing among Private Actors: A Tale of Evolving Balances* (2022) para 93.

59 *Supra*, European Commission Communication, *A European Strategy for Data*, Section 4.

60 *Supra*, Tombal, *Imposing Data Sharing among Private Actors: A Tale of Evolving Balances* (2022) para 93.

61 *Supra*, Tombal, *Imposing Data Sharing among Private Actors: A Tale of Evolving Balances* (2022) para 93.

62 *Supra*, European Commission, *Staff Working Document on Common European Data Spaces* (SWD/2022/45 final).

4.4 Obstacles to Data Sharing – the Need for EU Regulatory Intervention

The next section discusses the obstacles to data sharing, in terms of technical barriers, market failures and the lack of trust. As mentioned in the introduction, technical barriers are mostly tackled by the Common European Data Spaces project, rather than by the new cross-sectoral EU regulatory framework on data sharing. The discussion on technical barriers will therefore be rather short, while a deeper analysis will be devoted to the market failures and the lack of trust, which are the main justifications for the emerging EU regulatory framework on data sharing.

4.4.1 Technical Barriers

According to a survey conducted by the EU Commission in 2018, technical obstacles represent the main barrier to B2B data sharing,[63] and they are likely to have a negative effect on G2B and B2G data sharing too. The main technical barrier is the lack of 'interoperability' among different datasets. The lack of interoperability is a key problem in the ICT industry: without interoperability, different electronic devices cannot 'talk to each other' – e.g., mobile phones produced by different manufacturers can communicate because of common industry standards. In the context of the data economy, a lack of interoperability means that, even if the data holder agrees to share data with a third party in real-time, via a cloud-based solution, the recipient would not be able to gain access to the cloud, and thus to importing the dataset.[64]

In addition to the lack of interoperability, data sharing may be limited by the lack of 'compatibility' among the different datasets.[65] For instance, the data holder may collect and classify data in accordance with metadata which are not recognized by the data recipients. The different degree of 'granularity' of the datasets (i.e., the degree of data details) and potentially missing data, are also factors that are obstacles to the technical compatibility among different datasets.[66] While the lack of interoperability limits the sharing process, the lack of compatibility limits the ability of the data recipient to integrate the received data with their own dataset. Finally, security considerations may also undermine the data holder's incentives for sharing the data.[67] This is the case especially for the real-time and question-and-answer data sharing modalities, which are discussed in Section 2.3. In both scenarios, in fact, the recipient directly gains access to the data via a cloud solution;

63 *Supra*, European Commission, *Study on Data Sharing between Companies in Europe* (2018) ix.

64 *Supra*, European Commission, *Study on Data Sharing between Companies in Europe* (2018) 25.

65 Michal Gal and Daniel L Rubinfeld, 'Data Standardization' (2019) 94 New York University Law Review, NYU Law and Economics Research Paper No 19–17 737–769. https://www.nyulawreview.org/wp-content/uploads/2019/10/NYULAWREVIEW-94-4-GalRubinfeld-1.pdf(last accessed 21 February 2025).

66 *Ibid.*, 747.

67 *Supra*, European Commission, *Study on Data Sharing between Companies in Europe* (2018) 44.

the recipient thus gets direct access to the data holder's IT system, thus potentially creating cyber-security risks for the data holder's IT system.

Although technical barriers are widespread in the data economy, they may be solved only via *ad hoc* industry solutions. As discussed in Section 2.4, sharing platforms and technical enablers may design common Application Programming Interfaces (APIs) to facilitate the data exchange between the data holders and the recipients. Similarly, platforms and technical enablers can also harmonize the format of the metadata and prevent cyber-security risks. Since technical barriers may be solved only via *ad hoc* industry solutions, the EU legislator has decided to tackle these issues in the context of the Common European Data Spaces, rather than via the emerging cross-sectoral EU regulatory framework, discussed in the present chapter.[68] When established, the Data Spaces should solve the technical and security issues undermining data sharing in each industry. The recently established Data Spaces Support Centre (DSSC) will have the task of facilitating the elaboration of common industry standards to facilitate the sharing process.[69]

4.4.2 Market Failures

From an economic perspective, data is characterized by specific features, which have an impact on the sharing process. First, data is 'non-rival': many parties can use the same dataset for different purposes without creating any value loss for the original data collector.[70] Similarly, users can provide their data to multiple actors.[71] The latter is a major difference in comparison to 'physical' factors of production, which usually cannot be used by multiple parties at the same time. The non-rival nature of data has important legal implications: data cannot be subject to any *sui generis* IP right; rather than transferring the ownership of its dataset, in fact, the data holder grants either 'access' or 're-use' to a third party, without losing the right to the continuing use of the same dataset.

Secondly, data is characterized by important economies of scale and scope: the larger the amount and variety of the data collected, the better the accuracy of the AI predictions are, thus improving the quality of the digital service provided to consumers. According to Prüfer and Schottmüller,[72] this mechanism causes 'indirect network effects': the improved quality of the digital service, in fact, attracts further users, who feed the algorithm with further data (i.e., the user feedback loop), thus

68 Real-time Linked Dataspaces, http://dataspaces.info/#concepts (last accessed 25 January 2024).

69 https://dssc.eu/ (last accessed 25 January 2024).

70 Charles I Jones, Christopher Tonetti, 'Non-rivalry and the Economics of Data' (2020) 110(9) American Economic Review 2819–2858. https://christophertonetti.com/files/papers/JonesTonetti_DataNonrivalry.pdf (last accessed 21 February 2025).

71 The expression 'multi-homing' generally refers to the ability of users to provide their personal data to multiple online platforms to receive different digital services.

72 Jens Prüfer, Christoph Schottmüller, 'Competing with Big Data' (2021) 69(4) Journal of Industrial Economics 967–1008. https://onlinelibrary.wiley.com/doi/10.1111/joie.12259 (last accessed 21 February 2025).

self-reinforcing the economies of scale. Secondly, the larger number of users also increases the firm's revenues (e.g., a larger number of users increases the advertising revenues for social media and search engines).[73]

Thirdly, data may be defined as an 'infrastructural resource':[74] data is not an end-user product as such, but is, rather, an input that produces different types of services and improves the quality of goods. A dataset is simply a compilation of different data, which does not have any economic value as such. However, as discussed in the previous section, firms can rely on data to improve the quality of their services, as well as to cut their production costs. In the context of the digital economy, having access to certain datasets is essential for certain firms in order that they can remain competitive in the market. As Tombal argues, although data is non-rival and not subject to property rights, 'in practice, data may be technically and contractually excludable'. – i.e., the data holder may exclude third parties from having access to the data.[75] The large economies of scale and scope, as well as the indirect network effects, are major entry barriers that cause market concentration. In the context of the digital economy, data is controlled by few large incumbent data holders, which seem to be reluctant to share their datasets with third parties.[76]

As noted by a 2022 EU Commission study, two market failures may undermine B2B data sharing. On the other hand, when a single incumbent controls access to 'critical data' (i.e., data that is essential for the business models of certain firms, which cannot be replaced by comparable data), the incumbent may have an incentive to exclude competitors from getting access to the data by refusing to conclude a data-sharing agreement.[77] On the other hand, even when access is granted, the incumbent may have an incentive to impose unfair and discriminatory conditions on the data recipients.[78] These market failures resemble the refusal to deal/essential facility doctrine under EU competition law. However, most scholars agree that Art. 102 TFEU could hardly be used to sanction a refusal to grant access to data.[79]

73 Jan Krämer, Daniel Schnurr, Sally Broughton Micova, 'The Role of Data for Digital Markets Contextability: Case Studies and Data Access Remedies' (CERRE Report, 2020). The report is available at: https://cerre.eu/publications/data-digital-markets-contestability-case-studies-and-data-access-remedies/ (last accessed 25 January 2024).

74 Christian Reimsbach-Kounatze, 'Enhancing Access to and Sharing of Data: Striking the Balance between Openness and Control over Data' in Federal Ministry of Justice and Consumer Protection & Max Planck Institute for Innovation (eds), *Data Access, Consumer Interests and Public Welfare* (Nomos 2021) 27–68, 31.

75 *Supra*, Tombal, *Imposing Data Sharing among Private Actors: A Tale of Evolving Balances* (2022) 43.

76 Thomas Tombal, 'The Rationale for Compulsory B2B Data Sharing and Its Underlying Balancing Exercises' (2022) 84 Revue du Droit des Technologies de l'information 5–26. https://papers.ssrn.com/sol3/papers.cfm?abstract_id=3984873 (last accessed 21 February 2025).

77 *Supra*, European Commission, *Study on Model Contract Terms and Fairness Control in Data Sharing and in Cloud Contracts and on Data Access Rights* (2022) 7.

78 *Supra*, European Commission, *Study on Model Contract Terms and Fairness Control in Data Sharing and in Cloud Contracts and on Data Access Rights (2022)* 7.

79 Josef Drexl, 'Designing Competitive Markets for Industrial Data – between Propertisation and Access' (2016) Max Planck Institute for Innovation and Competition Research Paper, No 16–13 44.

Firstly, the data incumbent may have a strong bargaining position at a bilateral level, but it would not necessarily be 'dominant' in the relevant market in which it operates. In addition, conditions for the application of the essential facility doctrine can hardly be met in such a hypothetical case: first, the access denial may lead to the firm requesting the data to drop out of the market, but it would not be 'likely [to] eliminate all competition' in the relevant market.[80] Secondly, due to the data's non-rival nature and the lack of exclusive ownership rights, it would be hard to argue that dataset replication is 'impossible'[81] – i.e., it might be extremely costly and complicated, but is not impossible. Finally, it is doubtful that the 'new product' condition would be satisfied[82] – i.e., the requesting firm might need the data either to improve the quality of its products or to improve the efficiency of its production and supply chain, rather than to release a new product in the market.

To sum up, although data is non-rival and is not subject to exclusive ownership rights, its collection generates network effects that lead to market concentration. Although data sharing might foster innovation and facilitate the entry of new firms into the market, data incumbents might be reluctant to engage in B2B data sharing, which may undermine their market position. Refusal to grant access to the dataset/access under unfair conditions is a market failure that may undermine B2B data sharing. Since Art. 102 is generally considered unsuitable for solving these market failures, the EU legislator has opted for *ex-ante* regulation to solve them. As further discussed in Section 3, the mandated data access that is included in the DMA and in the sector-regulation aims to force the data holder to provide access to its dataset for its competitors, and, by doing so, thus solving these market failures.

Even in the absence of a data holder's strategic behavior to undermine the data-sharing process, the data holder may not have sufficient 'incentives' to encourage them to share the data.[83] As mentioned in the introduction, with the lack of a functioning market, firms may not be aware of the value of their dataset and thus they will not share their data.[84] The lack of economic incentives may affect B2B, as well as G2B, transactions that take place via a data platform, marketplace or technical enabler – i.e., G2B data sharing based on an economic rationale, as B2B data sharing. By contrast, other typologies of G2B and B2G data sharing, such as open data, civic data sharing, data prizes/awards and data philanthropy, may not be affected by the lack of economic incentives, since the data holder allows the

80 Case C-7/97, *Oscar Bronner GmbH & Co. KG v Mediaprint Zeitungs* [1998] ECLI:EU:C:1998:569, para 41.

81 *Ibid.*, para 41.

82 Case C-241/91, *Radio Telefis Eireann (RTE) and Independent Television Publications Ltd (ITP) v Commission of the European Communities* [1995] ECLI:EU:C:1995:98, para 29.

83 Bertin Martens, Néstor Duch-Brown, 'The Economics of Business-to-Government Data Sharing' (2020) JRC Digital Economy Working Paper 2020–04, Section 3.3.2. The report is available at: https://www.econstor.eu/bitstream/10419/227699/1/1691869767.pdf (last accessed 21 February 2025).

84 *Supra*, Reimsbach-Kounatze, 'Enhancing Access to and Sharing of Data: Striking the Balance between Openness and Control over Data' (2021) 43.

data's re-use to achieve an objective that is of general interest, rather than looking for compensation. The new EU regulatory framework has introduced general rules on compensation to solve the incentive problem. Since the degree of compensation varies, depending on the data's quality, and their value in both the supply chain and industry practices, the EU legislator has provided only general rules on compensation. As further discussed in Section 3, it is up to the parties to define the precise value of compensation in each transaction.

Finally, high 'transaction costs' and 'information asymmetries' might also represent market failures that undermine the data-sharing process. The expression transaction costs generally refers to the costs faced by the parties in order to engage in the transaction – e.g., the seller has to spend time looking for a buyer, while the buyer makes an effort to look for a seller.[85] On the other hand, the expression 'information asymmetries' generally refers to an imbalance in the ability of the buyer and seller to gain access to product information.[86] Information asymmetries create an imbalance between the seller and the buyer in relation to their bargaining positions, and this is an imbalance which usually favors the seller. For instance, the owner of a car usually has better information about the quality of his/her car than a potential buyer. Transaction costs and information asymmetries are also common in the data economy:[87] When there is the lack of a functioning data market, a potential buyer may have problems in identifying a suitable data provider, while a data supplier faces the challenging task of looking for an interested buyer. Similarly, since every dataset has features that are almost unique, it is rather difficult for a buyer to identify the dataset for which he/she is looking. Data platforms, marketplaces and technical enablers, improve the match between a buyer's demands and the seller's supply, thus reducing information asymmetries and transaction costs. From a regulatory perspective, the Common European Data Spaces announced by the EU Commission also aim to reduce transaction costs and information asymmetries:[88] in each data space, in fact, data providers and suppliers will gain better access to information. These market failures, therefore, will be tackled by future sector regulation, rather than by the overall EU data sharing legal framework that is discussed in this present chapter.

To sum up, strategic refusal to give access to critical data, a lack of economic incentives, high transaction costs and information asymmetries are the main market

85 OECD, 'OECD Glossary of Statistical Terms' (OECD, 1 September 2008) https://www.oecd.org/en/publications/oecd-glossary-of-statistical-terms_9789264055087-en.html (last accessed 25 January 2024).

86 Hayne E Leland and David H Pyle, 'Informational Asymmetries, Financial Structure, and Financial Intermediation' (1977) 32(2) The Journal of Finance 371–387.

87 Bertin Martens, Néstor Duch-Brown, 'The Economics of Business-to-Government Data Sharing' (2020) JRC Digital Economy Working Paper 2020–04, Section 3.3.2, Section 2.2. The report is available at: https://www.oecd.org/en/publications/oecd-glossary-of-statistical-terms_9789264055087-en.html (last accessed 25 January 2024).

88 Real-time Linked Dataspaces, 'Common European data spaces' http://dataspaces.info/common-european-data-spaces/ (last accessed 25 January 2024).

failures that affect the data-sharing economy. The EU legislator is currently tackling these barriers via different tools, while mandated sharing tackles the strategic refusal to share data by the data holder, the rules on compensation tackle the problems caused by a lack of incentives. Finally, the Common European Data Spaces act as matching platforms in certain industries, thus reducing transaction costs and information asymmetries.

4.4.3 Lack of Trust

Market failures and technical barriers are not the only factors that undermine data sharing. The 'lack of trust' in the data-sharing process is an additional factor that undermines the data holder's incentives to share its dataset. Lack of trust may be caused by several issues. First, a lack of trust may be caused by the 'lack of experience' of the data holder in relation to the data-sharing process. Data sharing is a rather new socio-economic phenomenon. Business operators, especially Small and Medium Enterprises (SMEs), still lack familiarity with B2B data sharing, since they have never previously engaged in this type of transaction.[89] Similarly, public institutions may be unaware of the public interest goals that they can achieve via open-access data re-use.[90] Finally, business operators that collect a large amount of data may be unaware of the possibility of sharing their data with public institutions in the context of data prizes/awards or data philanthropy.[91] Via the spread of data sharing, a larger number of public and private actors have become familiar, and thus less skeptical, about this process.

Secondly, a lack of trust in data sharing may also be caused by a 'reputational risk', a risk that is mostly perceived by business operators when sharing personal data.[92] Some business operators, in fact, may be concerned about losing their reputation if their consumers discover that their data, even if anonymized, have been shared with third parties. During recent years, the EU Data Spaces Support Centre (DSSC) has engaged in data sharing advocacy via the organization of conferences, thematic workshops, studies, the elaboration of best practices and marketing materials on the benefits of data sharing, such as podcasts and flyers. The DSSC has tried to increase the familiarity of private and public institutions with data-sharing benefits and has thus reduced the perceived risk of reputational loss.

Thirdly, the lack of trust in the data-sharing process may be caused by the current 'legal uncertainty' regarding this topic. Data sharing is a rather new socio-economic phenomenon; its regulatory framework is in its 'infancy'. During recent

89 *Supra*, European Commission, *Study on Data Sharing between Companies in Europe* (2018) 26.

90 *Supra*, European Commission, *Creating Value Through Open Data: Study on the Impact of Re-Use of Public Data Resources* (2015).

91 European Commission, Directorate-General for Communications Networks, Content and Technology, *Towards a European Strategy on Business-to-Government Data Sharing for the Public Interest* (Publications Office, 2020) 60. The text of the report is available at: https://op.europa.eu/en/publication-detail/-/publication/d96edc29-70fd-11eb-9ac9-01aa75ed71a1 (last accessed 25 January 2024).

92 *Supra*, European Commission, *Study on Data Sharing between Companies in Europe* (2018) 44.

years, EU Member States have adopted a number of laws to regulate different modalities of B2B, G2B and B2G data sharing.[93] Different national interventions may also cause legal uncertainty and restrict cross-border trade of data within the EU.[94] The recent legislative intervention by the EU legislator, which is further discussed in Section 3, aims to increase legal certainty and to reduce the divergences among the national regulatory frameworks.

Finally, lack of trust may also be caused by specific 'legal concerns'. Firstly, the 2018 EU Commission study on data-sharing practices showed that business operators were uncertain about the ownership rights over the data that they had collected.[95] In other words, data holders may be unaware of the fact that they control a dataset, but they do not have any ownership rights that they transfer, in an exclusive manner, to a third party. Similarly, data sharing may also be affected by privacy and liability concerns.[96] The data holder may be concerned with how the recipient party will process the acquired data. In particular, the data holder may be concerned with their liability *vis-à-vis* their own consumers/users, in relation to a possible breach of data protection rules by the data recipient.[97] Once again, the EU regulatory framework, discussed in the next section, aims to solve this problem.

To sum up, the lack of trust is a general problem that negatively affects data sharing. It includes several sociological dimensions, e.g., a lack of experience and the risk of reputational loss, as well as legal issues, such as legal uncertainty and specific legal concerns. While the sociological issues may be solved via advocacy programs to inform public and private institutions about the benefits of data sharing, the EU is trying to increase legal certainty via the common regulatory framework, which is further discussed in the pages that follow.

4.5 Compensation in the EU Data Sharing *Acquis*

4.5.1 B2B Data Sharing

B2B data sharing concerns the transactions between the data controller/holder, on the one hand, and the data recipient, on the other hand. In functioning markets, this typology of data sharing would be subject to the parties' contractual freedom. The data supplier and the recipient would define the conditions and compensation for data sharing in a contract. In the case of personal data, the transaction would take place only if one of the legal bases in Art. 6 GDPR was fulfilled (e.g., data subject provided his/her consent), or if the data were fully anonymized. However, as discussed in the previous, B2B data sharing may be undermined by a number

93 European Commission, *Staff Working Document Impact Assessment Report accompanying the document Proposal for a Regulation of the European Parliament and of the Council on harmonised rules on fair access to and Use of Data (Data Act)* 23.2.2022 (SWD/2022/34 final) Section 2.2.

94 *Ibid.*

95 *Supra*, European Commission, *Study on Data Sharing between Companies in Europe* (2018) 45.

96 *Supra*, European Commission, *Study on Data Sharing between Companies in Europe* (2018) 77.

97 *Supra*, Reimsbach-Kounatze, 'Enhancing Access to and Sharing of Data: Striking the Balance between Openness and Control over Data' (2021) 40.

of technical barriers, security concerns as well as market failures. At the core of the EU legal framework, therefore, there are provisions to encourage B2B data sharing. Such provisions, which are present in the GDPR, Data Act, DMA and sector-specific regulation, may be distinguished as falling into two categories: 'data portability' and 'mandated data sharing'. While data portability is a right enjoyed by the data subject/user, who can ask the data controller/holder to transfer the data to a third party, mandated data sharing is a legal obligation for the data controller/holder. Such an obligation is usually imposed to solve market failures, such as information asymmetries and excessive data concentration. To solve such market failures, the data controller/holder is usually required to share the dataset with their competitors.

4.5.1.1 Data Portability

Data portability is a right that can be exercised by the data subject. Under Art. 20(1) GDPR, in fact, the data subject has the right to obtain his/her personal data from the controller in a 'structured, commonly used and machine-readable format', to later 'transmit' such data to a different controller (i.e., a third party). In addition, under Art. 20(2) GDPR, the data subject may ask the controller to transmit his/her data directly to another controller 'where technically feasible'. The GDPR preamble points out that the data subject may exercise the right to data portability only in a case where the original data processing was due either to the performance of a contract, or due to the data subject's consent.[98] By contrast, data portability cannot be exercised in the case that the data controller is required by law to process the data.[99] By way of example, the user of a social media may require the platform to migrate its personal data to another social service. In practice, this possibility usually remains 'largely theoretical'.[100] Data portability represents one of the major novelties of the GDPR; it aims to strengthen the ability of data subjects to switch between different controllers, and thus to switch between services providers. However, data portability has rarely been exercised by any data subject. As discussed in the previous section, interoperability represents a major obstacle to B2B data sharing; data portability becomes ineffective with the lack of common technical standards.[101]

Although the expression 'data portability' usually refers to the data subject's right under Art. 20 GDPR, the Data Act includes a similar user's right to portability in relation to the non-personal data generated by a product's use. In particular, the user may ask the data holder to 'make available readily available data, as well as

98 *Supra*, para 68, GDPR preamble.

99 *Supra*, para 68, GDPR preamble.

100 *Supra, European Commission, Staff Working Document Impact Assessment Report accompanying the document Proposal for a Regulation of the European Parliament and of the Council on harmonised rules on fair access to and Use of Data (Data Act)* (SWD/2022/34 final) 4.

101 *Ibid.*

the relevant metadata necessary to interpret and use those data' to a third party.[102] The Data Act further provides that the data holder should share the data without delay; data should be shared in real-time, in an easy, secure, comprehensive manner, and structured in a machine-readable format.[103] Finally, the Data Act provides the user should not pay any compensation to the data holder; the data holder should share data of the 'same quality as is available to the data holder'.[104] The recipient cannot further share the data with any another third party,[105] neither can that recipient use the received data to develop products that compete with those of the data holder.[106] Finally, the proposed Data Act provides that a digital gatekeeper, within the scope of the DMA, may not be considered an eligible data recipient, in order to prevent the further strengthening of its market position.[107] By contrast, data holders that qualify as Small and Medium Enterprises (SMEs) are not requested to share data with third parties, while they can qualify as data recipients.[108]

According to Habic, the data portability regime introduced by the Data Act is positive for all the stakeholders who are involved in the process,[109] on the one hand, the users can access the data he/she has generated via the product's use, free of charge.[110] On the other hand, the data holder may rely on the generated data to improve the quality of a product; in this case, it would be asked by the user to grant access to the dataset to a third party, and it could ask for compensation on a FRAND basis, and it would still have access to the dataset.[111] Finally, the recipient may benefit from the shared data.

The GDPR and the Data Act radically diverge in terms of compensation for data portability. On the one hand, under the GDPR, data portability is considered a 'right', which can be exercised 'free of charge' by the data subject.[112] The GDPR provides for an exception to this regard: in case the portability request is 'manifestly unfounded or excessive',[113] especially of its 'repetitive character', the controller

102 *Supra*, Art 5(1), Data Act (2023).
103 *Supra*, Art 5(1), Data Act (2023).
104 *Supra*, Art 5(1), Data Act (2023).
105 *Supra*, Art 6(2)(c), Data Act (2023).
106 *Supra*, Art 6(2)(e), Data Act (2023).
107 *Supra*, Art 5(3), Data Act (2023).
108 *Supra*, Art 7, Data Act (2023).
109 Erik Habich (2022), 'FRAND Access to Data: Perspectives from the FRAND Licensing of Standard-Essential Patents for the Data Act Proposal and the Digital Markets Act'. 53 International Review of Intellectual Property and Competition Law: 1343-1373. https://link.springer.com/article/10.1007/s40319-022-01255-x (last accessed on 21 February 2025).
110 *Supra*, Art 4(1), Data Act (2023).
111 *Supra*, Art 9, Data Act (2023).
112 *Supra*, Art 20, GDPR.

Graef, Husovec and Purtova have pointed out that it is not clear, from the text of Art. 20 GDPR, whether re-use of ported data by receiving parties is also free of charge when data is protected by IP rights (e.g., copyright, trademark). Inge Graef, Martin Husovec, Nadezhda Purtova, 'Data Portability and Data Control: Lessons for an Emerging Concept in EU Law' (2018) 19(6) German Law Journal 1384.
113 *Supra*, Art 12(5), GDPR.

may either reject the portability request or charge a 'reasonable fee', covering the costs faced in implementing the portability request. On the other hand, the Data Act points out that the data holder and the recipient should agree on a non-discriminatory and reasonable compensation, which 'may include a margin' of profit for the data holder (i.e., FRAND compensation).[114] In particular, a 'reasonable' compensation should take into consideration the costs faced by the data holder in collecting and producing the data, and making it available to the recipient.[115] In its preamble, the Data Act further points out that the 'margin' would be influenced by a number of factors. In particular, the margin would decrease in case that the 'data holder has collected the data for its own business without any significant investments', and it may be excluded in case the shared data is not used by the data holder for its own business activities.[116] The data holder should inform the recipient about the criteria used to calculate the compensation, so that the recipient may verify whether the required compensation is indeed reasonable.[117] Finally, the Data Act reserves the possibility for the EU and national law to introduce, in separate legislation, a 'lower compensation' for sharing specific categories of data.[118]

According to Monti, Tombal and Graef, the Data Act grants a remuneration to the data holder to incentivize its efforts to collect and systematize the data.[119] According to the authors, the remuneration should cover the sharing costs faced by the data holder and a 'plus' elements. The 'costs' should include the technical costs faced by the data holder to make the requested data available (i.e., compiling, storage and formatting) and the human and organizational costs faced in arranging the data-sharing process.[120] By contrast, the data collection costs initially faced by the data holder should not be taken into consideration.[121] The 'plus' element implies a degree of profit for the data holder, which should be assessed on the basis of the amount and quality of shared data (e.g. whether the shared data are raw or inferred by the data holder), whether the initial data collection was at the core of the data holder's business model, rather than a side product of its business, and what is the follow-on use of the shared data.[122] While Monti, Tombal and Graef seem to support the idea that B2B data sharing should be remunerated, the compensation

114 *Supra*, Art 9(1), Data Act (2023).
115 *Supra*, Art 9(2), Data Act (2023).
116 *Supra*, para 47, Data Act preamble (2023).
117 *Supra*, Art 9(7), Data Act (2023).
118 *Supra*, Art 9(6), Data Act (2023).
119 European Commission: Directorate-General for Justice and Consumers, Giorgio Monti, Thomas Tombal, Inge Graef, *Study for Developing Criteria for Assessing "Reasonable Compensation" in the Case of Statutory Data Access Right* (Publications Office, 2022) 2. The study is available at: https://op.europa.eu/en/publication-detail/-/publication/599678d8-79d2-11ed-9887-01aa75ed71a1/language-en/format-PDF/source-277469567 (last accessed 25 January 2024).
120 *Ibid.*, 12–15.
121 *Ibid.*, 12–15.
122 *Ibid.*, 20–25.

mechanism introduced by the Data Act has been criticized by Kerber:[123] the author believes that compensation would not be needed, since the data controller would have enough incentives to continue collecting data, even in case it was forced to share data deriving from the product use. In addition, the third party receiving the data would likely pass the cost of compensation to final consumers, by thus defeating the legislator's intention to safeguard a free access to data for final users.

The Data Act also spells out the meaning of FRAND in relation to the possible discrimination against different data recipients. In particular, the data holder should not discriminate 'between comparable categories of data recipients'.[124] In the case of alleged discrimination, the data holder will have to prove that it has treated different recipients in a similar way – i.e., there is a reversed burden of proof relating to discrimination.[125]

The Data Act also includes specific provisions for facilitating data sharing with SMEs. First of all, in a case where the beneficiary was a SME, the compensation for data sharing should not exceed the costs faced by the data holder in order to arrange a specific transaction.[126] According to the Data Act's preamble, the direct costs include the technical costs faced by the data holder, but not of data collection and production costs faced by the data holder.[127] In addition, the data holder should provide 'sufficiently detailed information' to the recipient about the calculation of the compensation, to show that the latter has not exceeded the direct costs faced by the data holder.[128]

Finally, the Data Act provides for the establishment of new dispute settlement bodies, to solve disputes between the data holder and a third party in relation to the determination of FRAND conditions.[129] The bodies should be established in every Member State: they should be 'impartial and independent', and subject to 'non-discriminatory and fair rules of procedures';[130] they should have the 'necessary expertise' to solve FRAND compensation disputes;[131] the bodies should be accessible via electronic communications,[132] and they should be able to solve the dispute 'in a swift, efficient and cost-effective manner' (i.e., within 90 days).[133] The decision adopted by the new dispute settlements bodies does not prevent the right of the parties to seek judicial redress in the national courts of EU Member States.[134]

123 Wolfgang Kerber, 'Governance of IoT Data: Why the EU Data Act Will not Fulfill Its Objectives' (2023) 72(2) GRUR International 120–135.
124 *Supra*, Art 8(3), Data Act (2023).
125 *Supra*, Art 8(3), Data Act (2023).
126 *Supra*, Art 9(4), Data Act (2023).
127 *Supra*, para 49, Data Act preamble (2023).
128 *Supra*, para 51, Data Act preamble (2023).
129 *Supra*, Art 10(1), Data Act (2023).
130 *Supra*, Art 10(5)(a), Data Act (2023).
131 *Supra*, Art 10(5)(b), Data Act (2023).
132 *Supra*, Art 10(5)(c), Data Act (2023).
133 *Supra*, Art 10(5)(d) and Art 10(9), Data Act (2023).
134 *Supra*, Art 10(13), Data Act (2023).

The provisions discussed above represent one of the major innovations of the Data Act. They aim to encourage B2B data sharing to the benefit of SMEs, while preventing digital gatekeepers from further strengthening their market positions by acting as data beneficiaries.

Data portability has also been strengthened by the Digital Markets Act (DMA). Art. 6(9) DMA introduces an unconditional obligation for the gatekeeper to guarantee the portability of the collected data on the core platform service.[135] In particular, the data should be shared 'in real-time' with third parties.[136] According to the DMA preamble, the new obligation complements the right to data portability under the GDPR, 'facilitating switching and multihoming' for end users.[137] Since Art. 6(9) DMA refers to 'data', the new data portability right covers both personal and non-personal data, and the DMA thus bridges the current distinction between the legal regimes that now exist under the GDPR and the Data Act. On the other hand, unlike the Data Act, the DMA points out that the gatekeeper will not receive any compensation when the end user decides to exercise its right to data portability, even when the gatekeeper is required to transfer the data to one of its competitors.

4.5.1.2 Mandated B2B Data Sharing

Data portability is a right that is enjoyed by the data subject/user; consequently, B2B data sharing can be triggered only upon the request of the right holder. As mentioned in the previous section, the Data Act points out that the recipient may not use the shared data to develop products that are in competition with those of the data holder. By contrast, 'mandated' B2B data sharing refers to an obligation, on the part of the data controller/holder, to share data with third parties, which are usually its competitors.

4.5.1.2.1 MANDATED DATA SHARING IN THE DMA

The Digital Markets Act (DMA) includes a set of obligations that are applicable to those 'core platform services' that fulfill certain thresholds (i.e., in terms of the number of users and turnover) so that they can be considered 'gatekeepers', and are thus subject to the DMA obligations.[138] The DMA aims to ensure 'fairness' and 'contestability' in digital markets.[139] To achieve the market contestability goal, the DMA includes three B2B data-sharing obligations, which are aimed at encouraging the entry of new players into the market.

135 *Supra*, Art 6(9), DMA.
136 *Supra*, Art 6(9), DMA.
137 *Supra*, para 59, DMA preamble.
138 *Supra*, Art 3, DMA.
139 'the purpose of this Regulation is to contribute to the proper functioning of the internal market by laying down rules to ensure contestability and fairness for the markets in the digital sector'. *Supra*, para 7, DMA preamble.

Firstly, gatekeepers that operate in the field of digital advertising (e.g., social networks, search engines) shall provide, to advertisers and publishers, access to the performance measuring tools relied upon by the gatekeeper, as well as to the data necessary to measure the effectiveness of such tools.[140] The objective of this data-sharing obligation is to increase market transparency:[141] advertisers can compare the advertising costs with the remuneration granted by the gatekeeper to different publishers, so that advertisers can compare the offers provided by different platforms. Such increased transparency will also benefit publishers, who will be able to compare the potential advertising revenues granted by different platforms.

Secondly, gatekeepers should provide, to business users and to third parties, access to the data generated by consumers, in the context of the use of the core platform service.[142] For instance, business users selling products on Amazon marketplace should receive access to the data generated by the final consumers, while purchasing products on Amazon. The data-sharing obligation aims to prevent gatekeepers, like Amazon, from benefiting from preferential access to consumers' data due to their 'dual role' – i.e., as a platform operator and, at the same time, as a competitor, with business users relying on the platform to sell products.[143] Art. 6(10) DMA points out that the data-sharing obligation covers both 'aggregated and non-aggregated data, including personal data'. Personal data should be shared by the gatekeeper with business users only if that data is 'directly connected' with the products purchased by the consumer and provided that the consumer has provided his/her consent to such sharing.[144] Finally, data sharing should comply with specific quality standards; data sharing, in fact, should be 'effective, high-quality, continuous and in real-time"'.[145]

Thirdly, gatekeepers that are active as online search engines must provide to competitors access to the 'query, click and view data' that is generated by final users.[146] The gatekeepers shall share such data upon the request of the competitor. In the case that the shared data includes personal data, the latter shall be anonymized by the gatekeeper,[147] in such a way as to avoid any possible risks of the re-identification of the data subject.[148]

The three data-sharing obligations aim to 'cure' specific cases of excessive data concentration, usually affecting digital markets. It is worth bearing in mind that these mandated data-sharing obligations are included in Art. 6 DMA: their precise scope of application (e.g., the definition of the data recipients; the modality of sharing) will be further defined by the EU Commission decision which imposes specific

140 *Supra*, Art 6(8), DMA.
141 *Supra*, para 45, DMA preamble.
142 *Supra*, Art 6(10), DMA.
143 *Supra*, para 46, DMA preamble.
144 *Supra*, Art 6(10), DMA.
145 *Supra*, Art 6(10), DMA.
146 *Supra*, Art 6(11), DMA.
147 *Supra*, Art 6(11), DMA.
148 *Supra*, para 61, DMA preamble.

obligations on those firms with gatekeeper status.[149] These three obligations require the gatekeeper to share the data both with 'direct competitors' (e.g., a competing search engine) and third parties, using the platform ecosystem (e.g., advertisers, publishers and business users selling products on the platform marketplace). Secondly, the obligations underline the importance of 'real-time' data access. In terms of compensation, the gatekeeper shall share the data 'free of charge' with advertisers/publishers/business users. The only exception is represented by search engines, which shall share the query data with other search engines (i.e., 'direct competitors') based on FRAND conditions.[150]

4.5.1.2.2 MANDATED DATA SHARING BY SECTOR-SPECIFIC REGULATION

The DMA is not an isolated example of mandated data sharing in a specific sector. During recent years, mandated data sharing has been introduced in several EU Regulations and Directives.

The first example of B2B mandated data sharing can be found in the EU Regulation on Registration, Evaluation, Authorisation and Restriction of Chemicals (REACH).[151] One of the objectives of the Regulation is to stimulate the sharing of previous tests carried out by firms operating in the chemical sector, in order to limit the number of experiments with chemical substances on animals.[152] REACH identifies two typologies of data sharing: on the one hand, the firm requesting the registration of a new chemical substance can ask a previous registrant for access to data involving previous tests on animals.[153] Both the data holder and the potential recipient will 'make every effort' to reach a data-sharing agreement.[154] The cost of data sharing should be determined in a fair, reasonable and non-discriminatory way.[155] Reference to a FRAND basis is also present in Art. 303, REACH: the latter provision requires the firm that has registered a substance via the Substance Information Exchange Forum (SIEF) to share data concerning previous tests carried out on animals with potential registrants on a FRAND basis.

While the objective of mandated data sharing under REACH aims to achieve a public interest goal (i.e., safeguarding animals' welfare), data-sharing obligations under other EU legislation aim to solve market failures, such as information asymmetries and excessive data concentration, to stimulate the entry of new competitors

149 *Supra*, Art 8, DMA.

150 *Supra*, Art 6(11), DMA.

151 Supra, Regulation (EC) No 1907/2006 of the European Parliament and of the Council of 18 December 2006 concerning the Registration, Evaluation, Authorisation and Restriction of Chemicals (REACH), establishing a European Chemicals Agency, amending Directive 1999/45/EC and repealing Council Regulation (EEC) No 793/93 and Commission Regulation (EC) No 1488/94, as well as Council Directive 76/769/EEC and Commission Directives 91/155/EEC, 93/67/EEC, 93/105/EC and 2000/21/EC.

152 *Ibid.*, Art 25, REACH.

153 *Ibid.*, Art 27, REACH.

154 *Ibid.*, Art 27(3), REACH.

155 *Ibid.*, Art 27(3), REACH.

into the market. A well-known example, in this regard, is the second Payment Service Directive (PSD2).[156] The latter legislation, adopted in November, 2015, introduced the Access to the Account (XS2A) rule,[157] in order to stimulate the entry of FinTech operators into the banking sector and thus stimulating competition in the industry.[158] According to the XS2A rule, commercial banks should provide access to data on users' accounts to Third Party Providers (TPPs), as well as providing access to such accounts by executing payment orders.[159] The XS2A rule is applicable only in the case of online bank accounts,[160] and in a case where the consumer has provided his/her 'explicit consent' to such data sharing,[161] since the latter involves personal data. According to Feasey and de Streel, XS2A strengthens data portability if compared to Art. 20 GDPR:[162] data portability under the XS2A is unconditional, and it should take place on a continuous/real-time basis. The PSD2 points out that banks should grant data access to other financial operators 'without any discrimination'.[163] On the other hand, PSD2 does not provide any detail on whether data access should occur free of charge, or whether it should be subject to reasonable compensation. We might thus define this data-sharing framework as 'quasi-FRAND'.

A third example of B2B mandated data sharing can be found in the 2018 Motor Vehicles Regulation.[164] According to Art. 61, car manufacturers should provide access to independent operators to 'vehicle on-board diagnostic' (OBD) data.[165] Similarly to the XS2A rule, the access rule aims to encourage consumers to rely on the repair services offered by independent mechanics (i.e., who are competitors of the data holders), so that the consumers are not tied to the repair services provided by the car manufacturer. Taking into consideration the increasing amount of diagnostic data collected nowadays by cars, it is, in fact, important for independent

156 *Supra*, Directive (EU) 2015/2366 of the European Parliament and of the Council of 25 November 2015 on payment services in the internal market, amending Directives 2002/65/EC, 2009/110/EC and 2013/36/EU and Regulation (EU) No 1093/2010, and repealing Directive 2007/64/EC (PSD2).

157 *Supra*, Art 67, PSD2 (2015).

158 Oscar Borgogno, Giuseppe Colangelo, 'The Data Sharing Paradox: BigTechs in Finance' (2020) 16(2) European Competition Journal 492–511. https://heinonline.org/HOL/LandingPage?handle=hein.journals/eurcompet16&div=19&id=&page= (last accessed 21 February 2025).

159 *Supra*, Art 67, PSD2 (2015).

160 'That right shall not apply where the payment account is not accessible online'. *Supra*, Art 67(1), PSD2 (2015).

161 *Supra*, Art 67(2)(a), PSD2 (2015).

162 *Supra*, Feasey and de Streel, 'Data Sharing for Digital Markets' Contestability: Towards a Governance Framework' (2020) 49.

163 *Supra*, Art 67(3)(b), PSD2 (2015).

164 *Supra*, Regulation (EU) 2018/858.

165 '"Vehicle on-board diagnostic (OBD) information" means the information generated by a system that is on board a vehicle or that is connected to an engine, and that is capable of detecting a malfunction, and, where applicable, is capable of signalling its occurrence by means of an alert system, is capable of identifying the likely area of malfunction by means of information stored in a computer memory, and is capable of communicating that information off-board'. *Supra*, Art 3(49), Regulation (EU) 2018/858.

operators to have access to such non-personal data to provide their repair services. According to the Motor Vehicles Regulation, the car manufacturers shall provide data to the independent mechanic in an 'easily accessible manner in the form of machine-readable and electronically processable datasets'.[166] In terms of remuneration, the Motor Vehicles Regulation points out that the car manufacturer may charge 'reasonable and proportionate fees for access';[167] and such a fee may be calculated either on a time-basis (i.e., how long the mechanic had access to the dataset), or on a transaction-basis (i.e., the mechanic pays a fee each time s/he needs access to ODB).[168] Finally, the data should be provided 'on a non-discriminatory basis'.[169]

A fourth example of mandated data access can be found in the 2019 Electricity Directive.[170] In order to ensure competition in the retail market, but also to enable new emerging services, the eligible parties must be provided with access to data. Such data and information must be shared among the consumers, networks, systems and different applications. For example, Distribution System Operators (DSOs) and suppliers have to have access to 'metering and consumption data' in order to provide network management and supply services.[171] Since personal data is involved, the data sharing for other services may take place only in compliance with the GDPR requirements (e.g., the consumer has provided his/her consent to data sharing).[172] The Electricity Directive points out that data sharing should take place in a 'non-discriminatory manner and simultaneously' (i.e., multiple electricity suppliers can have access to the metering data).[173] In addition, the Directive points out that access to data 'shall be easy' and the relevant procedures to access data shall be publicly available.[174] On the other hand, final consumers should have access to the metering data without any additional cost (i.e., free of charge).[175] Unlike the Data Act, the Electricity Directive does not mention explicitly a right to data portability for final users in relation to their metering data. In addition, except for the non-discriminatory obligation, the Directive does not include any rule on data-sharing compensation. According to Art. 23(5), in fact, the energy regulatory authorities of the EU Member States shall be responsible 'for setting the relevant charges for access to data by eligible parties'.

Examples of mandated data sharing can also be found in the EU rules concerning the telecoms and postal sectors. According to the European Electronic

166 *Supra*, Art 61(1), Regulation (EU) 2018/858.
167 *Supra*, Art 63(1), Regulation (EU) 2018/858.
168 *Supra*, Art 63(2), Regulation (EU) 2018/858.
169 *Supra*, Art 61(7), Regulation (EU) 2018/858.
170 *Supra*, Directive (EU) 2019/944 of the European Parliament and of the Council of 5 June 2019 on common rules for the internal market for electricity and amending Directive 2012/27/EU.
171 *Supra*, Art 23(1), Directive (EU) 2019/944.
172 *Supra*, Art 23(3), Directive (EU) 2019/944.
173 *Supra*, Art 23(2), Directive (EU) 2019/944.
174 *Supra*, Art 23(2), Directive (EU) 2019/944.
175 *Supra*, Art 23(5), Directive (EU) 2019/944.

Communications Code (EECC),[176] telecoms operators providing 'number-based interpersonal communications services' should share data concerning telephone numbers and users with the providers of telephone directory enquiry services.[177] The data sharing should take place in accordance with 'fair, objective, cost oriented and non-discriminatory' terms.[178] The European Court of Justice (ECJ) has pointed out, in *KPN Telecom,* that the costs faced by the telecom operator in compiling, updating and providing relevant information on subscribers should not represent the basis for calculating 'cost-oriented' data-sharing compensation.[179] According to the ECJ, in fact, the compilation of these data is 'inextricably linked to the telephony service and does not demand any particular effort' from the side of the telecom operator.[180] As a consequence, telecoms operators may charge, to the providers of directory enquiry services only, the 'additional costs' faced in sharing the requested data.[181]

Finally, the 2008 Postal Service Directive requires the incumbent postal operator to share data concerning the postcode, address database, post office and delivery boxes, with other postal operators.[182] The incumbent operator should provide 'transparent, non-discriminatory access' to data.[183] On the other hand, the Directive does not provide for any specific remuneration for the data-sharing effort.

To conclude, sector-specific regulation in the chemical, banking, automotive, electricity, telecoms and postal sectors provide for specific obligations concerning mandated data sharing: industry incumbents are usually required to share relevant data about their customers with competitors, to encourage their entry into the market (e.g., PSD2, Motor Vehicles Directive, Postal Services Directive). Alternatively, industry incumbents may be forced to share relevant data with third parties to solve an information asymmetry, and thus to enable the third party to offer a service on the market (e.g., Electricity Directive, EECC). Finally, REACH imposes data sharing to achieve a public interest objective: to limit experiments on animals, and by doing so, increasing animals' welfare. These examples of mandatory data sharing usually include a non-discrimination obligation, whereby the data holder cannot discriminate against the different parties that require access to the dataset. On the other hand, these rules are not coherent in relation to the conditions and level of compensation granted to the incumbent in order to compensate for the data-sharing costs: the latter may be forced to share the data, either subject to

176 *Supra*, Directive (EU) 2018/1972 of the European Parliament and of the Council of 11 December 2018 establishing the European Electronic Communications Code (EECC).

177 *Supra*, Art 112(1), Directive (EU) 2018/1972.

178 *Supra*, Art 112(1), Directive (EU) 2018/1972.

179 Case C-109/03, *KPN Telecom BV v Onafhankelijke Post en Telecommunicatie Autoriteit* [2004] ECLI:EU:C:2004:749.

180 *Ibid.*, para 38.

181 *Ibid.*, para 40.

182 *Supra*, Art 11a, Directive 2008/6/EC of the European Parliament and of the Council of 20 February 2008 amending Directive 97/67/EC with regard to the full accomplishment of the internal market of Community postal services.

183 *Supra*, Art 11a, Directive 2008/6/EC.

a 'reasonable and proportionate fee' (e.g., Motor Vehicles Directive), or subject to a 'cost-oriented' fee (e.g., EECC). Finally, some legislation does not provide for any specific rules on the compensation for data sharing (e.g., PSD2 and the Postal Services Directive). Despite the industry specificities, the differences in the compensation levels are quite unsatisfactory; they show the lack of consistency in the EU regulatory framework on data sharing in relation to compensation. In addition, it remains unclear how the sector-specific rules on mandated data sharing will interact, in the future, with the Data Act entry into force.

4.5.2 G2B Data Sharing

A second typology of data sharing that is regulated by the EU legal framework is represented by the flow of personal and non-personal data from national governments/public agencies to the private sector (i.e., G2B data sharing). The 2019 Open Data Directive,[184] which replaced the 2003 Public Sector Information Directive,[185] and the Data Governance Act[186] are the two main pieces of EU legislation that regulate this typology of data sharing. Together, the Directive and the Regulation define a legal framework generally requiring public sector bodies to grant re-use of their data to business users.

The ODD covers the sharing of 'documents' held by 'public sector bodies' and 'public undertakings'.[187] The expression 'document' is rather broad; it covers 'any content whatever its medium' (i.e., including documents held in a digital format, and thus datasets held by the public administration of the EU Member States).[188] The general principle of the Directive is that public agencies should allow the re-use of documents, produced in the performance of their public tasks, for other commercial and non-commercial purposes, by private parties.[189] 'Where possible', public sector bodies shall make the documents available in 'open, machine-readable, accessible, findable and re-usable' format.[190] In general, public sector bodies shall share the requested documents 'free of charge',[191] eventually asking for the recovery of the marginal costs incurred in the 'reproduction, provision and dissemination of documents as well as for [the] anonymization of personal data' which is included in the document.[192] When charges are demanded, the public agency should disclose, in advance, the calculation basis for such charges.[193] The recipient

184 *Supra*, Directive 2019/1024 of the European Parliament and of the Council of 20 June 2019 on open data and the re-use of public sector information (ODD).
185 Directive 2003/98/EC of the European Parliament and of the Council of 17 November 2003 on the re-use of public sector information [2003] OJ L345/90.
186 *Supra*, Regulation (EU) 2022/868.
187 *Supra*, Art 1(1), ODD (2019).
188 *Supra*, Art 2(6), ODD (2019).
189 *Supra*, Art 3(1), ODD (2019).
190 *Supra*, Art 5(1), ODD (2019).
191 *Supra*, Art 6(1), ODD (2019).
192 *Supra*, Art 6(1), ODD (2019).
193 *Supra*, Art 7(1), ODD (2019).

should not benefit from any exclusivity right to the shared document.[194] Finally, the re-use of public documents shall be allowed in a non-discriminatory manner – i.e., the public agency should apply the same conditions of re-use (and remuneration) to comparable categories of documents and types of re-use.[195]

In addition to the general rules on the re-use of public documents, the ODD includes specific rules concerning 'research data' as well as 'High Value Datasets'. Research data include statistics, the results of experiments, measurements, survey results, interview recordings and images generated by universities and other research bodies, whenever the research has been financed by public funds.[196] To stimulate the re-use of scientific data, both by other research institutions and by the private sector, the research data should be made available in accordance with the FAIR principle – i.e., Findability, Accessibility, Interoperability and Reusability.[197] FAIR goes far beyond the general re-use principles that are included in the ODD, demanding that the public sector agencies make the research data 'findable' via a search database, and to allow for 'interoperability' in order to share the data with other datasets. Examples of high-value datasets are geospatial, meteorological and statistical data that are held by public sector bodies.[198] Similarly to the rules on research data, public sector bodies should provide access to high-value datasets via APIs (i.e., to allow interoperability with other datasets) and ensure that the data may be downloaded 'in a bulk'.[199] Public sector bodies should grant access to high value datasets 'free of charge',[200] with some exceptions that are related to public undertakings,[201] datasets held by libraries and museums[202] and in a case where the data disclosure would have a 'substantial impact on the budget' of the public body.[203]

In spite of the broad interpretation of the concept of documents and of the specific rules on the disclosure of research data and high-value datasets, the ODD does not cover documents that are protected by IP rights held by third parties (e.g., copyright), as well as documents including personal data.[204] The DGA complements the ODD, expanding data re-use to the categories of data that fall outside

194 *Supra*, Art 12(1), ODD (2019).

195 *Supra*, Art 11(1), ODD (2019).

196 *Supra*, para 27, ODD preamble (2019).

197 *Supra*, Art 10(1), ODD (2019).

198 Annex 1 includes a list of six high-value datasets. The EU Commission, via comitology decision, extends the list of high-value datasets subject to the specific rules of the Directive. *Supra*, Art 13(2), ODD (2019).

199 *Supra*, Art 14(1), ODD (2019).

200 *Supra*, Art 14(1), ODD (2019).

201 Public undertakings are not required to disclose high-value datasets if such disclosure would distort competition in the relevant market. *Supra*, Art 14(3), ODD (2019).

202 *Supra*, Art 14(4), ODD (2019).

203 In this case, the Member State may decide to exempt a public sector body from disclosing a high-value dataset for a period of up to two years. *Supra*, Art 14(5), ODD (2019).

204 *Supra*, para 6, DGA preamble (2022).

the scope of the Directive.[205] The conditions for the re-use of public data, mentioned by the DGA, are similar to the general conditions that are mentioned in the ODD. In particular, the recipient should not be entitled to any exclusivity right on the shared data;[206] conditions for re-use shall be 'non-discriminatory, transparent, proportionate and objectively justified';[207] personal data should be aggregated and anonymized before being shared.[208]

While the general re-use conditions are rather similar in the ODD and the DGA, the compensation conditions differ between the two pieces of legislation: while the Directive points out that public entities should allow the re-use of documents 'free of charge',[209] eventually asking for compensation for the marginal costs of the documents' production, the Regulation points out that public sector bodies 'may charge fees for allowing the re-use of such data'. The requested fee should be defined in advance (i.e., should be transparent), should be proportionate and objectively justified, and should be charged in a non-discriminatory manner among the different recipients. The DGA clarifies that the public sector agency should calculate the fee based on the costs faced in the reproduction of the data, as well as in the processes of anonymization and the seeking of consent from the data subject. Finally, the DGA provides that public sector bodies may make the data available 'at a discounted fee or free of charge' for non-commercial purposes (e.g., scientific research) or to SMEs.

The ODD and DGA diverge in relation to the compensation rules on data sharing: while, under the ODD, G2B data sharing should generally take place 'free of charge' (i.e., requesting the document disclosure costs would be an exception),[210] the DGA follows, as a general rule, the coverage of the marginal production costs;[211] by contrast, the 'free of charge' approach is rather an exception. Public sector bodies, in fact, may decide to share the data 'at a discounted fee or free of charge' in cases where the data is to be re-used for non-commercial purposes (e.g., scientific research) and if the beneficiary were an SME.[212] It is unclear if the EU legislators intentionally followed a different approach in the two pieces of legislation, either in order to generate further incentives for public sector bodies to share data under the DGA, or because 'data' sharing under the DGA would be more demanding for a public agency, if compared to 'document' disclosure under the DGA. In any case, the different compensation regime generates some degree of uncertainty, both for the public agencies and for the data recipients.

205 *Supra*, para. 10, DGA preamble and Art 3(1), DGA (2022).
206 *Supra*, Art 4, DGA (2022).
207 *Supra*, Art 5(2), DGA (2022).
208 *Supra*, Art 3(a), DGA (2022).
209 *Supra*, Art 6(1), ODD (2019).
210 *Supra*, Art 6(1), Art 10 and Art 14(1)(a), ODD (2019).
211 *Supra*, Art 6(1), DGA (2022).
212 *Supra*, Art 6(4), DGA (2022).

4.5.3 B2G Data Sharing

Business2Government is the most recent typology of data sharing. In the context of the COVID-19 pandemic, few online platforms voluntarily shared data with public authorities, in order to cope with the health care emergency.[213] In the aftermath of the coronavirus pandemic, the EU Commission has included rules on B2G data sharing in the context of the Data Act.

Art. 14 Data Act provides for a mandated data-sharing obligation in the context of 'exceptional need':[214] In particular, a public sector body, at the national or EU level, may order a data holder to share certain types of (personal and non-personal) data in order 'to respond to a public emergency'.[215] The Data Act preamble specifies that a 'public emergency' might be public health related (e.g., forecasting the emergence of new pandemic wave via Big Data analytics), as well emergencies represented by natural disasters and cyber-attacks.[216] Alternatively, in case of non-emergency situations, the public authority could require the data holder to share only non-personal data.[217] In particular, a public sector body might force a data holder to share non-personal data either to fulfill 'a specific task carried out in the public interest, that has been explicitly provided for by law',[218] or in case the public authority 'has exhausted all other means at its disposal to obtain such data' (e.g., buying the dataset in the market).[219]

In terms of compensation, in case of public emergency, the data holder shall provide the requested data 'free of charge'.[220] On the other hand, in case of non-emergency situations, the data holder should be entitled to receive a fair compensation. The latter should cover both the technical costs faced by the data holder (e.g. anonymization of personal data), as well as a reasonable margin of profit for the data holder. The data holder should inform the public authority about the calculation method of the costs incurred to share the data. and on the criteria used to assess the 'reasonable margin'.[221] Finally, SMEs should be entitled to receive a fair compensation when they are required to share data both in an emergency and non-emergency case.[222]

213 Via the COVID-19 Open Data initiative, for instance, Google shared, free of charge, relevant data concerning the COVID pandemic with scientists and health authorities. Chad W Jennings and Shane Glass, 'COVID-19 Public Dataset Program: Making Data Freely Accessible for Better Public Outcomes' (Google Cloud Blog, 31 March 2020) https://cloud.google.com/blog/products/data-analytics/free-public-datasets-for-covid19 (last accessed 25 January 2024).

214 *Supra*, Art 14, Data Act (2023).

215 *Supra*, Art 15(1)(a), Data Act (2023).

216 *Supra*, para 64, Data Act preamble (2023).

217 *Supra*, para 65, Data Act preamble (2023).

218 *Supra*, Art 15(1)(b)(i), Data Act (2023).

219 *Supra*, Art 15(1)(b)(ii), Data Act (2023).

220 *Supra*, Art 20(1), Data Act (2023).

221 *Supra*, Art 20(2), Data Act (2023).

222 *Supra*, Art 20(3), Data Act (2023).

The meaning of 'reasonable margin' is not completely clear. On the one hand, the Data Act's preamble points out that the compensation for the B2G data sharing should not constitute 'payment for the data itself'.[223] On the other hand, the reference to the reasonable margin implies that that the data holder may make a degree of profit from the data-sharing obligation. According to Richter, the data holder should not be entitled to receive only compensation of the marginal costs faced in the contest of data sharing, rather than enjoying a profit margin.[224] Since B2G data sharing should take place in case of purely exceptional circumstances, in fact, the lack of profit would not undermine the data holder's incentives to collect and process the data. Secondly, even if we accepted the idea that the data holder should be entitled to receive some degree of profit, it is worth noticing that the Data Act relies on 'costs + reasonable profit margin' for repeated B2G data sharing, rather than on the FRAND formula. As discussed in the previous sub-section, FRAND is the compensation formula provided by the chapter of the Data Act concerning B2B data portability. It is not fully clear why the legislation has opted for two different compensation formulae in relation to B2B and B2G data sharing.

4.6 Conclusions

As mentioned at the beginning of the chapter, data is the oil of the 21st economy: in the context of the digital economy, in fact, firms are competitive only if they have access to a large amount of high-quality data. Similarly, public institutions can provide more personalized services to citizens if they can access a large dataset. However, small firms and public institutions can often not collect a sufficiently large amount of data on their own; via data sharing, small firms and public institutions can have access to larger and more diversified sets of data, thus boosting their efficiency. Data access/re-use not only increases the efficiency of the data recipient; it is a win-win strategy for the data holder too. The latter, in fact, could gain remuneration for the shared data. In the case of data re-use, the dataset would represent a sort of 'waste product' for the data holder, since the latter would not further rely on such a dataset. By contrast, the recipient could 'recycle' the dataset to develop new and innovative services. As discussed throughout this chapter, the compensation received by the data holder would not be limited to monetary compensation: the recipient could also exchange its data with the data holder. Alternatively, the recipient could provide data analytics services to the data holder in exchange for the shared data. In a nutshell, data 'access' and 're-use', which are jointly defined in this chapter as 'data sharing', are efficient practices both for the data holder and the data recipient. This is the case in business2business (B2B) scenarios, as well

223 *Supra*, para 75, Data Act preamble (2023).

224 Heiko Richter, 'Access to Private Sector Data for the Common Good' (CERRE Report, 2023. The text of the paper is available at: https://cerre.eu/wp-content/uploads/2023/02/Data_Act_B2G_data_sharing.pdf (last accessed 25 January 2024).

as in government2business (G2B) and business2government (B2G) typologies of data sharing.

It is also worth pointing out that an increased degree of data sharing between public and private actors would not harm the privacy of individuals. The strict GDPR requirement on the collection and processing of personal data would continue to apply. In particular, the sharing of personal data may take place either if the data subject has provided his/her consent, or if the data has been anonymized, and has thus moved outside of the scope of data protection rules.

Despite its great benefits, the degree of data sharing is still limited. In spite of its growth during recent years, there are several firms/institutions that do not share their data with third parties. Data sharing is rather common among high tech firms, utilities and the providers of financial services, while public agencies, pharmaceutical companies and health care providers rarely grant access to their datasets to third parties. Several reasons explain the 'data-sharing paradox': interoperability and data portability obstacles, security and privacy concerns, uncertainty about the applicable legal framework, as well as a few market failures that are obstacles to the data-sharing process. Due to the lack of well-functioning data markets, firms/public institutions cannot assess the value of their datasets. They often prefer to 'seal' their data, therefore, rather than sharing with third parties.

In recent years, the European Union has developed a new legal framework to boost B2B, as well as G2B and B2G data sharing. The new legal framework includes two layers: on the one hand, the progressive establishment of Common European Data Spaces aims to introduce common standards in strategic sectors to foster interoperability and to solve security and privacy concerns via *ad hoc* industry solutions. On the other hand, a common cross-sectoral legal framework increases legal certainty and removes the market failures that hamper the sharing process. Within this new legal framework, while the Data Governance Act (DGA) and the Open Data Directive (ODD) aim to stimulate G2B data sharing, the recently adopted Data Act aims to foster B2B and B2G data sharing. Similarly, the right of data portability, under Art. 20 GDPR, also strengthens the B2B data sharing of personal data, and it thus complements the right of portability of non-personal data under Art. 5 Data Act. Finally, the EU has adopted an increasing number of pieces of legislation mandating B2B data sharing in specific sectors. The Digital Markets Act, for instance, includes a number of specific data-sharing obligations, mandating digital gatekeepers to share their data with competitors under certain circumstances. The DMA complements sector-specific rules, which mandate data sharing in specific industries, such as in the chemical, banking, automotive, electricity, telecoms and postal sectors.

It could be argued that the determination of the compensation terms and conditions should be left to the agreement of the parties, due to the multiplicity of scenarios that may arise in data sharing. In fact, it would be very difficult to define, *ex-ante,* a compensation mechanism for each data-sharing typology. The EU legal framework does not follow this approach: while leaving to the parties the precise determination of the compensation level, the EU legal framework defines general

Table 4.1 Compensation for Different Typologies of Data Sharing under EU Law

	Data Portability	*Mandated B2B Data Sharing*	*G2B Data Sharing*	*B2G Data Sharing*
GDPR	FREE			
Data Act	FRAND; COST			FREE; COST
DMA	FREE	FREE; FRAND		
REACH		FRAND		
PSD2		Quasi-FRAND		
Motor Vehicles		FRAND		
Electricity		Quasi-FRAND		
EECC		FRAND		
Postal Services		Quasi-FRAND		
ODD			FREE; COST	
DGA			COST	

FREE: free of charge.
COST: fee based on the marginal costs of data sharing.
FRAND: Fair, Reasonable and Non-Discriminatory terms.
Quasi-FRAND: compensation should be proportionate and non-discriminatory, BUT there is no reference to the actual FRAND formula.
Source: author's own illustration.

criteria to determine compensation, both in cases where the data sharing is freely agreed upon by the parties, and when it is mandated by law.

As can be noticed from Table 4.1, the EU legal framework refers to three main typologies of compensation: 'free access'; a fee based on the marginal costs of data sharing; and Fair, Reasonable and Non-Discriminatory (FRAND) compensation. A fourth typology, which can be defined as 'quasi-FRAND', refers to situations in which the EU legislation demands non-discriminatory and proportional compensation for the data holder; however, the FRAND formula is not fully and properly mentioned in the legislation.

This chapter has highlighted a few inconsistencies in the way data-sharing compensation is formulated in the different pieces of legislation. First, in the context of G2B data sharing, the ODD and the DGA diverge in relation to the compensation for the data provided by public sector agencies: in fact, while the ODD emphasizes that G2B data sharing should take place free of charge, eventually allowing the public institution to recover of the marginal costs of the documents' disclosure, the DGA opts rather for a costs compensation mechanism.

Secondly, in the context of B2B data sharing, while GDPR and the DMA point out that data portability should take place free of charge, while the Data Act stresses that compensation should be FRAND. The rationale followed by the three pieces of legislation is different: for the GDPR, the 'free' regime is justified by the fact that data portability is a right of the data subject, while, for the Data Act, the FRAND mechanism compensates for the data holders' efforts in terms of data collection. Finally, the 'free of charge' data portability regime covered in the DMA is justified by the need to tamper with the gatekeepers' market power. However, in relation to the 'blurred' distinction between personal and non-personal data and the overlaps between the different legislation, the compensation regime for data portability remains unclear; potentially generating disputes between data subjects/users and different business users in the future.

Finally, the compensation regime for mandated B2B data sharing is also unclear, and this is where we can find different FRAND variations. FRAND is a form of data-sharing compensation that is often referred to within the EU regulatory framework, especially in terms of data portability and mandated B2B data sharing. However, FRAND is never clearly defined in any EU data-sharing legislation. In particular, only the DMA, the Motor Vehicles Directive, REACH and the EECC openly refer to the FRAND principle, while the other pieces of legislation refer to quasi-FRAND formulas. Taking into consideration the different formula, it remains unclear how the sector-specific rules on mandated B2B data sharing will interact in the future with horizontally applicable rules, especially with the entry into force of the Data Act (Table 4.1).

Part II

Competition and Intellectual Property

5 Data Sharing's Competitive Impact and the Antitrust Response

Mariateresa Maggiolino

5.1 Introduction

In the grand narrative of business, the extraction of value from *information* is the epic tale of *informed decisions*, strategic prowess and the relentless pursuit of a competitive edge. Information illuminates the intricate nuances of consumer behavior. It unveils the desires that dwell in the hearts and minds of customers, enabling businesses to tailor their offerings with precision. Furthermore, information provides the lens through which firms scrutinize every move, product launch and market strategy of their rivals. It enables firms to identify competitive advantages, anticipate shifts in the industry and chart a course through the turbulent waters of market dynamics and developments. In summary, as has been known since *the dawn of the market economy*, information serves as a compass, guiding firms through the labyrinth of consumer preferences, rival maneuvers and the ever-evolving market landscape.

In the contemporary era, it is the leveraging of *digital technologies* that empowers firms to glean valuable information from extensive datasets. With a systematic approach, they adeptly collect, analyze and interpret large volumes of data – big data – unveiling intricate patterns, identifying trends and illuminating correlations. This nuanced process serves as the key to extracting meaningful insights about both present customers and competitors, allowing firms to peer into the crystal ball of the future, foreseeing trends and anticipated outcomes. Besides, it is the very same collection and use of data that enable firms to train and improve their own technologies, especially algorithms. Consequently, *data* have *now* become a catalyst for firms that are interested in both gaining a deep understanding of markets and controlling the innovative edge.

Hence, it should not be surprising that the antitrust discourse, once centered around information sharing, has now shifted its focus to the realm of data sharing – a term encompassing any practices whereby firms grant access to their datasets, transfer data or pool them together, either directly or indirectly.[1] Furthermore,

1 Indirect sharing happens through intermediaries like service providers, platforms, online tools or algorithms. It can also occur through a shared agency, such as a trade association, a market research organization or the suppliers, customers or online platforms associated with the parties involved in the sharing of data. Furthermore, data sharing can manifest through various channels, including

DOI: 10.4324/9781003248255-8

considering that information sharing among competitors was found to yield both the aforementioned procompetitive effects and anticompetitive effects, it should not be surprising that data sharing is also deemed to produce both types of effects. Specifically, data sharing can serve as a facilitator for the establishment and sustenance of cartels, empowering firms to identify and safeguard collusive equilibria against potential deviations.

Therefore, the role of a good antitrust legal expert is always to pinpoint the *factual circumstances* that make a particular exchange of data and information more anticompetitive than not. In essence, making a blanket argument that antitrust law should either encourage or hinder data sharing in general would be a gross mistake. Antitrust law must penalize the exchange of data in those specific market scenarios in which such a practice – or its refusal – has the potential to produce overwhelming anticompetitive effects.

But, there is more.

In the contemporary landscape, where data has emerged as a significant source of value, some scholars and institutions are beginning to ponder whether the inability to access certain datasets – or, more precisely, the exclusive access that a handful of firms may possess to those datasets – bestows upon them an unfair competitive advantage. While this aspect was not always a focal point in antitrust law, except for scenarios involving the essential facility doctrine,[2] the upcoming chapter will illustrate how the digital era has emphasized the necessity for antitrust regulations to ensure a level playing field among firms. Consequently, antitrust decision-makers have started interpreting *unilateral and/or exclusive access* to data as a potential tool of exploitation and are beginning to consider its potential as a tool of exclusion, even beyond the scope of the essential facility doctrine.

Additionally, and intersecting with the previously mentioned topics, the rise of the data economy has led antitrust law scholars to consider a question not previously addressed: namely, it has prompted them to explore the intersection between competition law and regulations such as the General Data Protection Regulation ("GDPR") that safeguard personal data.[3] These data, which enable the identification

websites or press releases. In all these instances, antitrust agencies and authorities must determine the liability not only of the firms sharing data but also of third parties, assessing whether they were aware of the data exchange or could reasonably have foreseen it. Put simply, having a third-party intermediary – whether it is another business entity or just a tool like an algorithm or platform – cannot be used as a way for companies to skirt the ban on exchanging sensitive information and avoid their responsibility for cartel-like behavior. *See*, in this regard, Case T-180/15 *ICAP and Others v European Commission* [2017] EU:T:2017:795, para 103; Case C-194/14 P *AC-Treuhand* v European *Commission* [2015] EU:C:2015:717, paras 27, 34–35; Case T-326/17 *Air Canada v European Commission* [2022] EU:T:2022:177, paras 370–371; Case C-542/14 *VM Remonts and Others v Konkurences padome* [2016] EU:C:2016:578, paras 30–31; and Case T-180/15 *ICAP and Others v European Commission* [2017] EU:T:2017:795, para 100.

2 For the explanation of the essential facility doctrine, *see* paragraph 4 of this chapter.

3 Regulation (EU) 2016/679 of the European Parliament and of the Council of 27 April 2016, on the protection of natural persons with regard to the processing of personal data and on the free movement of such data, and repealing Directive 95/46/EC [2016] OJ L119/1.

of individuals, constitute a portion of the data – whether a majority or not, depending on the industry – that companies generate, collect and transfer.

Thus, in light of the most recent case law and the new guidelines on the interpretation of Articles 101 and 102,[4] the chapter runs as follows. Section 2 explores how data sharing can potentially lead to collusion, reducing uncertainty about competitors' actions. Section 3 examines situations where (unilateral) data sharing enables exploitation, allowing a firm to harm its rivals using the information received. Section 4 assesses cases in which the refusal to share data by a group of firms or by a dominant firm puts rivals at a competitive disadvantage. Finally, for thoroughness, Section 5 explores the interface between the EU regulation ensuring the protection of personal data and competition law. Section 6 concludes.

5.2 Data Sharing as a Sword to Collude

The core tenet of neoclassical economics posits that each firm should independently and autonomously determine its economic activities. While this principle allows companies to adapt to rivals' actions, it strictly prohibits any direct or indirect interaction between businesses that could influence a competitor's market conduct or disclose the planned or contemplated strategies of a firm.[5] In other words, the competitive landscape thrives on *uncertainty*, requiring participants to be unsure about each other's strategic moves. Thus, the sharing of data among competitors becomes problematic when it diminishes this necessary uncertainty, essentially transforming data sharing into a tool for collusion.[6] Through data sharing, indeed, firms may gain the capability to pinpoint the terms of the collusive equilibrium they aim to achieve, such as the collusive price or output quota. Furthermore, data sharing may empower firms to detect and control any threat to the collusive outcome, be such a threat the result of deviation or the entry of potential competitors.

On the other hand, as the European Commission has recently acknowledged, data sharing may enable firms to benchmark their performance against best practices in the industry; and respond more quickly to changes in supply and demand and, thus, mitigate internal and external risks. In addition, data sharing has the potential to ignite innovation, cultivating a dynamic environment where diverse insights converge and flourish; and, in particular, this collaborative effort is

4 Communication from the Commission, *Guidelines on the applicability of Article 101 of the Treaty on the Functioning of the European Union to horizontal co-operation agreements* [2023] C(2023) 4752 final (hereinafter "Article 101 Guidelines"); and Communication from the Commission, *Amendments to the Communication from the Commission – Guidance on the Commission's enforcement priorities in applying Article 82 of the EC Treaty to abusive exclusionary conduct by dominant undertakings* [2023] C(2023) 1923 final (hereinafter "Article 102 Guidance Paper").

5 Case C-74/14 *Eturas and Others v Lietuvos Respublikos konkurencijos taryba* [2016] EU:C:2016:42, para 27; and Case C-8/08 *T-Mobile Netherlands and Others v Raad van bestuur van de Nederlandse Mededingingsautoriteit* [2009] EU:C:2009:343, paras 32–33.

6 Case C-286/13 P *Dole Food and Dole Fresh Fruit Europe v European Commission* [2015] EU:C:2015:184, para 121; and Case C-883/19 *HSBC Holdings and Others v European Commission* [2023] EU:C:2023:11, para 115.

especially pertinent in addressing new challenges, such as the pursuit of sustainable products, services and technologies.[7] Finally, data sharing helps consumers to reduce search and switching costs and to improve their choices.[8]

Therefore, over the years, EU institutions have identified certain factors that must be analyzed in order to assess the degree of anticompetitiveness of an exchange of data and information.

Firstly, one must consider whether the exchanged data or pieces of information are *commercially sensitive*. This is the case when the data/information at hand contain either details that are likely to impact competitors' commercial strategies or essential aspects that a business must safeguard in markets with effective competition to maintain or enhance its competitive standing.[9] In practice, in order to understand whether data and information are commercially sensitive, one must consider their *content*, their *level of aggregation*, their *age* and whether they are *private or public*. For example, data and information related to pricing, costs, capacity, production, quantities, market shares, customers and plans to enter or exit markets are deemed commercially sensitive, because they involve elements that, in a genuinely competitive market, no firms would have an incentive to reveal to each other. In contrast, data and information related to the general functioning of an industry, public policies or regulatory matters, non-confidential technical issues or general promotional opportunities are considered not commercially sensitive, because they cannot affect the strategic choices of any specific firm. Analogously, data pertaining to larger groups of companies, like averages and information expressed through percentage ranges, are not considered commercially sensitive.[10] On the flip side, personalized data and information are commercially sensitive as they enable the identification of the specific firm to which they relate.

Furthermore, the sharing of historical information is improbable to result in collusion, as it is unlikely to reveal competitors' planned behavior or foster a shared understanding of the market. Generally, the older the information, the less effective it is for promptly detecting deviations and, consequently, establishing a credible threat of swift retaliation.[11]

Finally, data and information that are public – that is to say, accessible to consumers and competitors at the same costs – are less sensitive than data and information that are said to be private because they available only to the firms taking part to the sharing.[12]

Now – clearly enough – the significance for antitrust law of commercially sensitive data/information as well as the several criteria used to detect it are not tied to

7 Giulia Schneider, 'Data Sharing for Collaborative Research under Art. 101 TFEU: Lessons from The Proposed Regulations for Data Markets' (2021) 17(3) European Competition Journal https://ssrn.com/abstract=3823191 (last accessed 30 January 2024).

8 Article 101 Guidelines, para 373.

9 *Ibid.*, paras 384 and 387.

10 *Ibid.*, paras 393 and 394.

11 *Ibid.*, para 390.

12 *Ibid.*, para 395.

the advent of digital technologies! The impact of current technologies lies somewhere else: in the *transition from data to information* and in the *tools employed to make this transition happen.*

Consider first the transition from data to information. Given that information can be inferred from data, there may be instances where the exchanged data themselves are not sensitive, but the information firms autonomously derive from it is.[13] In such a case, the *key policy question* to address is whether antitrust authorities should concentrate on the non-sensitive nature of the data exchanged and refrain from intervention, or if, in order to prevent elusive strategies, they should penalize the exchange of such data, as it facilitates the acquisition of the sensitive information derived. No institution has fully answered this question yet. However, it is likely that every antitrust authority and agency will decide based on whether the firms involved in the exchange knew or should reasonably have known that the specific data sharing would be used to infer commercially sensitive information enabling collusion. If that is the case, it is really not clear why companies should get a free pass on antitrust responsibility. If they did, they would have found a pretty cheap way to form cartels and bypass the enforcement of Article 101.

The reasoning remains unchanged when considering the technological tools used to exchange data and/or infer sensitive information. In a recent case about a pricing tool shared by several firms the Commission affirmed that, "*whilst using publicly available data to feed algorithmic software is legal, the aggregation of commercially sensitive information into a pricing tool offered by a single IT company to which various competitors have access could amount to horizontal collusion*".[14] In other words, the Commission clarified that the primary focus of the analysis was not to ascertain that firms were indirectly exchanging harmless data. The essence of this antitrust investigation was to determine whether, in this specific case, the involved firms were aware or could reasonably have been aware that the collected data together with the tool used to aggregate them and the resulting information made accessible to the firms could facilitate collusion. If so, the Commission would identify a violation of Article 101, preventing firms from using innocuous data and/or algorithmic methods to bypass the prohibition of anticompetitive agreements.

In summary, collusion is likely if firms end up sharing sensitive information, regardless of the raw data from which they derive that sensitive information and the tools they use to share it.

Secondly, in order to assess the competitive impact of data sharing, one must consider the structural features of the market at hand. The more these market characteristics are similar to those of an oligopoly, the more the data sharing is able to facilitate collusion.[15] This has always been the case because, since oligopolistic

13 *Ibid.*, para 392.
14 *Ibid.*, para 402.
15 *Ibid.*, para 412.

markets are already inclined towards collusion, increasing transparency further boosts firms' incentives for collusion.

Ultimately, the assessment of the competitive repercussions of data sharing hinges on a comprehensive analysis of the exchange itself. Specifically, antitrust authorities and agencies should consider the frequency of the exchange – whether it provides firms with regularly updated data that enhances rivals' awareness of their competitors' market positions. Additionally, they should analyze the nature of the exchange: whether it is private or public, plays a crucial role. Indeed, a private exchange increases horizontal transparency by involving only rivals, while a public exchange extends transparency vertically by involving suppliers, customers and consumers as well.

In essence, data sharing falls under the purview of Article 101, when it facilitates collusion. In particular, it consists in a restriction by object when the shared data are commercially sensitive and the exchange is capable of eliminating uncertainty among participants concerning the timing, scope and specifics of the conduct to be adopted in the market.[16] Away from this extreme scenario, data sharing may admit the aforementioned procompetitive justifications and, thus, be at most a restriction by effect that must be assessed in light of the above factors: data sensitivity, market structure and all the features of the exchange itself.

This implies that if one does not fall into the (irreversible) scenario of an information exchange that serves as a restriction by object, firms can engage in behaviors that mitigate the anticompetitive effects of the exchange, while still preserving the procompetitive ones. For example, a data pool where partially commercially sensitive information is shared, addressing information asymmetry in a dispersed market and resulting in consumer benefits, is unlikely to be deemed anticompetitive if participants ensure that any commercially sensitive data exchanged is essential and proportionate to achieve the procompetitive objective. Participants may, for instance, prioritize the use of aggregate and historical data; decrease the frequency of exchanges; and implement technical and practical measures to limit access and control the utilization of the shared information. It is crucial for participants to establish the arrangement transparently.

Likewise, suppose some firms are involved in an acquisition, in a merger or in a joint venture. Typically, they have a legitimate need to access detailed information about the other party's business in order to negotiate the deal and implement the concentration. However, some information of interest may be sensitive, such as current and future price information, strategic plans, costs and non-aggregated, customer-specific information. In such a scenario, the parties must establish a

16 In general terms, a multilateral practice qualifies as a restriction by object when it lacks any procompetitive justification. After all, there's no valid procompetitive rationale for two or more firms competing against each other to exchange information about their current and future commercial strategies. *See*, in this regard, Case C-883/19 P *HSBC Holdings and Others v European Commission* [2023] EU:C:2023:11 paras 115–116; Case T-758/14 *Infineon Technologies* v *Commission* [2020] EU:T:2020:307, para 156; and Case C-286/13 P *Dole Food and Dole Fresh Fruit Europe v European Commission* [2015] EU:C:2015:184, para 122.

protocol to monitor and control the information flow, ensuring competition among firms that, during the pre-merger period, remain independent economic agents and could continue as such if the merger does not materialize. For example, the parties should select the data to be shared so that they are strictly related to the needed due diligence, mask customer identities and aggregate them, as well as limit the access to the data room to select individuals – the so-called members of the clean team.

5.3 Data Sharing as a Sword to Exploit

Historically, data sharing was not considered a tool susceptible to exploitation, meaning a tool through which (dominant) firms could impose unfair terms and conditions on their customers, be they final consumers or other businesses.

However, the rise of digital intermediaries has fueled this potential.

Digital intermediaries serve as vast repositories of digital data, accumulating extensive information about not only their users, but also the companies engaging with them. Consider, for example, Amazon. It has a dual role: it runs a marketplace where independent sellers can sell products directly to consumers and, at the same time, it sells products on its platform as a retailer, in competition with those independent sellers. As a result, Amazon has access to large datasets about the independent sellers' activities on its platform, including non-public business data, whereas its rivals have not. Thus, Amazon – and only it – can use these data to identify new product opportunities and improve its own products, potentially undercutting the prices of third-party sellers or mimicking their best-selling items. For example, it has been said that Amazon is using data from third-party sellers to create its own private-label brands, such as AmazonBasics, which sell products like batteries, phone chargers and kitchen gadgets that are similar to those offered by third-party sellers on its platform.

What is wrong with that?

As mentioned in the introduction to this chapter, utilizing data to enhance products and customer experience and/or lower prices does not disrupt the proper functioning of the market. Instead, it enhances consumer welfare by motivating firms – including Amazon – to offer superior products and services at lower prices.

However, as recently highlighted by the Commission in the *Amazon Marketplace* case,[17] having exclusive access to data poses an *unfair advantage* for digital intermediaries like Amazon. While Amazon knew the nitty-gritty details of its rivals' strategies, those rivals were left in the dark about Amazon's game plan. So, only Amazon had the upper hand, not all the players, in finely-tuning their strategies to outdo rivals in terms of pricing or quality. Thus, while enabling Amazon to make competitive retail decisions, this unbalanced sharing of data disadvantaged Amazon's competitors by creating an uneven playing field.

17 European Commission, *Commission Decision of 20.12.2022 relating to a proceeding under Article 102 of the Treaty on the Functioning of the European Union (TFEU) and Article 54 of the EEA Agreement Cases AT.40462 – Amazon Marketplace and AT.40703 – Amazon Buy Box* [2022] (published 17 February 2023) C(2022) 9442 final.

To be sure, the Commission was not forced to take a decision in *Amazon Marketplace*, although it could have applied Article 102(a) to penalize the unfair terms and conditions under which Amazon's rivals were forced to share their data. Amazon was quick: it committed to refraining from using any non-public data that pertains to independent sellers' activities on its marketplace for its retail operations. More, it extended this commitment to both Amazon's automated tools and its employees, who are now prohibited from utilizing any data derived from Amazon Marketplace to make retail-related decisions.

The legacy of *Amazon Marketplace*, however, has not been lost. We can find it in the Digital Markets Act (DMA).[18]

As explained elsewhere,[19] the DMA serves as a leveler through which European institutions have chosen to (try to) narrow the gap that currently separates gatekeepers from their competitors, aiming to approximate equality among businesses at the starting points. Therefore, not only does the DMA include numerous provisions geared towards *rebalancing the allocation of resources* between gatekeepers and their competitors,[20] but the DMA also encompasses numerous provisions aimed at *ensuring equal opportunities* between gatekeepers and their rivals. Article 6(2) is one of them and it prohibits gatekeepers from unilaterally using data that cannot be universally shared with rivals and consumers.

5.4 Data Sharing as a Shield not to Be Left Behind

In the previous paragraph, it was mentioned how the DMA entails rules mandating gatekeepers to share their resources with competitors. This is the case of the provisions on interoperability, as outlined in Articles 6(7) and 7, along with the provisions mandating gatekeepers to provide competitors access to their assets, ranging from their platforms and software to *their data*, as stipulated in Articles 5(9), 5(10), 6(3), 6(4), 6(8), 6(9), 6(10), 6(11) and 6(12).

Indeed, it has been since the early days of the digital era that we have been discussing how certain firms – the well-known GAFAM, now referred to as "digital ecosystems" or "gatekeepers" according to DMA terminology – have managed to amass massive amounts of data, the so-called "big data".

Over time, this has created an undeniable competitive edge for them compared to their competitors. In the short term, this data has allowed them to better understand their customers' needs, leading to the development of superior products and

18 Regulation (EU) 2022/1925 of the European Parliament and of the Council of 14 September 2022 on contestable and fair markets in the digital sector and amending Directives (EU) 2019/1937 and (EU) 2020/1828 (Digital Markets Act) [2022] OJ L265/1 ("DMA").

19 Mariateresa Maggiolino, 'Is the DMA (Un)fair?' (2024) 12(2) Journal of Antitrust Enforcement. https://curia.europa.eu/juris/liste.jsf?num=C-377/20 (last accessed 30 January 2024).

20 Consider, for example, the rules on interoperability, as outlined in Articles 6(7) and 7, along with the rules mandating gatekeepers to provide competitors access to their assets, ranging from their platforms and software to their data, as stipulated in Articles 5(9), 5(10), 6(3), 6(4), 6(8), 6(9), 6(10), 6(11) and 6(12).

services, consequently driving their commercial success and resulting in a significant increase in market share. Looking ahead, this data has provided GAFAM with insights into potential market trends before their competitors, enabling them to innovate more efficiently and expand into new markets with novel products and services, shaping their unique ecosystems in the process. Altogether, over the years, these data-driven activities have fueled a continuous cycle of data accumulation, creating a virtuous loop that has increasingly widened the competitive gap between them and their rivals.

Therefore, despite what some have always said about these firms' success being rooted elsewhere – in the technologies they use to analyze those terabytes of data, along with the capital and human resources they invest – there has been an immediate concern about how to allow ecosystems' rivals access to their data. In other words, the recognition of data as crucial inputs for operating in digital markets has prompted the application of competition law and the adoption of *data sharing remedies*.[21] And this in order to ensure a level playing field for digital ecosystems and their competitors, thereby preventing the exclusion of the latter from the market or their relegation to a niche within it.

In general, antitrust law does not typically address resource sharing; its focus is primarily on market conduct rather than the initial endowments enjoyed by firms.[22] However, there exists an exception known as the *essential facility doctrine*, which may be applied to dominant firms under exceptional circumstances. In essence, while dominant firms are generally free to choose their business partners and utilize their resources as they see fit, the doctrine mandates that such firms must share their resources with rivals under specific conditions.[23]

If the resources in question are not covered by IPRS, such as datasets, three conditions must be met to apply a duty to deal: the refusal is likely to eliminate all competition in the secondary (non-monopolized) market; the refusal must lack any objective justification; and the resource in question must be essential. Only this final requirement, namely the indispensability of the requested resource, is decisive in the context of data.[24]

21 *See* Marco Botta, 'Shall we share? The Principle of FRAND in B2B Data Sharing' (RSC Working Paper 2023/30, 2023). Available at: https://ssrn.com/abstract=4422925

22 Actually, in Case C-377/20, *Servizio Elettrico Nazionale and Others v Autorità Garante della Concorrenza e del Mercato and Others* [2022] EU:C:2022:379, the Court has conveyed the notion that dominant firms are not credited for producing with resources that differ from those of their competitors, especially if the competitors do not have access to the same resources used by the dominant firm. In the same vein, *see* Case C-18/88, *Régie des télégraphes et des téléphones v GB-Inno-BM SA* [1991] EU:C:1991:474, para 25, quoting Case C-202/88, *French Republic v Commission of the European Communities* [1991] EU:C:1991:120, para 51. Of course, all these cases do not involve firms that acquired their dominant positions with merit, either previous state-owned monopolists or legal monopolists operating in the highly regulated industries subject to intensive liberalization processes.

23 Case C-7/97, *Oscar Bronner v Mediaprint* [1998] EU:C:1998:569.

24 To be sure, the EU document accompanying the Communication "Building a European data economy" mentions Magill, IMS Health, Microsoft and Huawei, all IP related cases, as cases providing

According to the Court of Justice, access to an input is indispensable if there are no "technical, legal or even economic obstacles capable of making it impossible, or even unreasonably difficult" to duplicate it.[25] The Court added that, in order to demonstrate the lack of a realistic potential alternative, it would be necessary at the very least to establish that it is not economically viable to create the resource on a scale comparable to that of the firm controlling the existing product or service.[26] In other words, in order to hold an input indispensable, the requesting firm should show that such an input and its fungible alternatives are not economically viable even for the firms that decide to undertake the same investments as the dominant firm.

This conclusion suggests that at least accessible data – that is, data that can be collected from the market for free or in exchange for money – should never be considered indispensable because, in our increasingly networked world, any firm can generate and gather data or buy them from data brokers.

Additionally, there are data that are not accessible to every firm on an equal basis, and brokers do not sell them. Consider user data from digital platforms and data generated by the Internet of Things: these data are not sold, and firms employ various strategies to lock in their clients, thereby maintaining their sole *de facto* control over them.[27]

However, inaccessible data are not necessarily indispensable ones within the meaning of *Bronner*, unless it is technically, economically or legally impossible to find substitutes. In more detail, a resource is not essential as such; it is essential *in relation to* "something" and *in comparison with* the other inputs that can be used in relation to that "something". It may be true that only a producer of smart fridges holds the data about the way homemakers use them. But for what purpose will producers of smart fridges analyze its exclusive data? If they are trying to guess individuals' dietary habits, even supermarkets may know individuals' dietary habits through consideration of credit card traces. Thus, the data of the producer of smart fridges are fungible with those of supermarkets. Likewise, if Meta explores its data to infer political trends, Google may do the same by considering the data coming from its search engines. In the same vein, if a public library processes its data to approximate individuals' book preferences, an association of editors can similarly learn people's likings by questioning the data about book sales. In short, exclusivity over data does not entail exclusivity over the pieces of information that can be

indications about the application of competition law to data. I am not sure about the accuracy of this reference, as big data as such cannot be protected with IPRs. However, for the discussion of the application to data of the peculiar conditions that must be met to impose a duty to deal when the resource at hand is the subject-matter of an IPR, *see* Giuseppe Colangelo, Mariateresa Maggiolino, 'Big data as Misleading Facilities' (2017) 13(2–3) European Competition Journal, 249.

25 *Supra*, Case C-7/97, *Oscar Bronner v Mediaprint*, para 44.

26 *Ibid.*, paras 45–46.

27 Kimberly A Houser, John W Bagby, 'The Data Trust Solution To Data Sharing Problems' (2023) 25 Vanderbilt Journal of Entertainment and Technology Law. Available at: https://ssrn.com/abstract=4050593 (last accessed 30 January 2024).

inferred from those data and that will change in relation with the products/services that could be produced by using those pieces of information.

Now, this reasoning does not assert that there can never be essential datasets. Rather, it asserts that big data as a whole are never essential. For instance, consider the case of a public administration that is the sole entity legally authorized to generate and collect certain data. Since these data have no lawful substitutes, they are deemed essential. However, the same cannot be said for the terabytes of data collected by digital ecosystems, as these data can potentially be replaced by other data depending on the intended purpose.[28] Taking a closer look, the focus of our reasoning and the essential facility doctrine should be on the information needed rather than big data.[29]

In summary, the essential facility doctrine is not particularly effective in compelling digital ecosystems to share their data. This is why, as said at the very beginning of this paragraph, the DMA has introduced new obligations aimed at achieving this goal.[30]

In addition, building upon the precedent set by *Slovak Telecom*,[31] in its recent guidelines[32] the Commission has introduced a new offense: the *constructive refusal to deal*. The Commission has established that a dominant firm abuses its power when it agrees to share its resources under unfair conditions that competitors could not afford or accept. Consequently, in this scenario, the unlawful conduct arises not due to the essential (or indispensable) nature of the resource in question, but rather due to the unjust nature of the burdensome conditions forced upon or offered to competitors. In light of this, if a rival of a dominant firm holding big data were permitted to access them under unfair terms and conditions, the latter could claim that the dominant firm is abusing its dominant position. Thus, if the Commission found the infringement, it would then require the dominant firm to share its data under fair, non-discriminatory and reasonable conditions.

So far, we have discussed situations where data sharing serves as a shield for competitors of dominant companies, helping them fend off the risk of market exclusion. However, there is a scenario where data sharing could instead be wielded as a sword to produce exclusion. This is the case when a company is denied access to specific data that result from a multilateral practice, such as an exchange of data or information among firms. In essence, antitrust law can address scenarios

28 Nils-Peter Schepp, Achim Wambach, 'On Big Data and its Relevance for Market Power Assessment' (2016) 7(2) Journal of European Competition Law & Practice, 120.

29 Rolf H Weber, 'Information at the Crossroads of Competition and Data Protection Law' (2014) 12(2) Zeitschrift für Wettbewerbsrecht, 169.

30 Xingyu Yan, Huaiwen He, 'Fine-Tuning the Ex-Ante Approach to Regulating Data Combination Practices' (Journal of Competition Law & Economics, 2021). Available at: https://ssrn.com/abstract=3842901

31 Case C-165/19 P *Slovak Telekom v European Commission (Slovak Telekom)* [2021] EU:C:2021:239, paras 50–51. *See* further Case C-42/21 P *Lietuvos geležinkeliai AB v European Commission* [2023] EU:C:2023:12, paras 81–84 and 91.

32 *See* Article 102 Guidance Paper, para 4.

where commercially sensitive information is exchanged and the exchange covers a substantial portion of that market, putting non-participating competitors at a significant disadvantage compared to those involved in the exchange.[33]

5.5 The Protection of Competition and Personal Data

Spanning across the aforementioned subjects, the emergence of the data-driven economy has compelled legal experts in antitrust to grapple with a previously unexplored issue: specifically, it has urged them to delve into the connection between competition law and regulations like the GDPR, which safeguard personal data. The latter constitute indeed a subset of the data that firms process to offer products and services.

Despite the heated debate surrounding the relationship between antitrust law and the protection of personal data,[34] there is a straightforward – almost simplistic – way to approach the issue.

Let us consider any unilateral or multilateral practice engaged in by one or more firms. By asking ourselves two straightforward questions about these actions – namely, whether they negatively impact the functioning of the market in terms of

33 *See* Article 101 Guidelines, para 382.

34 The debate can essentially be reduced to two main positions. Under a separatist approach, data protection and antitrust law are separated and not overlapping, since they protect different interests. *See* Maureen K Ohlhausen, Alexander P Okuliar, 'Competition, Consumer Protection, and the Right [Approach] to Privacy' (2015) 80(1) Antitrust Law Journal. Available at: https://ssrn.com/abstract=2561563; and James C Cooper, 'Privacy and Antitrust: Underpants Gnomes, the First Amendment, and Subjectivity' (George Mason Law & Economics Research Paper No 13–39, 2013), available at: https://ssrn.com/abstract=2283390, where he contends that "antitrust is the wrong vehicle to address privacy concerns". More moderate is the position of Eugene Kimmelman, Harold Feld, Agustín Rossi, 'The Limits of Antitrust in Privacy Protection' (2018) 8(3) International Data Privacy Law, 270, claiming that antitrust can be "one tool in the toolbox" for the protection of personal data.

On the other hand, under an integrationist approach, data protection considerations should be incorporated into antitrust analysis, because privacy is a non-price dimension of competition. *See* Peter Swire, 'Protecting Consumers: Privacy Matters in Antitrust Analysis' (*Centre For American Progress*, 19 October 2007) available at https://www.americanprogress.org/article/protecting-consumers-privacy-matters-in-antitrust-analysis/; and Robert H Lande, '*The Microsoft-Yahoo Merger: Yes, Privacy is an Antitrust Concern*' (University of Baltimore School of Law Legal Studies Research Paper No 2008-06, 2008) available at: https://ssrn.com/abstract=1121934. *See* also Maurice E Stucke, Allen P Grunes, 'No Mistake About It: The Important Role of Antitrust in the Era of Big Data' (University of Tennessee Legal Studies Research Paper No 269, 2015). Available at: https://ssrn.com/abstract=2600051

In more recent times, the integrationist theory has been partially reconsidered on the assumption that data protection and antitrust law might also be at odds. *See* Maurice E Stucke, 'The Relationship Between Privacy and Antitrust' (University of Tennessee Legal Studies Research Paper No 434, 2022) available at: https://ssrn.com/abstract=4042262. *See* also Giuseppe Colangelo, 'The Privacy/Antitrust Curse: Insights From GDPR Application in Competition Law Proceedings' (ICLE White Paper 2023–10–12, 2023) available at: https://ssrn.com/abstract=4599974, and Erika M Douglas, 'The New Antitrust/Data Privacy Law Interface' (2021) 130 Yale Law Journal, 647, both highlighting that data protection policies can be used as justification for anticompetitive behaviors and that behavioral remedies might have a detrimental impact on individual's privacy.

consumer welfare, and whether they adversely affect the level of privacy for the individuals of that market – we can identify the four scenarios in which the interface between antitrust law and the protection of personal data plays out.

The first two scenarios illustrate cases where the application of competition law inadvertently aligns with the protection of privacy. This alignment results in either the preservation of personal data as a consequential, albeit unintended, outcome of competition protection, or the punishment of privacy-decreasing conduct as a byproduct of safeguarding market well-functioning.

Imagine, for example, a dominant firm or a group of collaborating firms introducing a product, service or technology that is both innovative and privacy enhancing. This conduct is not restrictive to competition because the innovative offering enhances consumer welfare. Additionally, it does not violate privacy laws, including GDPR, as the innovation actually improves the level of privacy available in the market without involving any unlawful processing of personal data. In this case, hence, it is clear that the conduct poses no issues for those seeking to safeguard competition and personal data.

Next, consider the case of a dominant firm applying excessively high prices for the use of a privacy-friendly technology. Such conduct clearly violates Article 102(a) and, in addition, diminishes the level of privacy that consumers can afford. Similarly, consider a scenario where a dominant firm, interested in maintaining monopolistic prices in the market it dominates, excludes its horizontal rivals through a lengthy exclusive contract with a distributor holding a market share exceeding 40%. Suppose, in addition, that these foreclosed rivals happen to be companies capable of offering products, services or technologies that are more respectful of personal data than those of the dominant company. In this case, hence, the exclusionary and anticompetitive conduct evidently diminishes both competition and privacy levels in the market. Finally, ponder the case of two or more pharmaceutical companies exchanging data on the quantities of drugs they are preparing to sell for the treatment of a specific disease. Suppose that from reading those data, which are provided in a granular (non-aggregated) manner, one can trace back to the patients who will receive the drugs, either because the data has not been properly anonymized or because their anonymization can be easily bypassed. Suppose also that these patients have never consented to this data exchange between pharmaceutical companies. This conduct would constitute both a restriction by object under Article 101, as it would enable pharmaceutical companies to eliminate uncertainty regarding their future quantities (and thus prices), and a violation of Article 6 of the GDPR because – once again – the processing of patients' personal data could not be considered lawful, as it is not freely and expressly authorized. In short, hence, while there may be numerous examples, the key point in this second scenario is that it is equally clear that the practices at hand must be prohibited, because there will be no doubts about their harmful nature.

At most, in this second scenario, other types of issues may arise. Firstly, there is the question of whether a case of *ne bis in idem* could be at play, meaning whether it would be possible for one or more firms to face two sanctions for the same conduct.[35] Additionally, there is the matter of how the authorities responsible for enforcing antitrust law and the GDPR should coordinate. In this regard, the recent Judgment of the Court of Justice[36] regarding the *Bundeskartellamt v Facebook* case clarified that the "North Star" guiding relationships among an antitrust and a data protection authority is that of loyal cooperation. In concrete terms, this means that when an antitrust authority needs to assess whether a certain conduct respects the GDPR, it must verify, before anything else, if an authority responsible for the enforcement of the Regulation has already decided on that issue. Moreover, in case of doubt on a previous GPDR-authority decision (or when its proceeding has already started) the two authorities must consult each other. If consulted, the authority responsible for the enforcement of the GDPR must respond promptly and in any case within a reasonable timeframe.[37]

In summary, in the above scenarios, safeguarding personal data may be achieved through protecting a well-functioning market. But let us turn our attention to the other two, more complex scenarios: that where a behavior harms competition yet enhances privacy protection, and that where a behavior reduces privacy protection – or even infringes the GDPR – without impeding competition. In these cases, the questions that arise are as follows: should conduct that violates antitrust laws go unpunished because it promotes privacy levels in the market? And should conduct that does not infringe Articles 101 and 102 still be penalized by antitrust authorities because it diminishes the level of privacy guaranteed in the market?

Advocates of the notion that antitrust law should pursue multiple objectives simultaneously would firstly argue that if antitrust law safeguards both competition and personal data, privacy-related considerations should significantly influence the assessment of practices violating Articles 101 or Articles 102. They might even argue that such practices should be considered lawful in the interest of personal

35 Giuseppe Colangelo, Marco Cappai, 'Applying ne bis in idem in the Aftermath of bpost and Nordzucker: The Case of EU Competition Policy in Digital Markets' (a modified version is forthcoming in Common Market Law Review, 2023). Available at: https://ssrn.com/abstract=4344075 (last accessed 30 January 2024).

36 Case C-252/21 *Meta Platforms and Others v Bundeskartellamt* [2023] EU:C:2023:537.

37 This Judgment, which clarified, among other things, that the antitrust authority can ascertain a violation of the GDPR regulation only incidentally, for the sole purpose of applying the rules that protect the proper conduct of competitive games, can be interpreted in two ways. According to a broader interpretation, the Court of Justice has clarified the relationship between all administrative authorities in the European Union. This implies that also the authority responsible for enforcing the GDPR could incidentally identify violations of rules aimed at protecting competition, in coordination and consultation with the competent antitrust authority. Under a more restrictive interpretation, one could conclude that the aforementioned ruling pertains only to the scenario where a violation of the GDPR is incidentally detected by an antitrust authority, and not vice versa. Although contacts between different administrative authorities may occur, they should be considered merely occasional. For this topic, *see* Valeria Caforio, 'Molto rumore per nulla: la sentenza della Corte di giustizia sul rapporto tra diritto della concorrenza e tutela dei dati personali nell'Unione europea' (2023) Il diritto industriale, 404; Vincenzo Iaia, 'The Strengthening Liaison between Data Protection, Antitrust and Consumer Law in the German and Italian Big Data-Driven Economies' (2021) 26(2) Bialystok Legal Studies. Available at: https://ssrn.com/abstract=4533788

data protection. For example, this would be the case of a dominant firm, such as Google, planning to phase out third-party cookies – on which the entire online advertising industry relied on for tracking and collecting users' data – on Chrome, in order to substitute it with a new tool, known as "Privacy Sandbox". This initiative was investigated both by the CMA[38] and the European Commission.[39] The two competition authorities were worried that Google would have distorted competition and abused its dominant position, while the latter argued that its goal was to enhance privacy on the web. While the proceeding of the European Commission had not ended yet, the CMA accepted the commitments by Google:[40] the two will work together to modify the proposal of removing third-party cookies from Chrome, ensuring that both competition and privacy will be preserved.[41]

Secondly, those advocating for the multi-purpose approach would maintain that antitrust law should punish practices hindering privacy, even if they do not undermine competition, as the Bundeskartellamt did in the *Facebook* case. The German Competition Authority has argued that Facebook abused its dominant position in the social networking services market by collecting user data despite the rules of the GDPR. It was found that Facebook collected user data without disclosing and explaining to users why and how their data was being processed. Specifically, Facebook failed to disclose that it gathered data from various sources to combine them, a practice that enhanced Facebook's ability to profile users and, consequently, diminished the level of privacy provided to them. However, this way of collecting data was neither unfair in competitive terms, nor exclusionary. The German Competition Authority did not prove that in a competitive scenario

38 Competition and Markets Authority, 'Investigation into Google's "Privacy Sandbox" browser changes' (Gov.uk, 8 January 2021). Available at: https://www.gov.uk/cma-cases/investigation-into-googles-privacy-sandbox-browser-changes (last accessed 30 January 2024).

39 European Commission, Case AT.40670, Google - Adtech and Data-Related Practices [2021]. Available at: https://competition-cases.ec.europa.eu/cases/AT.40670

40 As far as the academic debate following Google's proposal and the antitrust authorities' investigations is concerned, *see* Damien Geradin, Dimitrios Katsifis and Theano Karanikioti, 'Google as a de facto Privacy Regulator: Analyzing Chrome's Removal of Third-party Cookies from an Antitrust Perspective' (TILEC Discussion Paper No DP2020–034, 2020). Available at: https://ssrn.com/abstract=3738107; and Mark Nottingham, 'Playing Fair in the Privacy Sandbox: Competition, Privacy and Interoperability Standards' (2021). Available at: https://ssrn.com/abstract=3891335

41 Along the same lines is the case of Apple's Tracking Transparency (ATT) Policy. Apple has required developers of its competitor apps that use the Apple Store to adopt a policy that provides greater protection for user privacy. This imposition was analyzed by a Market Study conducted by the CMA – https://www.gov.uk/cma-cases/mobile-ecosystems-market-study#launch-of-market-study, (Final Report, Appendix J, para 185) – which stated that, "we are concerned that Apple's current implementation of ATT is likely to result in harm to competition" and that "we consider that there are a number of ways in which the potential competition harms of ATT could be mitigated while retaining the benefits in terms of user choice and privacy". The Italian Competition Authority, as well as several other European authorities, has also initiated an investigation into this matter – *see* https://www.agcm.it/dettaglio?db=41256297003874BD&uid=8A27F73C4C9ADB7BC12589B00038A780&view=&title=A561-APP%20TRACKING%20TRANSPARENCY%20DI%20APPLE&fs=%20%2082_CE/102_CE-Abuso%20di%20posizione%20dominante

Facebook would have collected the data in a more transparent way. Furthermore, it did not show that Facebook's rivals were prevented from collecting data.[42]

Others contend that antitrust law ought to solely safeguard the market's functionality as reflected in changes to consumer welfare. They argue that in the first scenario, antitrust law should be applied, while in the second scenario, it should not. This stance, often referred to as "purist", is supported by various policy arguments, ranging from concerns about the wastage of resources that may result from the application of two separate pieces of law to the creation of a super antitrust authority tasked with double-checking prohibitions already covered by other pieces of legislation.[43] Nevertheless, there is a technical argument deserving of consideration in bolstering their position – an argument that is frequently disregarded and that is focused on consumers' willingness to pay for the protection of their personal data.

5.5.1 Willingness to Pay and Personal Data Protection

How does the market operate? In other words, how does the dynamic between supply and demand play out? When consumers are ready to pay for a product or service, businesses vie with one another to provide what consumers want.

So, if consumers in a certain market are willing to pay for safeguarding their personal data and ensuring privacy, businesses in that market will compete to offer products, services and technologies that meet consumers' privacy needs. Therefore, if a firm's practice in that market promotes privacy, the firm can not only justify its behavior, but also present it as beneficial to consumers, as firms usually do when their practices produce efficiency gains or quality improvements. Conversely, if a firm's action reduces privacy, it is possible to argue that it causes a consumer harm, because it is possible to imagine a scenario where without that action a more privacy-friendly equilibrium could have been achieved. Hence, in line with the "traditional antitrust approach", one could argue that in this second case the firm's action has resulted in an anticompetitive effect. All in all, if consumers are willing to pay for privacy, then the argument for incorporating the protection of personal data as an independent goal of competition law becomes irrelevant, because privacy increases result in consumer welfare increases, whereas privacy decreases result in consumer welfare decreases.

However, if consumers in a specific market are not keen on paying for the protection of their personal data – that is, ensuring a certain level of privacy – then the

42 See Giuseppe Colangelo, Mariateresa Maggiolino, 'Data Accumulation and the Privacy-Antitrust Interface: Insights from the Facebook Case for the EU and the U.S.' (Stanford Law School and the University of Vienna School of Law TTLF Working Paper No 31/2018. A modified version of the paper has been published in (2018) 8(3) International Data Privacy Law, 224). Available at: https://ssrn.com/abstract=3125490; and 'Antitrust Über Alles. Whither Competition Law After Facebook?' (2019) 42(3) World Competition Law and Economics Review. Available at: https://ssrn.com/abstract=3362428 (last accessed 30 January 2024).

43 Eugene Kimmelman, Harold Feld, Agustín Rossi, 'The Limits of Antitrust in Privacy Protection' (2018) and the arguments played out by Colangelo and Maggiolino in the papers quoted above.

argument just outlined lacks validity. Simply put, it is futile for firms to invest in efforts to enhance privacy by offering privacy-friendly products, services or technologies, when there is essentially no demand for privacy. Conversely, if consumers show no interest in safeguarding personal data and a firm's action lowers the privacy standard in the market, there is no scenario where a higher privacy level would naturally emerge. Therefore, the decline in privacy resulting from the firm's conduct cannot be considered a restriction of competition because competition was lacking from the outset.

This second scenario illustrates that advocating for antitrust laws to pursue additional goals beyond safeguarding competition, such as protecting privacy, presupposes that all consumers are consistently willing to pay for privacy, even when they are not. Consequently, it implies that all companies compete for privacy, even in cases where they do not.

This is why staunch advocates of antitrust law find it difficult to embrace the idea of antitrust law simultaneously serving various goals. Antitrust law is not the equivalent of a piece of top-down legislation that lawmakers use to protect one or multiple legal interests. Antitrust law aims to prevent companies from exploiting their power to manipulate competition, which naturally arises from businesses' drive to cater to consumers' needs. Therefore, using antitrust law to promote an objective like privacy when consumers – perhaps ignorantly or shortsightedly – are not actively seeking privacy measures, amounts to applying provisions that penalize competition restrictions in the absence of any real competition to restrict!

This is the fiction at the heart of the so-called multi-purpose approach that staunch antitrust scholars struggle to endorse.

5.6 Conclusion

Reading through this chapter, the reader may have mixed feelings.

On the one hand, the discussion about data sharing as a collusion tool does not appear particularly groundbreaking. It is still important, when assessing whether a data exchange among competitors falls under Article 101, to consider whether it eliminates or reduces the uncertainty that should naturally exist in their relationships. Similarly, the parameters to ponder when making this assessment remain the same: one must consider the sensitivity of the exchanged data, the market structure and the characteristics of the entire exchange.

On the other hand, the examination of data sharing as a means to either exploit rivals or level the playing field is a direct consequence of the increasing significance of data in digital society as valuable assets. What is strikingly evident is that antitrust law lacks the most effective tools to address the need for fair resource distribution and equal opportunities among companies operating within the market. In simpler terms, antitrust law typically focuses on how companies, through their actions that either consolidate or exploit market power, influence supply and demand, thereby impacting resource allocation and incentives for innovation. Antitrust law is not accustomed to enforcing prohibitions and obligations to ensure equal starting points among companies. Consequently, first, there has been some partial evolution in antitrust law in recent months, exemplified by cases like *Amazon Marketplace* and the establishment of the new offense of the constructive refusal to deal. Secondly, it was however necessary for European institutions to adopt the DMA.

Lastly, the chapter touched upon another potential development in antitrust law: the idea of making privacy protection a distinct objective. However, it was noted that this option seems unnecessary when consumers are willing to pay for privacy, and it involves accepting a fiction when they are not.

6 The Role of Intellectual Property Rights in Data-Sharing Obligations

Maria Lillà Montagnani

6.1 Introduction

As mentioned in many instances in the book, in the current era of digital technology growth, data has emerged as a crucial asset for companies. The accessibility of data and advanced techniques for mass data collection have increased, paving the way for more sophisticated analysis of unprecedented volumes of information. This progress is driven by the expanding sources of data collection, which are no longer confined to the digital realm. Emerging technologies now extend their influence across diverse aspects of life, making data-generating machines and technologies essential additions to our homes, health and lifestyle. This includes the integration of the Internet of Things (IoT), artificial intelligence (AI), robotics and various other autonomous systems.

Access to extensive datasets not only enables companies to gain a deeper understanding of consumers but is also vital for the ongoing development and innovation of technologies such as IoT and AI. Smart devices, engaging with both each other and the internet, generate, accumulate and share intricate details about their functionality and the surrounding world, thereby contributing to their refinement. For instance, sensors and devices within a smart home security system do not only gather data about the household's security status but also interact with each other and external services. A smart camera not only captures footage of any suspicious activity but also communicates with other security devices, such as motion sensors and door/window sensors, to provide a comprehensive overview of the situation. Additionally, this data could be shared with a central monitoring service or local law enforcement to enhance overall security measures. The insights derived from analyzing this data contribute to refining the system's performance, improving security protocols and optimizing the overall functionality of the smart home security ecosystem. Consequently, access to data has become indispensable for maximizing the potential of emerging technologies, serving as a crucial foundation for the development of new business models and advancing research across scientific and social domains.

Recognizing the significant correlation between data and market success, industry players heavily invest in the accumulation of data and contemporary data analytics techniques. Databases or data silos have evolved into pivotal economic assets for companies. Despite having access to substantial data volumes, it has

DOI: 10.4324/9781003248255-9

not become yet common for enterprises to share this information. The majority of companies tend to retain their data rather than share it,[1] to the point that a semi-property right on data was called.[2] This reluctance to share, however, may arise not only from a competitive strategy but also from legal uncertainties surrounding data transfer and use – concerns that proponents of an exclusive right over data considered mitigated by its introduction – as well as the need to comply with data protection regulations and intellectual property rights (IPRs).

On the other hand, over the last decade, the establishment of a free flow of data – i.e. the unrestricted movement of data across borders and IT systems in the EU – has been the objective of many EU institutions' policies aiming at fostering the data economy and a digital single market (DSM).[3] It is indeed through the fostering of the flow of data in the DSM – that is by making data the most accessible and usable possible across borders for all types of market players – that a well-functioning and dynamic data economy can be achieved. Similarly, the free flow of data is quintessential for the development of the European AI, which requires access to high-quality data and the "possibility to use, combine and re-use data from various sources".[4]

For this reason – and despite the initial reluctance to impose data-sharing obligations on private actors – the EU institutions – as discussed in detail in the book – introduced B2B data-sharing obligations in the Data Act (DA).[5] The DA presents various mechanisms for fostering the sharing of private data and lowering transaction costs linked to business-to-business (B2B) and customer-to-business (C2B) data sharing. It does so through the implementation of a framework for data intermediaries – that will handle the sharing of data by individuals, public bodies and private companies – and the establishment of the so called European common data spaces. At the same time, the Data Governance Act (DGA)[6] mandates data sharing among public authorities (G2B), businesses and users established in the EU as to data resulting from users' interaction with connected devices with the clear procompetitive rationale of fostering the creation of secondary and repairing markets.

1 European Commission, Communication to the European Parliament et al., *"Building a European Data Economy"* [2017] COM(2017) 9 final 8–9.

2 European Commission, Communication to the European Parliament et al., *A Digital Single Market Strategy for Europe* [2015] COM(2015) 192 final, 2015; European Commission, *Staff Working Document: A Digital Single Market Strategy for Europe – Analysis and Evidence* [2015] SWD(2015) 100 final, 2015; European Commission, *Staff Working Document on the free flow of data and emerging issues of the European data economy* [2017] SWD(2017) 2 final 33–38.

3 European Commission, *"Building a European Data Economy"* COM(2017) 9 final 2.

4 Annexes to the Communication from the Commission to the European Parliament, the European Council, the Council, the European Economic and Social Committee and the Committee of the Regions *Fostering a European approach to Artificial Intelligence* [2021] COM(2021) 205 final 11.

5 Regulation (EU) 2023/2854 of the European Parliament and of the Council of 13 December 2023 on harmonized rules on fair access to and use of data and amending Regulation (EU) 2017/2394 and Directive (EU) 2020/1828 (Data Act) [2023] OJ L, 2023/2854.

6 Regulation (EU) 2022/868 of the European Parliament and of the Council of 30 May 2022 on European data governance and amending Regulation (EU) 2018/1724 (Data Governance Act) [2022] OJ L152/1.

Both the DGA and DA address the issue of IPRs, emphasizing that the sharing of data must adhere to the existing legal framework and respect fundamental rights.[7] As a matter of fact, IPRs – coupled with data protection rules – have often been perceived as obstacles to the sharing of data, not just those held by companies but also by public sector bodies. Since the adoption of the first public sector information directive,[8] access and reuse of data held by public sector bodies (PSBs) became mandatory but should not interfere with any exclusive rights, namely it did not have the effect of limiting the exercise of IPRs that PSBs or third parties had on the data.[9] Over time, however, the reflection on how to accommodate compliance with IPRs protection within sharing obligation has developed. The DGA and DA mirror the shifting approach of the EU institutions to the matter.

In this chapter, I analyze how IPRs interact within the data realm and how the EU regulatory system accommodates IPRs in sharing/access and reuse obligations. To do this, I first briefly review the initial phase of the interplay between IPRs and data, highlighting the limited influence that the former has had on the latter, and the unsuccessful attempt to introduce a semi-property right on data – the data producer's right (Section 2). This includes considering the specific interaction between data and various IPRs: patents (Section 2.1), copyright (Section 2.2) and trade secrets (Section 2.3). In the second part of the chapter, I examine the EU's paradigmatic shift from reinforcing IP rights – or even semi-property rights – in the data realm to focusing on incentivizing data access and flows. This evolution in the relationship between IP and data is clearly reflected in the DGA and DA, which have already been analyzed in detail in this book, although without considering the dimension of IP interaction. In this context, I specifically discuss the role of data intermediaries, data spaces and the revision of the trade secrets and database directives. Finally, I conclude by assessing the change in the EU approach and by considering the actual role of IPRs in the EU regulatory framework relevant for data sharing.

6.2 The Initial Phase of the Relationship between Data and IPRs

The first phase of the relationship between IPRs and data is characterized by the idea that the latter could work as incentives for data-driven markets by providing that entitlement on data that would enable their licensing. This sparked a controversial debate in academia. Upon closer examination, however, this hypothesis failed to withstand scrutiny,[10] nor did it align with the approach adopted by the EU

7 See recitals 17, 20, 21 of Data Governance Act and recitals 13, 16, 30 of Data Act.

8 Directive 2003/98/EC of the European Parliament and of the Council of 17 November 2003 on the re-use of public sector information [2003] OJ L345/90 90–96.

9 Directive 2003/98/EC, recital 22, and Art 1.

10 Josef Drexl et al. 'Position Statement of the Max Planck Institute for Innovation and Competition of 26 April 2017 on the European Commission's "Public consultation on Building the European Data Economy"'. (Max Planck Institute for Innovation & Competition Research Paper No 17–08, MPI Munich, April 2017) https://www.ip.mpg.de/fileadmin/ipmpg/content/stellungnahmen/MPI

institutions since the Communication on a European strategy for data.[11] The idea of exclusive rights – particularly a new data producers' right – was left behind in favor of the principle of access and sharing of data for the better of the public good, as well as for technological optimization. The following subsections analyze the limits of IPRs in providing protection for data. For the sake of completeness, it also recalls the failed attempt to adopt a new *sui generis* right on data.

6.2.1 Patents and Data

Within the realm of IPRs, patents are typically associated with protection of technical entities like machinery or electronic devices such as autonomous vehicles. Consequently, one may consider them suitable for protecting the machine-generated data associated with these technologies. However, an invention, whether a product (instrument, machine or compound) or a process (industrial procedure or processing method), eligible for patent protection must meet certain criteria. It should not have been publicly disclosed before, must be original and not deducible in an obvious manner from existing technical knowledge at the time of patent application. When it comes to data, even if it is linked to an invention – as it is generated by a patented machine or collected through a patented process – it typically lacks the necessary features for patent eligibility. This is because the data primarily holds descriptive attributes, representing the output generated by a device (e.g., a patented sensor) or through a process and is generally observable by anyone with the appropriate means.

An argument for extending patent protection to include data suggests that not only the process but also its resulting product – the data generated by a patented technology – deserves protection. However, this argument was rejected in a notable case, *Rezeptortyrosinkinase II*,[12] by the German Federal Court of Justice (BGH). The court, in this instance, ruled against patent protection for the data sequence generated through a patented genetic test method.[13] The BGH emphasized that the

_Statement_Public_consultation_on_Building_the_EU_Data_Eco_28042017.pdf; P Bernt Hugenholtz, 'Against "Data Property"' in Hanns Ullrich, Peter Drahos and Gustavo Ghidini (eds), *Kritika: Essays on Intellectual Property* (Vol 3, Edward Elgar 2018) 48; Herbert Zech, 'A Legal Framework for a Data Economy in the European Digital Single Market: Rights to Use Data' (2016) 11(6) JIPLP 460; Bruno Zeller, Robert Walters, Leon Trakman, 'Is Privacy and Personal Data Set to Become the New Intellectual Property?' (2019) 50(8) IIC 937; Ciani Jacopo, 'Governing Data Trade in Intelligent Environments: A Taxonomy of Possible Regulatory Regimes between Property and Access Rights' in Ioannis Chatzigiannakis, Yoshito Tobe, Paulo Novais, Oliver Amft (eds), *Intelligent Environments* 2018 (London, IOS Press 2018) 285.

11 European Commission, Communication to the European Parliament et al., *A European strategy for data* [2020] COM(2020) 66 final.

12 BGH, Judgement of 27 September 2016, Case X ZR 124/15, *Rezeptortyrosinkinase II* (2017) GRUR 261.

13 This does, however, not account for the pharmaceutical sector; on data exclusivity in the pharmaceutical sector, *see* Maria Isabel Manley and Grant Strachan, 'Regulatory Data Protection' in Maria Isabel Manley and Marina Vickers (eds), *Navigating European Pharmaceutical Law* (Oxford, OUP 2015) 255.

information in the test results did not enjoy protection under the German Patent Law. For data to be covered by the patent protection granted to the process, it must exhibit factual-technical properties imparted by the process, making it a suitable subject for factual patenting. Hence, it is evident from legal precedents that patent protection does not extend to data produced by or generated from patented processes.

6.2.2 Copyright and Data

Among IPRs, copyright is renowned for offering the broadest scope of protection, encompassing a diverse array of works that have evolved and expanded over the years. Initially designed to safeguard publishers' interests in the realm of literature, copyright protection has continuously broadened its reach due to the recognition of new forms of human creativity deserving protection, such as computer programs and databases. It is this inherent expansiveness that makes copyright particularly compelling when seeking avenues for safeguarding newly developed concepts.

However, for an object to qualify for copyright protection, it must constitute a creative work, representing the original outcome of the author's intellectual creation.[14] To be granted protection such a criterion should be met by data, including both individual pieces of data and organized data, such as databases.

As to the former, the information generated through automated processes cannot be deemed a product of intellectual creation in itself, regardless of the intellectual effort invested in developing the technology that produces or processes the data. Consequently, data lacks the requisite level of originality. Even if copyright protection were applicable to the generated data, it would not address the question of determining the rightful owners among various potential actors – such as the machine designer, manufacturer or user – involved in data generation and collection activities.

As to the case of data in its accumulated form, that is, a set of information organized in the form of collections, compilations and lastly, databases, the scenario is more complicated.

First, collections of works receive explicit protection under international and European law. For instance, Article 2 of the Berne Convention safeguards "collections of literary or artistic works, such as encyclopedias and anthologies, which, due to the selection and arrangement of their contents, constitute intellectual creations". The definition of "literary or artistic work" has evolved to encompass productions in literary, scientific or artistic fields, irrespective of the mode or form of expression. This broader interpretation is affirmed internationally in both the TRIPS and the WCT, explicitly expanding the scope of copyright protection. Articles 5 of the WCT and 10(2) of TRIPS specifically mention "compilations of data or other material", whether in machine-readable or other forms, potentially

14 Eleonora Rosati, 'Originality in a Work, or a Work of Originality: The Effects of the Infopaq Decision' (2010–2011) 58(4) Journal of the Copyright Society U.S.A 795.

eligible for protection if they meet the creativity requirement in their selection and arrangement.

In the EU, the Directive 96/9/EC on the legal protection of databases[15] adopts this approach, defining a database as "a collection of independent works, data, or other materials arranged systematically or methodically and individually accessible by electronic or other means". This directive mandates EU Member States to ensure copyright protection for databases resulting from an author's intellectual creation, establishing databases as distinctive objects of copyright protection in Europe. However, due to databases' functional nature, concerns persist regarding their eligibility for copyright protection based on the requirement of "originality", initially designed for artistic creations. Recognizing these challenges and to foster information technology development in Europe, Directive 96/9/EC introduces a two-tier system: copyright protection for "original" databases and a *sui generis* database right for those not meeting the minimum originality standard but resulting from significant investment.[16] As far as the first layer is concerned, the existence of a "creative" database is rare in practice, particularly with the rise of big data, whose databases often lack a specific approach or strategy, being the product of purely technical considerations that exclude creative freedom. This also affects the second layer, that is the protection under the *sui generis* right, as randomly collected "big data" may not entail the necessary level of investment. In addition, for *sui generis* protection, legislation demands a "considerable human, technical, and financial" investment, focusing on qualitative and quantitative aspects.[17] Notably, this protection does not extend to investments solely for creating data, as clarified in court judgments related to the unauthorized use of sports event calendars.[18]

In any case, even where a database is awarded protection under copyright or the *sui generis* right, the object of protection remains only the "structure" of the

15 Directive 96/9/EC of the European Parliament and of the Council of March 11, 1996, on the legal protection of databases [1996] OJ L77/20.

16 On the ineffectiveness of the Directive in pursuing its objective *see* P Bernt Hugenholtz, 'Something Completely Different: Europe's Sui Generis Database Right' in Susy Frankel and Daniel Gervais (eds), *The Internet and the Emerging Importance of New Forms of Intellectual Property* (Netherlands, Kluwer Law International, Wolters Kluwer 2016) 205.

17 Estelle Derclaye, 'Database "Sui Generis" Right: Should We Adopt the Spin-Off Theory?' (2004) 26(9) EIPR 402.

18 Four landmark judgments issued by the European Court of Justice, each of them concerning the unauthorized use of sports event calendars by betting companies, specified that the *sui generis* right on databases does not protect investments made solely for the creation of data. *See* Judgments of the ECJ, November 9, 2004, Case C-46/02 *Fixtures Marketing Ltd v Oy Veikkaus Ab* [2004] EU:C:2004:694; Case C-203/02 *British Horseracing Board Ltd v William Hill Organization Ltd* [2004] EU:C:2004:695; Case C-338/02 *Fixtures Marketing Ltd v Svenska Spel AB* [2004] EU:C:2004:696; Case C-444/02 *Fixtures Marketing Ltd v Organismos Prognostikon Agonon Podosfairou AE* [2004] EU:C:2004:697. In general, the justification is that the objective of the *sui generis* right is to promote the establishment of storage and processing systems for existing information, not to protect the creation of further material, even if this may eventually become the content of a database. On the concept of creation of data *see* Mark J Davison, P Bernt Hugenholtz 'Football Fixtures, Horse Races and Spin-Offs: The ECJ Domesticates the Database Right' (2005) 27(3) EIPR 113.

database, referring to the selection or arrangement of the content. Both international treaties and European legislation are clear in this regard, as they expressly state that the protection "shall not extend to their contents" or "mere facts or data".[19]

6.2.3 Trade Secrets and Data

Another means of safeguarding information that has gained increasing relevance is the protection of commercial confidentiality concerning "business know-how" as a competitive asset. This scope also encompasses individual pieces of information, making trade secret protection one of the few legal mechanisms really capable of ensuring effective protection for data itself. However, instead of conferring an exclusive usage right, trade secrecy serves as a defense mechanism against third-party appropriation of the secret.[20]

Recent reforms in legislation regarding business confidentiality are reflected in the EU Directive 2016/943 on the protection of undisclosed know-how and business information (trade secrets).[21] For information to be considered a protectable "trade secret", it must, first and foremost, be "secret" in the sense that it is not generally known or readily accessible to individuals typically dealing with that kind of information. Additionally, it must possess "commercial value" due to its secrecy, and the confidentiality must be actively maintained by the person controlling the information through appropriate security measures.

To evaluate whether data fall within the category of protectable trades secrets, one should first question the secrecy of data – either as a whole or in the precise configuration and combination of their elements – and their accessibility by industry experts and operators. While certain digital data can undoubtedly be kept under a regime of secrecy and, consequently, remain unknown or not easily accessible to industry experts and operators, many of them, even if significant for the development of digital technologies, are certainly not born as secrets. This is always the case, for example, with data from public sources, and it is often the case with data collected through sensors. There are those who believe that if the data are inherently accessible – as is usually the case for data forming collections automatically within the Internet of Things – then protection is undoubtedly excluded.[22] Others, however, distinguish the accessibility of individual components of a data collection

19 Directive 96/9/EC, Art 3(2), recitals 45 f. *See* also Herbert Zech, 'Data as a Tradeable Commodity' in Alberto De Franceschi (ed), *European Contract Law and the Digital Single Market: The Implications of the Digital Revolution* (Cambridge, Intersentia 2016) 73.

20 Wolfgang Kerber, 'A New (Intellectual) Property Right for Non-Personal Data? An Economic Analysis' (2016) 65(11) GRUR International 994.

21 Directive (EU) 2016/943 of the European Parliament and of the Council of June 8 2016 on the protection of undisclosed know-how and business information (trade secrets) against their unlawful acquisition, use and disclosure [2016] OJ L157/1.

22 Josef Drexl, Reto Hilty et al., 'Data Ownership and Access to Data – Position Statement of the Max Planck Institute for Innovation and Competition of 16 August 2016 on the Current European Debate' (Max Planck Institute for Innovation & Competition Research Paper No 16–10, MPI Munich, August 2016) https://ssrn.com/abstract=2833165; Tanya Aplin, Alfred Radauer, Martin A

and the possibility of protecting the latter through secrecy, considering that individual accessibility of information does not compromise overall secrecy unless the easy reconstruction of the complex is possible through known data.[23]

Second, even if one were to demonstrate that data can be the subject of secrecy, its commercial value is also to be proved. This would be not the case, for example, of individual data. Already in the European Data Economy Staff Working Document of 2017, it was clearly stated that the value of data arises from the information "extracted" through the combination of data in the same dataset or in multiple aggregated datasets.[24] The observation that, in most cases, the commercial value does not come from a single piece of data but from the aggregation of digital data[25] further confirms that protection is not excluded by the fact that a single digital data, part of a broader configuration or combination of elements, is known or easily accessible by industry experts and operators. However, it must be proven that the commercial value of the data requiring protection through secrecy stems specifically from its status as secret information. This is because the value of secrecy – especially in the case of secret data – lies in the fact that it constitutes a competitive advantage, even if only potential, for those who keep it secret. It is certain that the economic value of data often derives from future extraction of yet-to-be-identified information, especially in the context of the IoT and, above all, with respect to non-(yet) processed data. Now, this potential economic value alone cannot be considered sufficient to ensure the protection of secrecy, precisely due to the essential need to simultaneously preserve the interest in the free circulation of information.

Third, regarding the requirement of measures reasonably suitable to maintain secrecy, the context of data confirms the difficulty of standardizing this aspect. It is not possible, in fact, to define *ex ante*, and independently of the specific case, what measures are considered suitable. In the case of data, the relativity of security measures is even more evident when considering the widespread heterogeneity of data, which, being vectors of information, can be the subject of secrecy. In other words, depending on the type of data, different security measures may be necessary compared to the information itself. For example, if the data subject to secrecy includes, even partially, personal data, it will be necessary to adopt all preventive measures to avoid the so called "data breach".[26]

Bader and Nicola Searle, 'The Role of EU Trade Secrets Law in the Data Economy: An Empirical Analysis' (2023) 54 IIC 826.

23 Cristiana Sappa, 'What Does Trade Secrecy Have to Do with the Interconnection-Based Paradigm of the Internet of Things?' (2018) EIPR 518.

24 European Commission, *Staff Working Document on the free flow of data* SWD(2017) 2 final.

25 Daniel Gervais, 'Exploring the Interfaces between Big Data and Intellectual Property Law' (2019) 10(1) JIPITEC 3.

26 European Commission, European Innovation Council and SMEs Executive Agency, Alfred Radauer, Martin Bader, Tanya Aplin et al., 'Study on the Legal Protection of Trade Secrets in the Context of the Data Economy – Final Report' (Publications Office 2022) 28. Available at: https://data.europa.eu/doi/10.2826/021443

In conclusion, it seems that the requirements for the protection of trade secrets certainly retain their relevance in the context of data. However, if their interpretation is already complex in traditional markets, this is even more true in this case due to the multifaceted and, above all, non-secret nature of much of the data, which, in turn, influences the assessment of their economic value and the adequacy of protection measures to be implemented. This is probably the reason why both the DGA and the DA focus mainly on the relationship between trade secret (among the IPRs) and data-sharing obligations.

As to the protectability of data under such right, one must consider that the category of data is certainly not homogeneous, and the distinction between raw data and processed data is particularly important. Only the latter serve as carriers of informational capital, whereas the former lack meaning as they are not analyzed in any way.[27] Consequently, data that has not undergone any form of processing cannot constitute the subject of a trade secret because they do not convey information; digital encoding is necessary to imbue them with meaning. On the other hand, "encoded" data can be the subject of a trade secret precisely because of the "informational" nature they have acquired.

6.2.4 The Data Producer's Right: A Failed Attempt

The discussed approaches on the issue of data ownership reflect what has often been perceived as a shortfall in legislation. In particular, IPRs have been incapable of providing sufficient protection for raw, machine-generated data. In light of the foregoing, some scholars have proposed the introduction of a new instrument which establishes an *ad hoc* protection for data producers, thereby awarding them specific rights on the generated data.[28] The proposal has initially been taken up in the European Commission's Communication on Building a European Data Economy, where a proprietary right on non-personal data, referring to anonymous machine-generated data, has been proposed under the title "data producer's right".[29] In this context, the data producer would be considered the owner or long-term user (as lessee) of the device and thus would be granted the exclusive right to use the generated data, as well as the right to award user licenses for a set price. However, the Commission also emphasized the need to provide exceptions to the exclusivity, in particular in the form of access for public authorities, for example, for traffic management or environmental reasons.[30]

27 Josef Drexl, 'Data Access and Control in the Era of Connected Devices' (Study on Behalf of the European Consumer Organisation BEUC, 2018). Available at: https://www.ip.mpg.de/fileadmin/ipmpg/content/aktuelles/aus_der_forschung/beuc-x-2018-121_data_access_and_control_in_the_area_of_connected_devices.pdf.

28 For a detailed analysis, *see* Herbert Zech, 'Data as a Tradeable Commodity' (2016) 19, 74.

29 European Commission, *"Building a European Data Economy"* COM(2017) 9 final. Available at: https://eur-lex.europa.eu/content/news/building_EU_data_economy.html

30 Ibid.

The proposal of awarding to someone the role of a data owner has given rise to lively debate, owing to the alleged absence of real evidence that it would help to resolve the detected problems of under-exploitation of data and "vendor lock-in".[31] In fact, there seems to be no lack of incentives for data producers, considering that the market for the exchange and use of machine-data has been progressively expanding, and the value of data has been growing exponentially.[32]

Conversely, many evaluated the proposal of an exclusive right for data producers as counterproductive with regard to the aim of encouraging data sharing.[33] Indeed, public consultation conducted by the European Commission among stakeholders in the data economy revealed that "the crucial question in business-to-business sharing is not so much about ownership, but about how access is organised".[34] Consequently, the majority rejected the idea of a new data ownership type of right.[35]

Another significant point of concern exists in the risky overlap between this new right and the (already existing) copyright and *sui generis* rights. The result would be a stratification of several levels of protection for machine-generated creations and could jeopardize the system of exceptions and free use stipulated by copyright (in particular that relating to data mining operations) and more generally undermine scientific development and progress.

Moreover, the allocation of data to a "rightful producer" leaves room for speculation since the Commission's proposal remains unclear as to which alternative should prevail in a situation where both the "owner or long-term user" are applicable. Further, in the era of IoT and connected devices, it is often questionable as to which manufacturer the data-generating item actually belongs.

What is more, the adoption of a property right for data producers, despite being designated to stimulate the data market, would run the risk of increasing the difficulty in licensing aggregated data, that is, data held by different producers, as

31 Josef Drexl, Reto Hilty et al., 'Data Ownership and Access to Data' (2016) 3; P Bernt Hugenholtz, 'Against "Data Property"' (2018) 48.

32 Petroc Taylor, 'Value of the Data Economy in the European Union (EU) and United Kingdom from 2016 to 2020 and in 2025' (2022). Available at: www.statista.com/statistics/1134993/value-of-data-economy-eu-uk/

33 See also Wolfgang Kerber, 'A New (Intellectual) Property Right for Non-Personal Data?' 994; Daniel Gervais, 'Exploring the Interfaces between Big Data and Intellectual Property Law' 3; Josef Drexl, 'Data Access and Control in the Era of Connected Devices' 3; Francesco Banterle, 'The Interface between Data Protection and IP Law: The Case of Trade Secrets and the Database Sui Generis Right in Marketing Operations, and the Ownership of Raw Data in Big Data Analysis' in Mor Bakhoum, Beatriz Conde Gallego, Mark-Oliver Mackenrodt, Gintarė Surblytė-Namavičienė (eds), *Personal Data in Competition, Consumer Protection and Intellectual Property Law: Towards a Holistic Approach?* (Berlin, Heidelberg, Springer 2018) 438.

34 European Commission, Communication from the Commission to the European Parliament et al., *"Towards a common European Data Space"* COM(2018) 232 final 9; European Commission, 'Public Consultation on Building the European Data Economy' (European Commission, 10 January 2017) https://ec.europa.eu/digital-single-market/en/news/public-consultation-building-european-data-economy (last accessed 30 January 2024).

35 European Commission, Communication from the Commission to the European Parliament et al., *"Towards a Common European Data Space"* COM(2018) 232 final 9.

it would greatly raise transaction costs caused by the need to acquire rights from different parties. Using the example of automated or autonomous driving, an on-board computer not only draws on data generated by the vehicle itself, but also on data provided by external sources. Hence, data generation and analysis occur within a much more complex network of multiple actors, all of which contribute to the generation of additional data and the creation of overall economic value. Under these circumstances, transaction costs which result from the acquisition of aggregated data could only be avoided if the driver is the owner of all data collected and processed by the on-board computer. However, this is neither technically nor economically feasible as the concept does not take into account the fact that much of the data in a vehicle are linked to, or based on, external data gathered by other parties.

6.3 From IPRs Protection on Data to Data Access and Flow: A Paradigmatic Shift in the EU Approach

The second phase of the relationship between IPRs and data is the result of a paradigmatic shift of the EU institutions, turning away from data ownership as the means to foster data circulation and focusing on the need to incentivize data access and sharing. The 2020 Communication on a European strategy for data leaves behind the idea that an exclusive right on data was needed to foster the data-driven markets. It instead highlights the need to foster data access and flow for the better of the public good, as well as for technological optimization.[36] In pursuing the objective of higher productivity and more competitive markets, what is recognized as essential is free circulation and reuse of private and public data.[37]

In essence, the 2020 European strategy for data (hereinafter also "2020 Data Strategy") consists of four pillars: (a) the introduction of a horizontal (cross-sectoral) governance system for data access and usage; (b) investment actions aimed at strengthening the Union's capabilities and infrastructures required for data processing and use; (c) the development of skills in the field of data, regarding individuals' control over their own data as well as generating more data literacy among European citizens and European small and medium-sized enterprises; and lastly, (d) the creation of common spaces in strategic sectors and according to domains of public interest, complementary to the horizontal common European data space.[38]

The first and the latter are those relevant to the matter at hand. In order to create a horizontal governance system for the access to, and usage of, data, the Commission has foreseen three different actions: firstly, the introduction of a legislative framework for the governance of Common European Data Spaces, adopted by the Commission on 25 November 2020, as the already mentioned DGA. The

36 European Commission Communication, *A European strategy for data* COM(2020) 66 final 12.

37 European Commission Communication, *A European strategy for data* COM(2020) 66 final 8 f.

38 For an overview *see* Ginerva Bruzzone, Koenraad Debackere, 'As Open as Possible, as Closed as Needed: Challenges of the EU Strategy for Data' (2021) 56(1) les Nouvelles – Journal of the Licensing Executives Society.

measures aim at facilitating the cross-border and cross-sector usage of data by arranging interoperability requirements and standards. Secondly, the revision of the PSI framework through the adoption of the Open Data Directive[39] that introduces a list of "high value" datasets held by the public sector which are supposed to become re-usable for free, in machine-readable format and downloadable in bulk, opening up the use of specific categories of private data. Thirdly, the adoption of a legislative instrument, on harmonized rules on fair access to and use of data, the above mentioned DA, aiming to exploit the full potential of data-driven innovation in the EU by easing the data usage and phasing out of legal uncertainties for market participants as to data-sharing.

In this context, a huge role is played by the access and sharing of data held by private companies that has been mainly left to contractual arrangements between the concerned parties.

According to the Commission's communication, voluntary data sharing should remain the general principle, on the basis of corporate social responsibility or out of bare "data philanthropy",[40] and only be punctuated where specific circumstances dictate to take other, namely, compulsory actions.[41] In order to oblige a private entity to share its data with a third party, a strong legislative justification is required that adheres to the principles of necessity and proportionality. What could provide such a basis is competition. "Data producers" who have a strong bargaining position due to extensive data silos could be required to provide access to SMEs, which otherwise would encounter difficulties in competing for data and thereby be hindered in their own development of data-based technologies.[42] Indeed, a large part of raw data is concentrated in the hands of globally established platforms such as Google, Amazon, Alibaba or Facebook, also acting as gatekeepers in the European Union.[43] The fact that usage of their collected data is often restricted to in-house analysis means they are able to extend their technological lead, which may evolve into a negative effect on the entire market. The trust placed in the economy by settling for a voluntary-based policy in B2B data access may be misplaced. Indications of this restrained interest in data sharing can already be drawn from the current situation, where a large portion of companies do not share or exchange data.[44] For this reason, the DA introduces sharing obligations that have a procompetitive aim, intending

39 Directive (EU) 2019/1024 of the European Parliament and of the Council of 20 June 2019 on open data and the re-use of public sector information (recast) [2019] OJ L172/56 56–83.

40 European Commission, *Staff Working Document on the free flow of data* SWD(2017) 2 final 14.

41 European Commission Communication, *A European strategy for data* COM(2020) 66 final 13.

42 This proposal had already been made at an early stage of the European Data Strategy in the already mentioned Commission's *Staff Working Document on the free flow of data* 21.

43 The Digital Services Act (Regulation (EU) 2022/2065 of the European Parliament and of the Council of 19 October 2022 on a Single Market For Digital Services and amending Directive 2000/31/EC [2022] OJ L277/1 1–102) specifically regulates these very large platforms, formulating additional obligations that aim to increase transparency and accountability.

44 Extensively: European Commission: Directorate-General for Communications Networks, Content and Technology, Everis Benelux et al., 'Study on Data Sharing between Companies in Europe' (Final Report, Publications Office 2018). Available at: https://op.europa.eu/de/publication-detail/-/

to improve consumers' conditions. However, the compulsory sharing of privately held data may introduce friction into an already delicate system. In this context, IPRs, such as trade secrets or copyright on databases, need to be considered when mandating data access. It is essential to strike a balance between access and sharing rules and the protection of IPRs, as the DA seeks to do. In addition to clarifying the application of the trade secrets protection directive,[45] the DA includes a (residual) revision of the database directive.[46]

Complementary to the first pillar, the fourth pillar provides for the introduction of a series of European common spaces in strategic economic sectors and domains of public interest. These "domains" are selected on the basis of whether the use of data will have systemic impact on the entire ecosystem, as well as on citizens.[47] The horizontal framework will thus be complemented by sector-specific rules and platforms, which shall improve the EU-wide availability and interoperability of data. Differences across various sectors will depend on the maturity of discussions – for example, the progress already made in public administration, from the PSI Directive to the current Open Data Directive,[48] as well as problems encountered with regard to data availability in a particular sector (e.g. sensitive data in the health sector). Sector-specific legislation may, in this context, offer the possibility of customized compliance rules from a data protection viewpoint, allowing the authorities to take into consideration the level of sensitive data and the accordingly necessary safeguards. The degree of public interest and involvement may play an important role, which could be higher in sectors such as health and lower in areas such as manufacturing.

Against this background, the following subparagraphs address the concrete handing of IPRs in the DGA (3.1) and DA (3.2), respectively – while relying on Chapters 2 and 4 of the book for the overview of the content of the two Acts.

6.3.1 Data-Sharing Obligations vis-à-vis IPRs Protection in the DGA

The DGA fosters the sharing of data not by imposing direct obligations, rather by requiring the establishment of data intermediaries – that will handle the sharing of data by individuals, public bodies and private companies – and by contributing at

---

publication/8b8776ff-4834-11e8-be1d-01aa75ed71a1/language-en; European Commission, *Staff Working Document on the free flow of data* SWD(2017) 2 final 15.

45 As required by Commission, European Commission Communication, *A European strategy for data* COM(2020) 66 final 13 https://eur-lex.europa.eu/legal-content/EN/TXT/?uri=celex:52020DC0066

46 As anticipated by the European Commission in its Communication to the European Parliament et al., *Making the most of the EU's innovative potential – An intellectual property action plan to support the EU's recovery and resilience* COM(2020)760 final 15.

47 The Commission identifies nine common spaces, including mobility, health, manufacturing, financial, agricultural and public administration sectors.

48 See further in detail Mireille Van Eechoud, 'A Serpent Eating its Tail: The Database Directive Meets the Open Data Directive' (2021) 52 IIC 375; for an overview *see* also Maria Lillà Montagnani, Antonia von Appen, 'IP and Data (Ownership) in the New European Strategy on Data' (2021) 43(3) EIPR 156.

the advancement of the so called European common data spaces that found their roots in the 2020 Data Strategy and that are also interested by the Data Act.

The former – also called "data-sharing service providers" – come as a European alternative to the existing major tech platforms. To uphold trust in these new entities, they will have to notify public authorities of their intention to provide data-sharing services; commit to the protection of sensitive and confidential data; and observe requirements to ensure their neutrality. These providers will have to distinguish their data-sharing services from other commercial operations, and are prohibited from using the data exchanged for any other purposes. Certain services that have been excluded from becoming new data intermediaries as part of the regulation include cloud service providers and data advertising brokers, data consultancies or providers of data products. In addition, data intermediaries also face transparency and security obligations, enhancing the level of trust towards the data-sharing framework and indirectly contributing to the increase of private data-sharing initiatives. Through these mechanisms the DGA aims at establishing an ecosystem that will lead to increased sharing and reuse of public, private, personal and non-personal data.

The latter – the European data spaces[49] – are intended as interoperable frameworks in strategic sectors and public interest domains. At their core, data spaces facilitate trusted data relationships among partners who adhere to stringent standards for data storage and sharing. The overarching goal is to accelerate digital transformation by surmounting legal and technical barriers to voluntary data sharing. This initiative also aims to build trust through clear, equitable rules for data usage, empowering organizations to share data while retaining control over their own generated data.[50]

As mentioned, already in the 2020 Data Strategy ten initial sectoral data spaces were outlined, spanning areas such as manufacturing, healthcare, finance and energy. These spaces were then expanded further, encompassing sectors like media and cultural heritage.[51]

A key feature of these data spaces is interoperability. This ensures that data can flow seamlessly across different sectors and initiatives. For instance, the Green Deal data space will collaborate with other sectoral spaces, promoting synergy and maximizing data utility across domains.[52] The DA includes provisions for

49 Margherita Corrado, Laura Zoboli, 'Are Data Spaces a "Silver Bullet" for the EU Data Economy?' in Kalpana Tyagi, Anselm Kamperman Sanders and Caroline Cauffman (eds), *Digital Platforms, Competition Law, and Regulation: Comparative Perspectives* (London, Bloomsbury Publishing 2024) 105.

50 European Commission, *Commission Staff Working Document on Common European Data Spaces* [2022] SWD(2022) 45 final (hereinafter *Staff Working Document on Data Spaces*) 16.

51 European Commission, *Staff Working Document on Data Spaces* SWD(2022) 45 final. Available at: https://data.consilium.europa.eu/doc/document/ST-6532-2022-INIT/en/pdf

52 Within the framework of the Common European Green Deal data space, the European Strategy for Data mentions an action for the creation of a common European data space for Smart Circular Applications in order to make available the most relevant data for enabling circular value creation along supply chains.

establishing common technical standards and guidelines to facilitate this interoperability, aiming to harmonize data-sharing practices across the EU.[53] Additionally, these data spaces will rely on shared technical infrastructures and governance frameworks.[54] These frameworks will provide a basis for coordinating data-pooling and data-sharing activities among stakeholders. A horizontal governance structure will be established to define administrative and contractual rules, ensuring transparent rights for accessing, processing and sharing data.[55] These rules will be complemented by sector-specific regulations to cater to unique industry needs.[56]

Crucially, data owners will maintain control over their data, dictating who can access it, for what purposes and under what conditions.[57] This control is expected to bolster trust among businesses and individuals, encouraging more extensive data sharing and fostering a competitive European data economy.[58] Participation in data spaces will be open to organizations and individuals adhering to EU regulations and values.[59] This openness aims to promote competition among service providers by reducing barriers to entry and preventing monopolistic practices, particularly relevant in sectors like repair services where data access can be monopolized by product manufacturers.[60]

Moreover, compliance with existing European rules, including the General Data Protection Regulation (GDPR),[61] IPRs and competition laws, is paramount. In particular, data spaces must ensure secure data exchange and robust personal data protection measures. Specific provisions, such as anonymization for sensitive data, will facilitate safe and ethical data-sharing practices.

As far as IPRs are concerned, instead, the DGA lacks specific indications as to make possible sharing data in the limited cases in which it is under IPR protection. What is sure it that any of the DGA obligations should apply only insofar as they are compatible with international agreements on the protection of intellectual property rights, such as the Berne Convention, the TRIPS Agreement and the WIPO Treaties.[62]

53 European Commission, *Staff Working Document on Data Spaces* SWD(2022) 45 final 43.

54 European Commission, *Staff Working Document on Data Spaces* SWD(2022) 45 final 4.

55 Johan Bodenkamp, 'Common European Data Spaces and The Data Economy' (Online Expert Seminar, 3 November 2022).

56 Data Governance Act, Art 26 (2022). In particular they are commissioned to propose guidelines on data spaces and, more generally, to advise the Commission on security requirements, access procedures and cross-industry standards for data sharing.

57 European Commission, *Staff Working Document on Data Spaces* SWD(2022) 45 final 3.

58 European Commission, *Staff Working Document on Data Spaces* SWD(2022) 45 final 4.

59 Ibid.

60 Data Act (2023) 13.

61 Regulation (EU) 2016/679 of the European Parliament and of the Council of 27 April 2016 on the protection of natural persons with regard to the processing of personal data and on the free movement of such data, and repealing Directive 95/46/EC (General Data Protection Regulation) [2016] OJ L119/1.

62 Data Governance Act, recital 17.

In conclusion, the plan for the establishment of EU data spaces seeks to form a framework for efficient, secure and ethical data sharing across diverse sectors. Certainly, clear guidelines and robust governance mechanisms will be essential to navigate legal complexities and promote fair competition within the European data ecosystem.

Within the data spaces realm, the data space for cultural heritage deserves specific attention in this chapter due to its strong connection with the IP realm, being directed towards advancing the digital transformation of cultural heritage institutions and promoting the reuse of cultural content in other domains, such as tourism and education. Unlike the health data space, which currently has a regulatory proposal,[63] the data space for cultural heritage is not established by a Regulation, instead, it relies on the November 2021 Commission's Recommendation on a common European data space for cultural heritage[64] that encourages Member States to accelerate the digitization of cultural heritage assets and provides guiding principles on data spaces for cultural heritage. Therefore, such common space currently relies on two main work strands. The first work strand involves deploying the data space for cultural heritage through procurement. This aims to establish and operate the data space, building on the existing *Europeana* digital service infrastructure platform and, where possible, the *Simpl* smart cloud-to-edge middleware platform. Continuation of this effort may be addressed through actions in the future years.[65] The second work strand consists of grants that support cultural heritage institutions in utilizing technologies and connecting to the data space. This strand focuses on leveraging advanced technologies to enhance the quality, sustainability and reuse of data, while also building digital capacity in the cultural sector. This is achieved through collaboration with existing and relevant European, national and regional initiatives and platforms.[66]

6.3.2 Data-Sharing Obligations vis-à-vis IPRs Protection in the DA

To evaluate the interaction between IP and data sharing, it is crucial to examine the DA, which was also highlighted as the designated framework to clarify the scope of applying the trade secrets directive.[67] Specifically, the Commission noted that

63 European Commission, *Proposal for a Regulation of the European Parliament and of the Council on the European Health Data Space* [2022] COM(2022)197 final.

64 Commission Recommendation (EU) 2021/1970 of 10 November 2021 on a common European data space for cultural heritage [2021] C(2021)7953 OJ L401/5 5–16.

65 European Commission, *Second Commission Staff Working Document on Common European Data Spaces* [2024] SWD(2024) 21 final, https://digital-strategy.ec.europa.eu/en/library/second-staff-working-document-data-spaces

66 European Health and Digital Executive Agency, 'Call for Proposals: Data Space for Cultural Heritage' (*European Commission*, 14 September 2023) https://hadea.ec.europa.eu/calls-proposals/data-space-cultural-heritage_en (last accessed 30 January 2024).

67 European Commission, Communication to the European Parliament et al., *Making the most of the EU's innovative potential An intellectual property action plan to support the EU's recovery and resilience* [2020] COM(2020) 760 final 15 ss.

while the directive seemed to provide effective protection tools, it might be necessary to specify the types of data qualifying as trade secrets. Additionally, clarity was sought on whether current exceptions adequately supported data-driven and green economies and how these tools could combat illicit data acquisition, use and disclosure effectively.

Broadly, the DA aims to ensure fair distribution of data value among operators and promote data access and use. It introduces new possibilities for user access to and utilization of data from connected devices, imposing obligations on data holders.[68] For instance – as explored more in detail in Chapter 2 of this book – it mandates sharing data generated by connected products or related services, such as medical devices or sensor-equipped agricultural machinery,[69] with users and potentially third parties upon request.

Regarding data covered by trade secrets, the DA stipulates that data holders cannot refuse access requests solely on grounds of trade secrecy.[70] However, if third-party access involves trade secret-protected data, disclosure is contingent upon demonstrating that such disclosure is strictly necessary for the agreed-upon purpose between the user and the third party.[71]

In balancing these interests, the DA introduces exceptions to the trade secret holder's right to decide on access and use by third parties.[72] It aims to increase data circulation while preserving the confidentiality of trade secrets, safeguarding their economic value. The DA requires data holders and users to adopt necessary measures to preserve data confidentiality before disclosure,[73] such as through contractual terms, confidentiality agreements and technical standards.

However, amendments introduced in subsequent versions of the DA, confirmed in the current text, provide additional exceptions and safeguards. These amendments aim to better balance conflicting interests and protect the legal position of trade secret holders. They require trade secret holders to identify protected data and allow them discretion in decisions related to data sharing, including scenarios where economic harm from disclosure is likely.[74]

68 Ulla-Maija Mylly, 'Transparent AI? Navigating between Rules on Trade Secrets and Access to Information' (2023) 54 IIC 1013.

69 Para 15, Data Act Preamble (2023).

70 Para 31, Data Act Preamble (2023).

71 Josef Drexl et al., 'Position Statement of the Max Planck Institute for Innovation and Competition of 25 May 2022 on the Commission's Proposal of 23 February 2022 for a Regulation on Harmonised Rules on Fair Access to and Use of Data (Data Act)' (Max Planck Institute for Innovation & Competition Research Paper No 22–05, MPI Munich, May 2022) 288 https://www.ip.mpg.de/en/research/research-news/position-statement-on-the-eu-data-act.html

72 Ulla-Maija Mylly, 'Transparent AI? Navigating between Rules on Trade Secrets and Access to Information' (2023) 1013 ff.

73 Alfred Radauer, Martin Bader, Tanya Aplin et al., 'Study on the Legal Protection of Trade Secrets in the Context of the Data Economy' (2022) 91.

74 For a more in depth analysis: Laura Zoboli, 'Il segreto commerciale e le politiche europee in materia di dati/Trade secret and European Data Policies' (2023) 32 AIDA, Italian Annals of Copyright, Culture and Entertainment.

In conclusion, while the Data Act facilitates greater openness to trade secret-protected data within defined parameters, it introduces complexities and uncertainties, such as ambiguities in regulatory language and challenges in harmonizing trade secret protection with data circulation imperatives. This detailed regulatory framework, while protective, may inadvertently hinder data circulation and potentially conflict with the inherently flexible nature of trade secret protection.[75]

A quick mention should also be made to the impact that the DA produces on the so called *sui generis* (database) right provided for by the already mentioned Directive 96/9/EC. In particular, Article 35 of the Data Act stipulates that the *sui generis* right does not apply to databases containing data obtained or generated from the use of a related product or service.[76] This provision aims to ensure that users' rights to access and use such data, as established in Articles 4 and 5 of the Data Act, are not hindered. These articles grant users the right to access, use and share data generated by their use of related products or services.

This new provision addresses the digital economy's need to facilitate data circulation and sharing, as highlighted in the impact assessment report on the Data Act. Specifically, recital 84 of the proposal's preamble clarifies that Article 35 was designed to prevent data holders from claiming *sui generis* rights over databases containing data generated by connected products or services.

The goal is to prevent data lock-in for user-generated data through automated processes within the IoT ecosystem. However, the scope of Article 35 is notably limited in terms of its objectives and the types of data it affects.[77]

To understand the significance of Article 35, it is crucial to assess whether the exclusion it prescribes was already implicit in the Database Directive, established through jurisprudence, or if it is a new development introduced by Article 35 itself. Recital 84 indicates that the exclusion applies when such databases are not already eligible for *sui generis* protection. The Commission frames Article 35 as a means to resolve legal uncertainty regarding *sui generis* rights over databases that would not qualify for such protection under existing rules.

This suggests that the lack of *sui generis* rights was a pre-existing condition, not a consequence of Article 35, which serves to clarify this point. Previous CJEU rulings had already excluded databases created through data-generation investments from *sui generis* protection. Article 35 thus has an important clarifying role, even if it merely reiterates existing exclusions.

75 Thomas Margoni, Charlotte Ducuing, Luca Schirru, 'Data Property, Data Governance and Common European Data Spaces' (2023) 3 Computerrecht: Tijdschrift voor Informatica, Telecommunicatie en Recht 202–211; Josef Drexl et al., 'Position Statement of the Max Planck Institute for Innovation and Competition of 25 May 2022 on the Commission's Proposal of 23 February 2022 for a Regulation on Harmonised Rules on Fair Access to and Use of Data (Data Act)' 101 ff.

76 European Commission, *Commission Staff Working Document Impact Assessment Report Accompanying the document Proposal for a Regulation of the European Parliament and of the Council on harmonised rules on fair access to and use of data* (Data Act) [2022] SWD(2022) 34 final.

77 Inge Graef, Martin Husovec, 'Seven Things to Improve in the Data Act' (2022). Available at: https://ssrn.com/abstract=4051793 (last accessed 30 January 2024).

However, suggesting that Article 35 is merely a clarification might be reductive. IoT data may not always fall under the category of created and generated data excluded from *sui generis* protection. Scholars argue that if a database creator can prove that the database results from data acquisition (not creation) and that the investment is substantial, *sui generis* claims could be legitimate. Therefore, Article 35 might represent a real reduction in the *sui generis* right's scope, emphasizing the need for more open data to support IoT and emerging technologies.[78]

Supporting this broader interpretation, the Commission designed Article 35 to address the German Supreme Court's Autobahn-Maut decision,[79] which favored the inclusion of machine-generated data under *sui generis* protection.[80] Article 35 also aims to resolve conflicts between the Database Directive and Articles 4 and 5 of the Data Act, which grant users control over data they generate. This conflict was not initially resolved by the Database Directive, thus necessitating Article 35 to align with the objectives of promoting data sharing and circulation.[81]

6.4 Conclusions

The evolution of the relationship between IPRs and data within the EU reflects a significant paradigmatic shift from a focus on data ownership to a prioritization of data access and flow. This shift is encapsulated in the transition from the initial phase, where there was an attempt to reinforce IP rights and even propose a semi-property right on data, to the current approach that emphasizes the necessity of facilitating data access and sharing to foster innovation and competition.[82]

In this sense, the much welcomed 2020 Communication on a European strategy for data marked a departure from the idea that exclusive rights on data were necessary to stimulate data-driven markets. Instead, it underscored the importance of fostering data access and flow for the public good and technological optimization. The strategy identified four key pillars: establishing a horizontal governance framework for data access and usage; investing in data processing and infrastructure capabilities; enhancing data literacy and control; and creating sector-specific common data spaces. This holistic approach aims to maximize the economic and societal benefits of data by promoting its free circulation and reuse.

78 Ibid.

79 BGH, Judgment of 25 March 2010, Case I ZR 47/08, *Autobahnmaut* (2010).

80 Josef Drexl et al., 'Position Statement of the Max Planck Institute for Innovation and Competition of 25 May 2022 on the Commission's Proposal of 23 February 2022 for a Regulation on Harmonised Rules on Fair Access to and Use of Data (Data Act)'.

81 Thomas Margoni, Thomas Gils, Eyüp Kun, 'Chapter X of the Data Act and the Sui Generis Database Right' (*Centre for IT & IP Law Blog*, 14 June 2022) https://www.law.kuleuven.be/citip/blog/chapter-10-of-the-data-act-and-the-sui-generis-database-right/.

82 Wolfgang Kerber, 'A New (Intellectual) Property Right for Non-Personal Data?' 994; Francesco Banterle, 'The Interface between Data Protection and IP Law 438; Daniel Gervais, 'Exploring the Interfaces between Big Data and Intellectual Property Law' 3; Josef Drexl, 'Data Access and Control in the Era of Connected Devices' 3.

The DGA and DA are central to this new regulatory landscape. The DGA takes two steps further by establishing data intermediaries and European common data spaces to enhance data sharing across various sectors, while ensuring trust and compliance with data protection standards. These intermediaries, also known as data-sharing service providers, are designed to serve as neutral entities that facilitate data exchanges without commercial bias. The common data spaces, in turn, provide interoperable frameworks that encourage voluntary data sharing and collaboration across strategic sectors.

The DA, on the other hand, introduces specific obligations and rights to ensure fair access and use of data generated by connected devices. It mandates data sharing between users, third parties and data holders while addressing the complexities associated with trade secrets and database protection. In particular, the DA provides mechanisms to protect trade secrets while still enabling necessary data disclosures for innovation and competition. Additionally, it addresses the limitations of the *sui generis* database right, ensuring that data generated in the IoT ecosystem is not locked in by proprietary claims.

Although the EU's shift towards prioritizing data access and flow over data ownership represents a forward-thinking approach to harnessing the full potential of the digital economy, by creating a robust legal framework that promotes data sharing, the interface with IPRs protection remain in fact still to be fully understood. As a matter of fact, how this framework will actually work remains to be seen. While the legislation sets ambitious goals for data sharing and protection, its success will depend on effective implementation, compliance by stakeholders and the resolution of potential conflicts between data access and IPR protections. Continuous monitoring, stakeholder engagement and possible regulatory adjustments will be essential to achieving the desired balance between fostering innovation and safeguarding intellectual property in the rapidly evolving digital economy.

Part III

Conclusions

7 The Interplay of Data Protection, Competition Law, IP Law and Data Sharing

Laura Zoboli and Maciej Bernatt

7.1 Introduction

The EU's commitment to promoting data sharing through legislative initiatives such as the Open Data Directive, the Data Governance Act, the Digital Services Act, the Digital Markets Act and the Data Act underscores the vital importance of creating an environment that supports data-driven innovation while upholding transparency, accountability and privacy. These regulatory efforts address challenges related to data access, interoperability and fairness, aiming to foster thriving and inclusive digital and data markets throughout Europe.

Despite these initiatives, a critical gap seems to persist in the realm of B2B data sharing. This book has highlighted how, despite its recognized potential to drive innovation and create value, B2B data sharing is subject to several legal limitations and – as seen in Chapter 1 remains limited – which significantly impacts the competitiveness and innovation potential of firms. The scarcity of B2B data-sharing initiatives underscores the need for focused attention and strategic interventions to unlock the full potential of data-driven collaboration among businesses.

By delving into the regulatory frameworks affecting B2B data sharing and revealing their lack of coherence, this book has provided valuable insights and actionable strategies for businesses, policymakers and other stakeholders. Navigating the complex landscape of data sharing in the digital age is no small feat, but understanding these dynamics is crucial for fostering collaboration, innovation and value creation.

As we conclude this exploration of B2B data sharing, we recognize the pivotal role it plays in shaping the future of the digital economy. By promoting collaboration and innovation, B2B data sharing has the potential to unlock new opportunities and drive societal progress. Thus, this book contributed to the discourse on aligning relevant regulatory frameworks and harnessing the full benefits of data-driven collaboration in the business world.

In this context, this conclusive chapter proceeds on two critical fronts that should be addressed to advance the public debate in the direction of contributing to an effective data-sharing system in the EU. First, general regulatory frameworks – specifically, competition law, intellectual property law and personal data protection law – impose limitations on the extent to which firms can share data. The following sections will explore the dynamics between these laws and consider how to

DOI: 10.4324/9781003248255-11

enhance the existing legal framework to better incentivize data sharing especially at the B2B level, while ensuring that values associated with competitive markets, innovation and privacy are duly protected in the data-sharing process. Second, the possible need for greater coherence among the new legislation adopted by the EU, which are designed to facilitate data sharing within the data economy and digital market. Data spaces are proposed as an intermediate solution that could harmonise horizontal and vertical regulatory frameworks, that aims to align with fundamental interests and rights while, at the same time promoting data sharing and, consequently, data-driven innovation.

7.2 IP, Competition and Personal Data Protection Laws as Limitations to Data Sharing

This section seeks to identify the limitations to data sharing imposed by intellectual property, competition and data protection laws. By focusing on how these regulatory frameworks may hinder or fail to incentivize data sharing, this section sets the stage for the subsequent section, which will explore the complementary aspects and consider how the same regulations can, under certain conditions, also facilitate data sharing. As framed in the following subsections, these three areas of law establish principles that can limit data sharing ("limiting principles"), which must be considered when interpreting new EU legal acts designed to promote data sharing within the EU internal market.

7.2.1 IP Perspective

While new pieces of EU legislation, discussed later, aim to facilitate data sharing, intellectual property law may sometimes contradict this objective. These limitations can be expressed in two dimensions: (i) the limited role of IPRs concerning data, which, as will be seen in section 3.1, primarily pertains to data collections; and (ii) the interference between IP protection and regulations promoting data sharing.

Regarding the first dimension, as discussed in detail in Chapter 6, IPRs can certainly be seen as a tool to reinforce the position of data holders, making it necessary to scrutinize the intersection between data assets and IPRs. However, patents and copyrights cannot protect data per se. For data to be covered by patent protection, it must exhibit factual-technical properties imparted by the patented process, making it suitable for patenting. Legal precedents clearly indicate that patent protection does not extend to data produced or generated from patented processes. Similarly, copyright cannot protect information generated through automated processes because it is not considered a product of intellectual creation, regardless of the intellectual effort invested in developing the technology that produces or processes the data. Consequently, data lacks the requisite level of originality required for copyright protection. Trade secret protection, however, retains its relevance in the context of data. The interpretation of trade secret requirements is already complex in traditional markets, and this complexity increases in the realm of data due to its multifaceted and often non-secret nature. This influences the assessment of the economic value of data and the adequacy of protection measures. This complexity is a likely explanation as to why both the Data Governance Act and the Data Act focus primarily on the relationship between trade secrets and data-sharing obligations. The protectability of data under trade secret law depends on recognizing that data is not a homogeneous category. The distinction between raw data and processed data is particularly significant. Only processed data serve as carriers of informational capital, whereas raw data lack meaning until analyzed. Consequently, unprocessed data cannot constitute a trade secret because they do not convey information; digital encoding is necessary to imbue them with meaning. Conversely, "encoded" data can be subject to trade secret protection precisely because of the "informational" nature they acquire.

Regarding the second dimension, while new pieces of EU legislation aim to facilitate data sharing, IPRs can sometimes create obstacles. First, the DGA lacks specific indications on sharing data under IPR protection. It is clear, however, that DGA obligations apply only if compatible with international intellectual property agreements, such as the Berne Convention, the TRIPS Agreement and the WIPO Treaties. Second, to assess the interaction between IP and data sharing, the Data Act is crucial, particularly as it clarifies the scope of the Trade Secrets Directive. There certainly was a need for clarity on whether current exceptions adequately support data-driven and green economies and how these tools can combat illicit data acquisition, use and disclosure effectively and this – as it will be seen in section 5 below – has been addressed by the Data Act only in part.

7.2.2 Competition Law Perspective

Competition law may in certain circumstances impose limitations on the scope of permissible data sharing. Generally, since competition law aims at elimination of business practices which restrict competition, it makes such kinds of B2B (business-to-business) data-sharing illegal which would amount to restriction of competition. As explained in detail in Chapter 5, two principal scenarios in this respect can be mentioned.

First, within the ambit of Article 101 TFEU, data sharing is prohibited by competition law when it facilitates collusion between firms. This happens once data shared is in itself sensitive or can be used to infer information that is sensitive and in result facilitates the coordination of firms' behavior on the market. The Commission Horizontal Guidelines[1] explain, for example, that "aggregation of commercially sensitive information into a pricing tool offered by a single IT company to which various competitors have access could amount to horizontal collusion".[2] However, the exchange of raw data in itself will not be problematic. It is when data collected feeds in the sensitive information which is shared between firms when competition law prohibitions kick in. The background rationale is the

1 Communication from the Commission, *Guidelines on the applicability of Article 101 of the Treaty on the Functioning of the European Union to horizontal cooperation agreements* [2023] C(2023) 4752 final (hereinafter "Horizontal Guidelines"). https://eur-lex.europa.eu/legal-content/EN/TXT/?uri=oj:JOC_2023_259_R_0001

2 *Ibid.*, para 402.

reduction of uncertainty among firms on the market with respect to the timing, scope and specifics of the conduct to be adopted in the market:[3] uncertainty is a key feature of competitive markets, and its reduction may have negative consequences for the ways in which markets operate.

Second, competition law limits data sharing once potential violation of Article 102 TFEU is at stake. In short, a dominant firm can be subject to antitrust investigation for forcing its business customers or individual consumers to share their respective business or personal data. The European Commission investigation in *Amazon Marketplace*[4] and the Bundeskartellamt investigation in *Meta* case[5] are illustrations here. The former case suggests that such practices should not be merely perceived from the exploitation perspective: accumulation of data by a firm that is already dominant may lead to further entrenchment of such a firm's position on the market by giving it advantage over its actual and potential competitors.

7.2.3 Personal Data Protection Perspective

The personal data protection regime in the EU imposes a broad and diverse set of limitations on data sharing. Indeed, the principal rationale behind personal data protection is to impose limits on how personal data can be processed and by doing so to safeguard fundamental rights, i.e. right to privacy. As explained in detail in Chapter 3, sharing of personal data is strictly restricted due to, among others, (i) broad, functional definition of personal data, which consequently also includes pseudonymized data; (ii) far-reaching protection of such personal data which are sensitive or concern children; (iii) strict requirement of freely given consent of data subject for processing of his or her data; (iv) purpose limitation (in principle personal data cannot be further processed in a way incompatible with the initial purpose); (v) data minimization rules (as a result of which only the necessary amount and category of data can be shared to achieve the purpose of data sharing). What's more, EU data-related laws tend to refer to GDPR to limit its scope of application (as it often also does for IPRs). On one hand, the Regulation on the free flow of non-personal data[6] states in Article 2(2) that where personal and non-personal data in a dataset are inextricably linked, the Regulation does not prejudice the application of GDPR. On the other hand, Article 7(8) of the DMA regulates the exchange of data between the gatekeeper and the provider of number-independent interpersonal communication services which makes a request for interoperability. It provides that only personal data of end users which are necessary to provide effective

3 See Mariateresa Maggiolino, Chapter 5.

4 European Commission, *Commission Decision of 20.12.2022 relating to a proceeding under Article 102 of the Treaty on the Functioning of the European Union (TFEU) and Article 54 of the EEA Agreement Cases AT.40462 – Amazon Marketplace and AT.40703 – Amazon Buy Box* [2022] (published 17 February 2023) C(2022) 9442 final.

5 Case C-252/21 *Meta Platforms and Others v Bundeskartellamt* [2023] EU:C:2023:537.

6 Regulation (EU) 2018/1807 of the European Parliament and of the Council of 14 November 2018 on a framework for the free flow of non-personal data in the European Union [2018] OJ L303/59.

interoperability can be shared between these two entities, and only if such sharing is compliant with the GDPR. In this direction, Joanna Mazur argues in Chapter 3 that gatekeepers are likely to rely on the GDPR to deny the implementation of data-sharing obligations listed in the DMA.[7]

7.3 IP, Competition and Personal Data Protection Laws in Service Data-Sharing

This section aims to explore how intellectual property, competition and data protection laws can facilitate data sharing. By examining the potential of these regulatory frameworks to promote data sharing under certain conditions, it sets the stage for understanding how these laws can complement new EU legal acts designed to encourage data sharing within the EU internal market. As outlined in the following subsections, these three areas of law establish principles that, when interpreted and applied thoughtfully, can enhance data sharing while still protecting exclusivity, innovation, competition and privacy ("fostering principles").

7.3.1 IP Perspective

Reflecting the structure used to address the role of IP as an obstacle to B2B data sharing in section 2.1 above, this section considers IP as a potential facilitator in two dimensions: (i) the role of IPRs in the data realm and (ii) the interaction between the IP regulatory framework and regulations promoting data sharing.

Regarding the first dimension, the protection of databases or data collections is paramount. Collections of works receive explicit protection under international and European law. For example, Article 2 of the Berne Convention safeguards "collections of literary or artistic works, such as encyclopedias and anthologies, which, due to the selection and arrangement of their contents, constitute intellectual creations". This definition has expanded to include productions in literary, scientific or artistic fields, irrespective of their form of expression. The TRIPS Agreement and the WIPO Copyright Treaty reinforce this broader interpretation, specifically mentioning "compilations of data or other material", whether in machine-readable or other forms, as potentially eligible for protection if they exhibit creativity in selection and arrangement. In the EU, Directive 96/9/EC on the legal protection of databases adopts this approach, defining a database as "a collection of independent works, data, or other materials arranged systematically or methodically and individually accessible by electronic or other means". This directive mandates EU Member States to ensure copyright protection for databases resulting from an author's intellectual creation, establishing databases as distinct objects of copyright protection in Europe. However, concerns persist regarding databases' eligibility for copyright protection based on the requirement of "originality", initially designed for artistic creations. To address these challenges and foster information

7 See Joanna Mazur, Chapter 3.

technology development, Directive 96/9/EC introduces a two-tier system: copyright protection for 'original' databases and a sui generis database right for those that do not meet the minimum originality standard but result from significant investment. The first layer of protection – copyright for "creative" databases – is rare in practice, especially with the rise of big data, where databases often lack a specific approach or strategy, being products of purely technical considerations. This also affects the second layer – *sui generis* protection – as randomly collected "big data" may not meet the necessary investment level. For *sui generis* protection, legislation requires a "considerable human, technical, and financial" investment, focusing on qualitative and quantitative aspects. Notably, this protection does not extend to investments solely for creating data, as clarified in court judgments related to the unauthorized use of sports event calendars. Even when a database is awarded protection under copyright or the *sui generis* right, the object of protection remains only the "structure" of the database, referring to the selection or arrangement of the content. Both international treaties and European legislation are clear that protection "shall not extend to their contents" or "mere facts or data".

As per the second dimension, the key regulation to look at is the Data Act that impacts on both trade secret and *sui generis* protection in the data realm. It is true DA stipulates that data holders cannot refuse access requests solely on the grounds of trade secrecy. However, if third-party access involves trade secret-protected data, disclosure is contingent upon demonstrating that such disclosure is strictly necessary for the agreed-upon purpose between the user and the third party. In balancing these interests, the DA introduces exceptions to the trade secret holder's right to decide on access and use by third parties. It aims to increase data circulation while preserving the confidentiality of trade secrets and safeguarding their economic value. The DA requires data holders and users to adopt necessary measures to preserve data confidentiality before disclosure, such as through contractual terms, confidentiality agreements and technical standards. Amendments in subsequent versions of the DA provide additional exceptions and safeguards to better balance conflicting interests and protect trade secret holders. These amendments require trade secret holders to identify protected data and allow them discretion in decisions related to data sharing, especially where economic harm from disclosure is likely. In conclusion, while the Data Act facilitates greater openness to trade secret-protected data within defined parameters, it introduces complexities and uncertainties. These include ambiguities in regulatory language and challenges in harmonizing trade secret protection with data circulation imperatives. This detailed regulatory framework, while protective, may inadvertently hinder data circulation and potentially conflict with the inherently flexible nature of trade secret protection. Additionally, the DA impacts the *sui generis* database right provided by Directive 96/9/EC. Article 35 of the Data Act stipulates that the *sui generis* right does not apply to databases containing data obtained or generated from the use of a related product or service. This provision ensures that users' rights to access and use such data, as established in Articles 4 and 5 of the Data Act, are not hindered. While many see this provision as not introducing a novel element, as it could be inferred from Directive 96/9/EC, it addresses the digital economy's need for clarity in facilitating data circulation and sharing, particularly by preventing data lock-in from user-generated data in the IoT ecosystem.

7.3.2 Competition Law Perspective

In section 2.2 competition law was considered to stay in the way of such data sharing which facilitates collusion and such use of data by a dominant firm that amounts to abuse of its dominant position. The former situation, which constitutes a 'by object' restriction of competition, must be distinguished from data sharing among competitors. While the latter may potentially restrict competition, it lacks the 'by object' characteristics and may qualify for either an individual exemption under Article 101(3) TFEU or one of the group exemptions provided in EU secondary law, such as exemptions for standardization or R&D agreements.[8] Data pools[9] are a key example here. In particular, data pool agreements under which undertakings licence specific datasets to a central administrator in order to fully exploit its whole value by means of big data analytics,[10] are likely to escape Article 101 TFEU prohibition[11] if data pool agreements are correctly built and abide by the participating undertakings.[12] In other words, data pools can facilitate data-sharing without raising substantive competition law related risks.

8 Please note that "by object" restrictions are unlikely to meet either individual or group exemption conditions.

9 A data pool is a data sharing system between companies, which involves an element of reciprocity, whereby at least some companies contribute data, *see* Martina Anzini, Anne-Carine Pierrat, 'Data Pools as Information Exchanges between Competitors: An Antitrust Perspective' (CEP 2020). Available at:: https://www.cep.eu/fileadmin/user_upload/cep.eu/Studien/cepInput_Data_pools/cepInput_Data_Pools_as_Information_Exchanges_between_Competitors_An_Antitrust_Perspective.pdf.

10 Oscar Borgogno, Giuseppe Colangelo, 'Data sharing and interoperability: Fostering Innovation and Competition through APIs' (2019) 35(5) Computer Law & Security Review.

11 If necessary measures are implemented, they cannot be classified as "by object" restrictions. The Horizontal Guidelines underline that "a data pool in which (partly) commercially sensitive data is exchanged which addresses information asymmetry in a non-concentrated market and that will result in benefits for consumers is unlikely to be considered as a restriction by object if the participants ensure that any commercially sensitive data that they exchange through the pool is necessary and proportionate to achieve the pro-competitive aim" (Sec 418). The Guidelines explain that participants can, for instance, rely as much as possible on aggregate and historical data, reduce the frequency of the exchange and implement measures to restrict access to the information exchanged and/or to control how it is used (ibid.). The participants should ensure that the arrangement is set up in a transparent manner (ibid.).

12 The 2023 Horizontal Guidelines explain that (i) participants in a reciprocal data-sharing arrangement such as a data pool should in principle only have access to their own information and the final, aggregated, information of other participants; (ii) technical and practical measures ensure that a participant is unable to obtain commercially sensitive information from other participants individually (Sec 408). In addition, the Guidelines encourage that (i) the management of a data pool can be assigned to a trustee that is subject to strict confidentiality rules as regards the information received from participants in the data pool; and (ii) undertakings that manage a data pool should also ensure that only information that is necessary for the implementation of the legitimate purpose of the data pool is collected (Sec 408).

Such a neutral scenario must be distinguished from situations where competition law (and, more recently, the DMA) actively promotes data sharing – namely, when access to data held by a dominant firm (or a gatekeeper, in the case of the DMA) is mandated or when fair terms for data access are ensured. Three approaches can be considered here. First, and most controversially, is to mandate access to the dominant firm's data by relying on the essential facility doctrine. A principle challenge which needs to be overcome by competition authority is to prove that access to the dominant firm's data is indeed indispensable and in particular that it cannot be accessed in different ways in an economically viable way (for example by means of its duplication).[13] Second, this approach aligns with the conditions set out in the *Slovak Telekom* ruling,[14] where access to a dominant player's data – while not denied in principle – would need to be mandated if the dominant firm's behavior is found to be contrary to this obligation, ensuring that access is granted under fair, non-discriminatory, and reasonable terms. The third approach, which is applicable in case of gatekeepers are various data-sharing obligations imposed by virtue of Article 6 and Article 7 DMA that will be considered more in detail in section 5 below. In particular, prohibitions applicable to gatekeepers, particularly Article 6(2), serve as an additional safeguard against the excessive use of other firms' or consumer data and play a complementary role vis-à-vis competition law. Last, one may consider that merger scrutiny can also play a role in preventing excessive market power, also in data-rich industries, to ensure that these consolidations do not lead to monopolistic control over vast amounts of data, which could stifle competition and innovation. In a nutshell, examining the potential impacts of mergers on market dynamics, regulatory bodies can also prevent the creation of data monopolies that could abuse their dominance, contributing to ensuring that data remains accessible and not overly concentrated in the hands of a few entities.

7.3.3 Personal Data Protection Perspective

While the regime of personal data protection is often perceived as a main obstacle for data sharing in the EU, the rules contained in GDPR offer a certain space for data sharing. First, the GDPR applies to personal data, and while it defines personal data very broadly, it does not impose limits on sharing of anonymized data and other kinds of data which are not personal (such as industrial data). Other, less restrictive legal regimes such as the Regulation on the free flow on non-personal data impose the rules under which such data is shared.

Second, the GDPR does not prohibit, as such, sharing of personal data by a data controller with third parties for commercial purposes. While in practice this is likely to be difficult, an interested data controller (a firm) should not rule out such a scenario completely. In this case such a firm should ask a data subject for consent[14] and offer a data subject an effective right to withdraw such a consent even

13 See more Maggiolino, Chapter 5.

14 Data sharing is in such a case a specific purpose within the meaning of Article 6(1)a of the GDPR. Such a consent would have to meet the criteria of being sufficiently specific and informed enough.

after his or her personal data was shared with third parties. The controller may also consider relying on grounds other than consent which are listed in Article 6 GDPR, for example a contract between data controller and data subject [Article 6(1)(b)].

Third, a potential for the GDPR compliant data sharing can be identified in the data-portability right contained in Article 20 of the GDPR. One can imagine that a data holder is approached by firms to encourage him or her to rely on his/her data-portability right to ask the data controller to share his/her data with such a firm or to upload such data directly to a platform used by such a firm.

7.4 Limiting and Fostering Principles of IP, Competition and Data Protection Laws

The analysis shows that IP, competition law and data protection law establish principles and rules that limit and foster data sharing that must be considered when creating a coherent data-sharing regime in the EU. Data sharing cannot occur in contravention of the interests these laws protect, namely the exclusivity and incentive of innovation via IPRs, competition and privacy. The table below illustrates these principles and confirms the need to balance them when creating a coherent data-sharing regime in the EU (Table 7.1).

Table 7.1 Limiting and Fostering Principles of Data Sharing

Regulatory Framework	*Limiting Principles*	*Fostering Principles*
Intellectual Property	• No copyright and patent on data, limiting the reinforcement of the data holders' position. • IPRs as a limit pro-data sharing regulation.	• (Residual) protection through trade secrets. • Copyright and *sui generis* right on databases. • Integration with the Data Act.
Competition Law	• Article 101 TFEU: risk of facilitating collusion via data sharing. • Article 102 TFEU: risk of imposition of data-sharing obligations by dominant firms.	• Article 101(3) TFEU: possible exemptions for data pooling and standardization or R&D agreements. • Integration with the Digital Markets Act. • Merger scrutiny can potentially contribute to preventing excessive data concentration.
Data Protection	• Data protection as a limit pro-data sharing regulation. • Broad, functional definition of personal data, with mixed datasets falling under GDPR. • Strict requirement for freely given consent for data use. • Purpose limitation and data minimization rules.	• Facilitation through anonymization. • Consent mechanism. • Data portability. • Increased trust in data sharing.

7.5 Coherence of EU Data Sharing Acquis

While intellectual property, competition law and data protection law may, in some respects, incentivize data sharing, a key role is to be played by pro-data-sharing regulations. Indeed, the EU has introduced a plethora of new regulations aimed at governing data access, transfer and sharing, creating a complex and often overlapping legal framework. This book has dissected this system, highlighting where these overlaps cause issues in coherence and legal certainty, and providing clarity on which rules firms should follow in various data-sharing scenarios. In other words, we can certainly talk today about an EU data-sharing acquis which aims to promote data sharing in the EU. However, the question remains whether these new legislation are coherent with one another and have the actual potential to stimulate data sharing in the EU. The following analysis intends to frame the pros and cons of the current scenario, trying to envisage paths for reflection on how to make it more conducive to pro-data sharing, especially among private entities.

As addressed in Chapters 2 and 4 of the book, the new EU legal framework covers B2B, G2B and B2G data sharing. It aims to stimulate data sharing by introducing a common EU regulatory framework, thus increasing legal certainty, rather than imposing a sharing obligation. Mandated data sharing is introduced only in specific circumstances where the EU legislator identifies either a specific market failure (e.g. in a specific sector, vis-à-vis gatekeepers, etc.) or a public interest reason, such as the B2G data-sharing obligation in the case of a public emergency, justifying direct intervention in market dynamics. Therefore, mandated data sharing is the exception, not the general rule, also within the new EU regulatory framework. More in detail, the 2019 Open Data Directive (ODD), replacing the Public Sector Information (PSI) Directive, introduces new rules to stimulate the sharing of data held by public authorities with the private sector, facilitating government-to-business (G2B) data sharing. The Data Governance Act (DGA) introduces a governance framework to stimulate both G2B and business-to-business (B2B) data sharing. Recently adopted, the Data Act introduces rules to stimulate B2B data sharing and to grant users' access to IoT generated data also in favor of third parties and data sharing from the private sector to the public sector in case of a public emergency, addressing also B2G data sharing. The Digital Market Act (DMA) includes specific data-sharing obligations, mandating digital gatekeepers to share their data with competitors under certain circumstances. It complements sector-specific rules that mandate data sharing in industries such as chemical, banking, automotive, electricity, telecom and postal services. Additionally, the right to data portability, as outlined in Article 20 of the General Data Protection Regulation (GDPR), allows data subjects to request the transfer of their personal data to a third party, resulting in B2B data sharing. In addition to the aforementioned regulations, there are sectoral regulations, such as the Directive on Payment Services (PSD2), which stipulates a right for third parties to access the banking data of consumers under certain circumstances.

Without attempting to cover all the discussions from Chapter 2 and Chapter 4 of the book, it is important to highlight some uncertainties regarding the relationship between pro-data sharing regulations. Generally, the need to protect personal data, ensure exclusivity guaranteed by IPRs and prevent anti-competitive market distortion are external limits to these regulations and, in addition, what we can define as the EU data sharing acquis sometimes lacks internal coherence.

First, the Data Act (DA) makes significant strides in data sharing by setting up obligations to share data and a more general framework for data access and sharing. However, it fails to fully integrate with public sector information regulations like those in the Data Governance Act and the Open Data PSI Directive. Moreover, it does not sufficiently address issues such as manufacturers harvesting data from publicly purchased devices, leaving public procurement bodies to manage these concerns.

Second, the Data Governance Act (DGA) aims to facilitate the reuse of public sector data, including personal, confidential and IP-protected data, provided it respects existing rights. It establishes intermediaries for data-sharing facilities and data spaces but does not override third-party rights, requiring a methodology for resolving rights issues before granting access.

Third, the Digital Markets Act (DMA) focuses on gatekeepers (namely, undertaking providing core platform services designated pursuant to Article 3), imposing obligations to provide access and portability rights. However, it lacks a standalone right for business users to access and port data, potentially leading to litigation over inferred data. The DMA also mandates that advertisement repositories be accessible via APIs, with provisions for regulatory access for enforcement and research purposes. As is known, the DMA is part of the Digital Services Act Package together with the Digital Services Act, that applies to providers of intermediary services including online platforms.

Fourth, the Open Data Directive (ODD) governs access to public sector information for commercial use, creating a level playing field. Operating independently from the Data Act, it is limited by intellectual property rights and business confidentiality restrictions, focusing on public-good data.

Fifth, if it is true that general regulations related to the data realm – primarily the GDPR and the Regulation on the Free Flow of Non-Personal Data (FFD) – address the movement of personal and non-personal data within the EU internal market, at the same time they create obstacles to data sharing by requiring full compliance with their (sometimes) complex provisions and by prevailing on pro-data sharing provisions.

Lastly, considering one of the sectoral frameworks as an example, the PSD2 introduces specific rules for the payment services sector, including provisions for data access and transfer aimed at enhancing competition and innovation in financial services (Table 7.2).

In more general terms, firms may face uncertainties regarding which regulations apply in specific situations. The interplay between general and specific laws complicates compliance, particularly when specific rules do not provide clear guidance. For instance, if the DMA does not offer a coherent solution, businesses might turn to the general principles of the Data Act or other sector-specific laws. The DMA imposes obligations on gatekeepers to provide data access

Table 7.2 Data Sharing Regulations in the EU

Regulation	*Data Type*	*Pro-Sharing Objective*	*Main Tools*
DA	Private data.	Private data sharing.	Obligations to share data (B2C, B2B, B2G) + general framework for data access and sharing.
ODD/DGA	Public data.	Public data reuse ("as open as possible").	Obligation on Public Sector Bodies to offer public data for reuse (G2B).
DMA	Private data.	Private data access and portability.	Obligation on gatekeepers to provide access and portability rights.
GDPR	Personal data.	Free flow and data protection.	Framework for digital trust + portability + transfer, etc.
FFD	Non-personal data.	Free flow.	Ban on data localization measures.
Other	Various.	Sector-specific.	Sector-specific legislation (e.g. PSD2) and sectoral data spaces.

but does not specify which data is covered, potentially limiting business users' rights. Gatekeepers may also claim *sui generis* database rights, further restricting access. The DGS encourages the reuse of public sector data, but the ODD limits it to non-IP-protected data, while one can believe that public sector bodies must facilitate access while navigating intellectual property and confidentiality concerns.

Therefore, in order to improve the regulatory landscape, simplifying and harmonizing overlapping regulations can provide better legal certainty. In this direction, clearer integration of public sector information rules within the DA is needed. In addition, the DMA could be refined to explicitly grant access and portability rights to business users, not just end users. This would empower businesses to leverage data more effectively against gatekeepers. Establishing clearer guidelines for data intermediaries and data spaces can enhance data sharing. Ensuring that these entities cater to small businesses as well as large platforms is crucial for fostering innovation and competition. Moreover, developing frameworks that explicitly address the tensions with data protection, IP and competition law – as it is for example the case of DA and trade secrets – can be more conducive to a vibrant data economy.

7.6 Data Spaces as the Possible Place to Balance the Regulatory Frameworks

As discussed in various chapters of this book (2, 4 and 6), the EU is actively supporting the creation of Common European Data Spaces in strategic sectors to overcome technical, privacy and security barriers that currently hinder data sharing in specific industries. Announced in the 2020 Data Strategy, the European

Commission detailed these Common European Data Spaces further in a Staff Working Document published in February 2022 and the DGA and the DA contributed to define their structure. Each Data Space aims to create a single market for data, encouraging data sharing among firms in specific strategic sectors (e.g. healthcare, industrial manufacturing, agriculture, finance, mobility, the Green Deal, energy, public administration). The Commission will introduce common interoperability standards and sectoral data governance rules, such as model contracts, licenses and access rights, while the EU budget will fund the development of common IT infrastructures for each Data Space.

For the purposes of this chapter, data spaces can be viewed as an intermediate scenario where various EU regulatory frameworks converge to facilitate data sharing. These spaces can help balance the need to protect IPRs, personal data and competition while promoting data sharing in both B2B contexts and with public sector bodies. They also provide a platform to address the inconsistencies and lack of communication among existing EU pro-data sharing regulations. Additionally, it is essential to note that obstacles to data sharing are not only legal but also technical and cultural, and data spaces aim to overcome these by creating an interoperable and secure framework. EU data spaces aim to promote the availability of large pools of data in specific sectors and domains of public interest, combined with the technical tools and infrastructures necessary for data use and exchange, and appropriate governance mechanisms.

Despite being sector-specific, data spaces share common features. Even though only the health data space proposal has been released, insights into their governance mechanisms can be inferred from EU policy documents on data spaces in general.[15] Structurally, data spaces involve data relationships between trusted partners who adhere to high-level standards and guidelines related to data storage and sharing.[16] The goal is to accelerate digital transformation in identified fields by overcoming legal and technical barriers to voluntary data sharing and addressing trust issues through the development of fair, practical and clear rules for data use.[17] Data spaces aim to create an environment where market participants feel empowered to share more data for economic and societal use while retaining control over the data they generate. By making available large pools of good-quality and interoperable data in specific sectors, combined with the necessary infrastructure for data use and exchange, and appropriate governance mechanisms, data spaces should facilitate increased data movement across Member States and sectors.[18]

15 In addition to the policy documents, starting from 2021 the EU has launched a series of preparatory actions in the various sectors. *See*, for example, European Commission, 'Digital Europe Programme (DIGITAL) Call for proposals – Preparatory actions for Data Spaces' (2021). https://ec.europa.eu/info/funding-tenders/opportunities/docs/2021-2027/digital/wp-call/2021/call-fiche_digital-2021-prepacts-ds-01_en.pdf

16 Gaia-X, 'What is a data space?', White Paper 1&2022, https://gaia-x-hub.de/wp-content/uploads/2023/11/GX-White-Paper-Data-Space.pdf (last accessed 30 January 2024).

17 European Commission, *Commission Staff Working Document on Common European Data Spaces* [2022] SWD(2022) 45 final 16.

18 Ibid., 21.

To address the crucial interoperability requirement, the Data Act allows the Commission to adopt guidelines specifying interoperability standards for the functioning of data spaces. This includes architectural models and technical standards implementing legal rules and arrangements fostering data sharing, such as access rights and technical translations of consent or permission.[19] Through Article 33 on data interoperability, the Data Act aims to contribute to developing common data spaces. However, the vagueness of some provisions in the Data Act risks hindering rather than promoting the creation of data spaces.[20] In particular, the Data Act makes no reference to interoperability across data spaces. It is crucial to specify whether the requirements for operators also apply to interoperability across sectors and how they align with each data space's features. Data spaces will rely on common technical infrastructures to facilitate coordination and ensure fair data pooling and sharing among actors.[21] Common elements across sectors will be implemented through a horizontal governance structure encompassing administrative and contractual rules that establish rights to access, process, use and share data transparently and reliably.[22] These common elements will be complemented by sector-specific rules.[23] According to the DGA, a European Data Innovation Board will be established to assist the Commission in developing data spaces, among other tasks.[24]

An important feature of data spaces is data control: data holders will control the data they generate and share, whether for payment or free.[25] Data owners can decide who accesses their data, for what purpose and under what conditions.[26] Increased trust will incentivize both businesses and individuals to share data, fostering an interconnected and competitive European data economy.[27] Moreover, data spaces should be open to organizations and individuals who respect EU rules and values.

19 European Commission, *Proposal for a Regulation of the European Parliament and of the Council on harmonised rules on fair access to and use of data* (Data Act), COM(2022) 68 final Art 28(6).

20 Josef Drexl and others, 'Position Statement of the Max Planck Institute for Innovation and Competition of 25 May 2022 on the Commission's Proposal of 23 February 2022 for a Regulation on Harmonised Rules on Fair Access to and Use of Data (Data Act)' (2022) SSRN Electronic Journal 81.

21 European Commission, *Commission Staff Working Document on Common European Data Spaces* SWD(2022) 45 final 4.

22 Johan Bodenkamp, 'Common European Data Spaces and The Data Economy' (Online Expert Seminar, 3 November 2022).

23 Governance frameworks must also comply with the relevant EU legislation (e.g. the GDPR, ePrivacy Directive, Platform to Business Regulation).

24 Regulation (EU) 2022/868 of the European Parliament and of the Council of 30 May 2022 on European data governance and amending Regulation (EU) 2018/1724 [2022] OJ L152/1 Art 26. In particular they are commissioned to propose guidelines on data spaces and, more generally, to advise the Commission on security requirements, access procedures and cross-industry standards for data sharing.

25 European Commission, *Commission Staff Working Document on Common European Data Spaces* SWD(2022) 45 final 3.

26 Johan Bodenkamp, 'Common European Data Spaces and The Data Economy'.

27 European Commission, *Commission Staff Working Document on Common European Data Spaces* SWD(2022) 45 final 4.

This openness will foster competition among product and service providers requiring data sharing, avoiding potential competition lock-in due to manufacturers' specific protocols.[28] This is particularly relevant for the repair sector, where manufacturers often control data generated by their products, creating lock-in effects and hindering the market entry of after-sales service providers.[29]

For what is of specific interest in this chapter, data spaces are also crucial for ensuring compliance with European rules and cross-sectoral measures. They must operate fully within existing rules on personal data protection provided by the GDPR.[30] This means, for example, that health data can be processed for secondary use only for specific purposes established by the Regulation.[31] Data exchange must occur in a secure environment that guarantees adequate protection of personal data. Specific measures are established for sensitive data categories, where anonymization mechanisms can facilitate data sharing.

Additionally, data spaces must respect existing competition law and IP provisions. The Staff Working Document on Data Spaces states that data spaces shall comply with Articles 101 and 102 TFEU, the related Guidelines for Horizontal Cooperation Agreements,[32] and the Block Exemption Regulations.[33] Similarly, the Data Act ensures that its provisions do not prejudice the application of competition rules. However, neither the Staff Working Document on Data Spaces nor the Data Act thoroughly analyzes potential anti-competitive issues or measures to prevent collusion among competitors involved in data spaces. Regarding IPRs, data spaces – also thanks to data intermediaries – can balance the rights of IPR holders with the need for openness. For example, they can contribute to reconciling the data holders' interest in protecting trade secrets with the legitimate interests of users and third parties in accessing and using data. Indeed, data holders benefit from control over the data and the ability to determine trade secrecy prior to data sharing,

28 Ibid.

29 European Commission, *Proposal for a Regulation of the European Parliament and of the Council on harmonised rules on fair access to and use of data* (Data Act), COM(2022) 68 final 13.

30 Regulation (EU) 2016/679 of the European Parliament and of the Council of 27 April 2016 on the protection of natural persons with regard to the processing of personal data and on the free movement of such data, and repealing Directive 95/46/EC (GDPR) [2016] OJ L119/1.

31 'Questions and Answers – EU Health: European Health Data Space (EHDS)' (*European Commission*, 3 May 2022) ec.europa.eu/commission/presscorner/detail/en/qanda_22_2712&gt (last accessed 30 January 2024).

32 European Commission, 'Communication from the Commission Guidelines on the applicability of Article 101 of the Treaty on the Functioning of the European Union to horizontal cooperation agreements' [2011] (2011/C 11/01) ("Horizontal Guidelines"). As is well-known, the Guidelines are intended to assist market participants in self-assessing whether an agreement restricts competition and, if so, whether it fulfills the criteria for an exemption. https://eur-lex.europa.eu/legal-content/EN/TXT/PDF/?uri=CELEX:52023XC0721(01)

33 Commission Regulation (EU) No 1218/2010 of 14 December 2010 on the application of Article 101(3) of the Treaty on the Functioning of the European Union to certain categories of specialisation agreements [2010] OJ L335/43 ("Specialisation Block Exemption Regulation"); and Commission Regulation (EU) No 1217/2010 of 14 December 2010 on the application of Article 101(3) of the Treaty on the Functioning of the European Union to certain categories of research and development agreements [2010] OJ L335/36 ("Research & Development Block Exemption Regulation").

which can lead to power asymmetries, and this poses a risk that data holders might preemptively determine data-sharing terms in a conflict of interest position.

Even if data spaces seem promising for resolving conflicts among regulatory frameworks, they might also fall short by requiring strict compliance or excessively relaxing critical rules, potentially facilitating competitor collusion. To truly support systematic data-driven innovation through increased sharing, these balancing acts should be integrated into the general regulatory framework, ensuring their relevance extends beyond specific industry-related initiatives.

7.7 Conclusions

The interplay of intellectual property IP law, competition law and personal data protection within the context of data sharing, particularly in the realm of B2B interactions, presents a multifaceted challenge that necessitates a balanced and nuanced approach. This chapter has provided a comprehensive examination of these intersecting legal domains, shedding light on both their limiting and facilitating roles in the pursuit of a robust data-sharing ecosystem. From the IP perspective, the tension between protecting proprietary data and promoting open access is palpable. IP laws, while essential for safeguarding innovation and rewarding creators, often create barriers to data sharing by restricting access to valuable datasets. This can stifle collaboration and limit the potential for new, data-driven innovations.

Competition law, designed to eliminate competition restrictive practices, can also act as a double-edged sword. On one hand, it aims to dismantle data silos and promote data accessibility; on the other, stringent regulations can inadvertently discourage data-sharing agreements that might be viewed as anti-competitive. Thus, striking a balance between fostering competition and facilitating cooperation is crucial. Personal data protection laws, epitomized by the GDPR in the EU, prioritize the privacy and security of individuals' data. While these laws are fundamental in building trust and ensuring ethical data use, they can complicate data sharing by imposing stringent compliance requirements. Businesses often find themselves navigating a complex legal landscape where the protection of personal data conflicts with the imperative to share and utilize data for innovation.

Conversely, these legal frameworks also provide pathways to support and enhance data sharing. IP law, through mechanisms such as licensing agreements and data pooling, can foster a collaborative environment where data is shared under agreed-upon terms that protect the interests of all parties involved. This promotes innovation while respecting intellectual property rights. Competition law, by advocating for open markets and dismantling anti-competitive practices, can create a level playing field that encourages data sharing. Policies that prevent data monopolies and promote interoperability are instrumental in ensuring that data flows freely and equitably among businesses, driving collective growth and innovation. Data protection laws, although stringent, offer a foundation for trust in the digital economy. By ensuring that personal data is handled responsibly, these laws build consumer confidence, which is essential for the widespread adoption of data-sharing practices. Additionally, frameworks such as the GDPR encourage the development of privacy-preserving technologies, which can facilitate secure and compliant data sharing.

The coherence of the EU's data-sharing acquis remains a critical issue. The plethora of legislative initiatives – ranging from the Open Data Directive to the Data Act – reflects the EU's commitment to a thriving data economy. However, the challenge lies in harmonizing these frameworks to create a seamless regulatory environment. Inconsistencies and overlaps among these laws can create confusion and hinder the effective implementation of data-sharing strategies.

The concept of data spaces emerges as a promising solution to the regulatory complexities of data sharing. By creating structured environments where data can be shared under clear and consistent rules, data spaces can harmonize the various legal frameworks and facilitate cooperation. These spaces aim to balance the protection of fundamental rights and interests with the promotion of data-driven innovation, thereby providing a practical pathway to achieving the EU's data economy objectives. However, while data spaces show promise in resolving conflicts among regulatory frameworks, they may also prove inadequate by imposing overly strict compliance or excessively relaxing critical rules, potentially facilitating competitor collusion. To genuinely support systematic data-driven innovation through enhanced sharing, these balancing acts should be integrated into the broader regulatory framework, ensuring their relevance extends beyond sector-specific initiatives. In other words, it is crucial to recognize that while data spaces are important, we cannot invest everything in them alone; instead, we must strive for a harmonious and collaborative regulatory scenario.

In doing so, it is worth examining experiences beyond the EU system, such as those in India, the United Kingdom and Poland since they reveal diverse approaches to establishing nationwide data sharing schemes.[34] Typically, these efforts involve a central body tasked with approving datasets, managing data-sharing requests and arbitrating disputes among custodians and processors. While this centralized model offers security by allowing state oversight, it can strain under increasing data volumes and hinder cross-border initiatives within the EU. India's exploration of decentralized data custodians and blockchain verification represents an alternative approach. Empowering data subjects to control anonymization of their personal data further exemplifies India's progressive stance, surpassing even the stringent standards of the EU's GDPR. Meanwhile, the data trust model, extensively explored in India, Poland and the UK, presents an attractive regulatory alternative. Yet, it risks tech giants like Google and Facebook influencing data ethics and standards. Even with the adoption of data trust models, as observed in the UK, effective data

34 *See* Marcin Z Zieliński, 'Non-Personal Data Sharing Initiatives. A Comparative Approach' (2023). Available at: https://cars.wz.uw.edu.pl/images/konferencje/konferencje_miedzynarodowe/DATA%20SHARING/Non-personal%20data%20sharing%20initiatives.%20A%20comparative%20approach.pdf.

sharing demands robust legal frameworks like contracts, equitable trusts, corporate structures or regulatory oversight. Such frameworks often necessitate significant legislative intervention to be implemented effectively. Poland's innovative concept of placing unprocessed raw data in the public domain, thus bypassing legal protections, could bolster data-sharing popularity. However, reluctance from major data producers may hinder widespread adoption of this approach.

Moving back to the EU dimension, it is clear that the future of B2B data sharing in the internal market hinges on the ability that the EU institutions will have to navigate and reconcile the intricate interplay of IP, competition and data protection laws. By fostering an environment where these legal frameworks complement rather than conflict with each other, we can unlock the full potential of data-driven innovation. This chapter underscores the need for ongoing dialogue and strategic alignment among businesses, policymakers and other stakeholders to create a coherent and supportive regulatory landscape.

In conclusion, the journey toward an effective and inclusive data-sharing ecosystem is complex but attainable. By leveraging the strengths of IP, competition and data protection laws, and by exploring innovative solutions such as data spaces, we can pave the way for a vibrant digital economy that benefits all. This chapter contributes to the broader discourse on aligning regulatory frameworks, ultimately aiming to harness the transformative power of data for societal progress and economic growth.

Bibliography

Books, Chapters and Articles

Agrawal, Ajay, Joshua Gans, and Avi Goldfarb. *Prediction Machines: The Simple Economics of Artificial Intelligence.* Harvard Business Press, 2018.

Aichholzer, Georg, and Herbert Burkert, eds., *Public Sector Information in the Digital Age. Between Markets, Public Management and Citizens' Rights.* Edward Elgar Publishing, 2004.

Alemanno, Alberto. "Big Data for Good: Unlocking Privately Held Data to the Benefit of the Many." *European Journal of Risk Regulation* 9, no. 2 (July 2018): 183–191. https://doi.org/10.1017/err.2018.34.

Alovisio, Mauro. "Criticità Privacy nel riuso dei dati pubblici." *Informatica e Diritto* 1–2 (October 2011).

Anderson, Tore. "Datatilsynet (Norway) - 20/02319 (gdprhub.eu)." https://gdprhub.eu/index.php?title=Datatilsynet_(Norway)_-_20/02319.

Aplin, Tanya, Alfred Radauer, Martin A. Bader, and Nicola Searle. "The Role of EU Trade Secrets Law in the Data Economy: An Empirical Analysis." *International Review of Intellectual Property and Competition Law* 54 (May 2023): 826–858. https://doi.org/10.1007/s40319-023-01325-8.

Banterle, Francesco. "The Interface Between Data Protection and IP Law: The Case of Trade Secrets and the Database *sui generis* Right in Marketing Operations, and the Ownership of Raw Data in Big Data Analysis." In *Personal Data in Competition, Consumer Protection and Intellectual Property Law: Towards a Holistic Approach?*, edited by Mor Bakhoum, Beatriz Conde Gallego, Mark-Oliver Mackenrodt, and Gintarė Surblytė-Namavičienė, 411–443. Springer, 2018. https://doi.org/10.1007/978-3-662-57646-5_16.

Blackman, Colin, and Simon Forge. *In-depth Analysis Real- ized for the European Parliamentary Research Service, Data Flows – Future Scenarios*. P/A/ITRE/ IC/2017-04, 12 (2017).

Borgogno, Oscar, and Giuseppe Colangelo. "Data Sharing and Interoperability: Fostering Innovation and Competition through APIs." *Computer Law & Security Review* 35, no. 5 (October 2019): 105314. https://doi.org/10.1016/j.clsr.2019.03.008.

Borgogno, Oscar, and Giuseppe Colangelo. "The Data Sharing Paradox: BigTechs in Finance" *European Competition Journal* 16, no. 2–3 (October 2020): 492–511. https://doi.org/10.1080/17441056.2020.1812285.

Botta, Marco. "Shall We Share? The Principle of FRAND in B2B Data Sharing." *Robert Schuman Centre for Advanced Studies Working Paper* 2023, no. 30 (April 2023). http://dx.doi.org/10.2139/ssrn.4422925.

Brouwer, Evelien. "Legality and Data Protection Law: The Forgotten Purpose of Purpose Limitation." In *The Eclipse of the Legality Principle in the European Union*, edited by Leonard F. M. Besselink, Frans Pennings, and Sacha Prechal, 273–294. Kluwer Law International, 2011.

Bruzzone, Ginevra, and Debackere Koenraad. "As Open as Possible, as Closed as Needed: Challenges of the EU Strategy for Data." *les Nouvelles* (March 2021): 41–49.

Bygrave, Lee A., and Luca Tosoni. "Article 4(1). Personal Data." In *The EU General Data Protection Regulation (GDPR): A Commentary*, edited by Christopher Kuner, Lee A. Bygrave, Christopher Docksey, and Laura Drechsler, 103–115. Oxford University Press, 2020. https://doi.org/10.1093/oso/9780198826491.003.0007.

Bygrave, Lee A., and Luca Tosoni. "Article 4(7). Controller." In *The EU General Data Protection Regulation (GDPR): A Commentary*, edited by Christopher Kuner, Lee A. Bygrave, Christopher Docksey, and Laura Drechsler, 145–156. Oxford University Press, 2020. https://doi.org/10.1093/oso/9780198826491.003.0013.

Bygrave, Lee A., and Luca Tosoni. "Article 4(8). Processor." In *The EU General Data Protection Regulation (GDPR): A Commentary*, edited by Christopher Kuner, Lee A. Bygrave, Christopher Docksey, and Laura Drechsler, 157–162. Oxford University Press, 2020. https://doi.org/10.1093/oso/9780198826491.003.0014.

Cabral, Luis, Justus Haucap, Geoffrey Parker, Georgios Petropoulos, Tommaso Valletti, and Marshall Van Alstyne. *The EU Digital Markets Act*. Publications Office of the European Union, 2021. https://doi.org/10.2760/139337.

Caforio, Valeria. "Molto rumore per nulla: la sentenza della Corte di giustizia sul rapporto tra diritto della concorrenza e tutela dei dati personali nell'Unione europea." *Il diritto industriale* 5 (2023): 405–413.

Cappai, Marco, and Giuseppe Colangelo. "Applying ne bis in idem in the Aftermath of bpost and Nordzucker: The Case of EU Competition Policy in Digital Markets." *Common Market Law Review* 60, no. 2 (2023): 431–456. https://doi.org/10.54648/cola2023026.

Carolan, Eoin. "The Continuing Problems with Online Consent under the EU's Emerging Data Protection Principles." *Computer Law & Security Review* 32, no. 3 (June 2016): 462–473. https://doi.org/10.1016/j.clsr.2016.02.004.

Casalini, Francesca, and Javier López González. "Trade and Cross-Border Data Flows." *OECD Trade Policy Working Papers* 220 (January 2019). https://doi.org/10.1787/b2023a47-en.

Cate, Fred H., and Viktor Mayer-Schönberger. "Notice and Consent in a World of Big Data." *International Data Privacy Law* 3, no. 2 (May 2013): 67–73. https://doi.org/10.1093/idpl/ipt005.

Ciani, Jacopo. "Governing Data Trade in Intelligent Environments: A Taxonomy of Possible Regulatory Regimes between Property and Access Rights." In *Intelligent Environments 2018: Workshop Proceedings of the 14th International Conference on Intelligent Environments*, edited by Paulo Novais, Ioannis Chatzigiannakis, Yoshito Tobe, and Oliver Amft, 285–297. IOS Press, 2018.

Cimina, Vera. "The Proposal for a European Health Data Space: Between Pursued Objectives and Data Protection Challenges." *ERA Forum* 24 (October 2023): 343–359. https://doi.org/10.1007/s12027-023-00764-7.

Clifford, Damian, and Jef Ausloos. "Data Protection and the Role of Fairness." *Yearbook of European Law* 37 (January 2018): 130–187. https://doi.org/10.1093/yel/yey004.

Colangelo, Giuseppe. "The Privacy/Antitrust Curse: Insights from GDPR Application in Competition Law Proceedings." *ICLE White Paper* (October 2023). http://dx.doi.org/10.2139/ssrn.4599974.

Colangelo, Giuseppe, and Mariateresa Maggiolino. "Antitrust *Über Alles*. Whither Competition Law After Facebook?" *World Competition* 42, no. 3 (2019): 355–376.

Colangelo, Giuseppe, and Mariateresa Maggiolino. "Big Data as Misleading Facilities." *European Competition Journal* 13, no. 2–3 (June 2017): 249–281.

Colangelo, Giuseppe, and Mariateresa Maggiolino. "Data Accumulation and the Privacy-Antitrust Interface: Insights from the Facebook Case." *International Data Privacy Law* 8, no. 3 (August 2018): 224–239. https://doi.org/10.1093/idpl/ipy018.

Comandè, Giovanni, and Giulia Schneider. "Differential Data Protection Regimes in Data-Driven Research: Why the GDPR Is More Research-Friendly Than You Think." *German Law Journal* 23, no. 4 (May 2022): 559–596. https://doi.org/10.1017/glj.2022.30.

Cooper, James C. "Privacy and Antitrust: Underpants Gnomes, the First Amendment, and Subjectivity." *George Mason Law Review* 20, no. 4 (2013): 1129–1146.

Corrado, Margherita, and Laura Zoboli. "Are Data Spaces a 'Silver Bullet' for the EU Data Economy?" In *Digital Platforms, Competition Law, and Regulation Comparative Perspectives*, edited by Kalpana Tyagi, Anselm Kamperman Sanders, and Caroline Cauffman, 105–123. Bloomsbury Publishing, 2024.

Custers, Bart, and Helena Uršič. "Big Data and Data Reuse: A Taxonomy of Data Reuse for Balancing Big Data Benefits and Personal Data Protection." *International Data Privacy Law* 6, no. 1 (February 2016): 4–15. https://doi.org/10.1093/idpl/ipv028.

Davison, Mark J., and Hugenholtz P. Bernt. "Football Fixtures, Horse Races and Spin-offs: The ECJ Domesticates the Database Rights." *European Intellectual Property Review* 27, no. 3 (2005): 113–118.

De Terwangne, Cécile. "Article 5 Principles Relating to Processing of Personal Data." In *The EU General Data Protection Regulation (GDPR): A Commentary*, edited by Christopher Kuner, Lee A. Bygrave, Christopher Docksey, and Laura Drechsler, 309–320. Oxford University Press, 2020. https://doi.org/10.1093/oso/9780198826491.003.0034.

Derclaye, Estelle. "Database "Sui Generis Right: Should We Adopt the Spin Off Theory?" *European Intellectual Property Review* 26, no. 9 (January 2004): 402–413.

Derclaye, Estelle. *The Legal Protection of Databases: A Comparative Analysis*. Edward Elgar, 2008.

Demetzou, Katerina. "Data Protection Impact Assessment: A Tool for Accountability and the Unclarified Concept of 'High Risk' in the General Data Protection Regulation." *Computer Law & Security Review* 35, no. 6 (November 2019): 105342. https://doi.org/10.1016/j.clsr.2019.105342.

Douglas, Erika M. "The New Antitrust/Data Privacy Law Interface." *Yale Law Journal Forum* 130 (January 2021): 647–684.

Drechsler, Laura. "Practical Challenges to the Right to Data Portability in the Collaborative Economy." In *Collaborative Economy: Challenges and Opportunities* (Actas del 14° Congreso Internacional Internet, Derecho y Política. Universitat Oberta de Catalunya, Barcelona, 21–22 de junio de 2018), 219–235, at 227–228, 232, 2018. https://scholar.google.at/citations?view_op=view_citation&hl=en&user=HUWJo-sAAAAJ&citation_for_view=HUWJo-sAAAAJ:mVmsd5A6BfQC

Drechsler, Laura, and Irene Kamara. "Chapter 13: Essential Equivalence as a Benchmark for International Data Transfers after Schrems II." In *Research Handbook on EU Data Protection Law*, edited by Eleni Kosta, Ronald Leenes, and Irene Kamara, 314–352. Edward Elgar Publishing, 2022. https://doi.org/10.4337/9781800371682.00022

Drexl, Josef. "The Changing Role of Personal and Non-Personal Data." In *Digital Revolution: Data Protection, Smart Products, Blockchain Technology and Bitcoins Challenges for Law in Practice*, edited by Alberto De Franceschi, and R. Schulze, 19–41. C.H. Beck, 2019.

Drexl, Josef. "The Competition Dimension of the European Regulation of Public Sector Information and the Concept of an Undertaking." In *State-Initiated Restraints of Competition*, edited by Josef Drexl and Vicente Bagnoli, 64–100. Edward Elgar, 2015. https://doi.org/10.4337/9781784714987.00013.

Drexl, Josef. "Designing Competitive Markets for Industrial Data – between Propertisation and Access." *Max Planck Institute for Innovation and Competition Research Paper* 16–18 (2016).

Forge, Simon. *Optimal Scope for Free-Flow of Non-Personal Data in Europe*. Policy Department for Economic, Scientific and Quality of Life Policies. Directorate-General for Internal Policies PE 618.988 (April 2018).

Forgó, Nikolaus, Stefanie Hänold, and Benjamin Schütze. "The Principle of Purpose Limitation and Big Data." In *New Technology, Big Data and the Law*, edited by Marcelo Corrales, Mark Fenwick, and Nikolaus Forgó, 17–42. Springer Singapore, 2017. https://doi.org/10.1007/978-981-10-5038-1_2.

Frischermann, Brett M. *Infrastructure: The Social Value of Shared Resources. Infrastructure: The Social Value of Shared Resources*. Oxford University Press, 2012.

Gal, Michal, and Daniel L. Rubinfeld. "Data Standardization." *New York University Law Review* 94 (October 2019): 737–770.

Georgieva, Ludmila, and Christopher Kuner. "Article 9 Processing of Special Categories of Personal Data." In *The EU General Data Protection Regulation (GDPR): A Commentary*, edited by Christopher Kuner, Lee A. Bygrave, Christopher Docksey, and Laura Drechsler, 373–375. Oxford University Press, 2020. https://doi.org/10.1093/oso/9780198826491.003.0038.

Geradin, Damien, Dimitrios Katsifis, and Theano Karanikioti. "Google as a de facto Privacy Regulator: Analyzing Chrome's Removal of Third-party Cookies from an Antitrust Perspective." *TILEC Discussion Paper* 2020, no. 34 (November 2020). http://dx.doi.org/10.2139/ssrn.3738107.

Gervais, Daniel. "Exploring the Interfaces between Big Data and Intellectual Property Law." *Journal of Intellectual Property, Information Technology and E-Commerce Law* 10, no. 1 (2019): 3–19.

Gobbato, Sara. "Open Science and the Reuse of Publicly Funded Research Data in the New Directive (EU) 2019/1024." *Journal of Ethics and Legal Technologies* 2, no. 2 (November 2020): 145–161.

González Fuster, Gloria. "Article 18 Right to Restriction of Processing." In *The EU General Data Protection Regulation (GDPR): A Commentary*, edited by Christopher Kuner, Lee A. Bygrave, Christopher Docksey, and Laura Drechsler, 486–487. Oxford University Press, 2020. https://doi.org/10.1093/oso/9780198826491.003.0050.

González Fuster, Gloria. *The Emergence of Personal Data Protection as a Fundamental Right of the EU*. Law, Governance and Technology Series 16. Springer International Publishing, 2014, https://doi.org/10.1007/978-3-319-05023-2.

Graef, Inge, and Martin Husovec. "Seven Things to Improve in the Data Act." (March 2022) http://dx.doi.org/10.2139/ssrn.4051793.

Graef, Inge, Martin Husovec, and Nazehda Purtova. "Data Portability and Data Control: Lessons for an Emerging Concept in EU Law." *German Law Review* 19, no. 6 (November 2018): 1359–1398. https://doi.org/10.1017/S2071832200023075.

Graef, Inge, and Jens Prüfer. "Governance of Data Sharing: A Law & Economics Proposal." *Research Policy* 50, no. 9 (November 2021): 104330. https://doi.org/10.1016/j.respol.2021.104330.

Graef, Inge, Thomas Tombal, and Alexandre de Streel. "Limits and Enablers of Data Sharing. An Analytical Framework for EU Competition, Data Protection and Consumer Law." *TILEC Discussion Paper* 2019, no. 24 (November 2019): 1–35. https://doi.org/10.2139/ssrn.3494212.

Houser, Kimberly A., and John W. Bagby. "The Data Trust Solution to Data Sharing Problems." *Vanderbilt Journal of Entertainment and Technology Law* 25, no. 1 (2023): 113–180.

Hugenholtz, P. Bernt. "Against 'Data Property'." In *Kritika: Essays on Intellectual Property*, edited by Hanns Ullrich, Peter Drahos, and Gustavo Ghidini, 48–71 (2018). https://doi.org/10.4337/9781788971164.00010.

Hugenholtz, P. Bernt. "Database Directive." In *Concise European Copyright Law*, edited by Thomas Dreier and Bernt Hugenholtz, 405, 2nd ed. Kluwer Law International, 2016.

Hugenholtz, P. Bernt. "Something Completely Different: Europe's Sui Generis Database Right." In *The Internet and the Emerging Importance of New Forms of Intellectual Property*, edited by Susy Frankel and Daniel Gervais, 205–222. Wolters Kluwer, 2016.

Iaia, Vincenzo. "The Strengthening Liaison between Data Protection, Antitrust and Consumer Law in the German and Italian Big Data-Driven Economies." *Bialystock Legal Studies* 26, no. 5 (December 2021): 63–74. https://doi.org/10.15290/bsp.2021.26.05.04.

Janssen, Katleen. *The Availability of Spatial and Environmental Data in the European Union.* Kluwer Law International, 2010.

Janssen, Katleen, and Jos Dumortier. "Towards a European Framework for the Re-use of Public Sector Information: A Long and Winding Road." *International Journal of Law and Information Technology* 11, no. 2 (January 2003): 184–201. https://doi.org/10.1093/ijlit/11.2.184.

Jones, Charles, and Christopher Tonetti. "Nonrivalry and the Economics of Data." *American Economic Review* 110, no. 9 (September 2020): 2819–2858.

Kerber, Wolfgang. "Governance of IoT Data: Why the EU Data Act Will Not Fulfill its Objectives." *GRUR International* 72, no. 2 (February 2023): 120–135. https://doi.org/10.1093/grurint/ikac107.

Kerber, Wolfgang. "A New (Intellectual) Property Right for Non-Personal Data? An Economic Analysis." *Gewerblicher Rechtsschutz und Urheberrecht, Internationaler Teil* 11 (2016): 989–999.

Kerber, Wolfgang. "Rights on Data: The EU Communication 'Building a European Data Economy' from an Economic Perspective." In *Trading Data in the Digital Economy: Legal Concepts and Tools,* edited by Sebastian Lohsse, Reiner Schulze, and Dirk Staudenmayer, 159–160. Namos/Hart Publishing, 2017.

Kerber, Wolfgang, and Jonas Frank. "Data Governance Regimes in the Digital Economy: The Example of Connected Cars." (November 2017). http://dx.doi.org/10.2139/ssrn.3064794.

Kimmelman, Eugene, Harold Feld, and Agustin Rossi. "The Limits of Antitrust in Privacy Protection." *International Data Privacy Law* 8, no. 3 (August 2018): 270–276. https://doi.org/10.1093/idpl/ipy015.

Kokott, Juliane, and Christoph Sobotta. "The Distinction between Privacy and Data Protection in the Jurisprudence of the CJEU and the ECtHR." *International Data Privacy Law* 3, no. 4 (November 2013): 222–228. https://doi.org/10.1093/idpl/ipt017.

Kosta, Eleni. "Article 35 Data Protection Impact Assessment." In *The EU General Data Protection Regulation (GDPR): A Commentary*, edited by Christopher Kuner, Lee A. Bygrave, Christopher Docksey, and Laura Drechsler, 665–679. Oxford University Press, 2020. https://doi.org/10.1093/oso/9780198826491.003.0072.

Kosta, Eleni. *Consent in European Data Protection Law*, Nijhoff Studies in European Union Law 3. Martinus Nijhoff Publishers, 2013.

Kotschy, Waltraut. "Article 6 Lawfulness of Processing." In *The EU General Data Protection Regulation (GDPR): A Commentary*, edited by Christopher Kuner, Lee A. Bygrave, Christopher Docksey, and Laura Drechsler, 321–344. Oxford University Press, 2020. https://doi.org/10.1093/oso/9780198826491.003.0035.

Kuner, Christopher. "Article 46 Transfers Subject to Appropriate Safeguards." In *The EU General Data Protection Regulation (GDPR): A Commentary*, edited by Christopher Kuner, Lee A. Bygrave, Christopher Docksey, and Laura Drechsler, 797–812. Oxford University Press, 2020. https://doi.org/10.1093/oso/9780198826491.003.0086.

Lande, Robert H. "The Microsoft-Yahoo Merger: Yes, Privacy Is an Antitrust Concern." *FTC: WATCH* 714, no. 9 (February 2008). https://ssrn.com/abstract=1121934.

Leland, Hayne E., and David H. Pyle. "Informational Asymmetries, Financial Structure, and Financial Intermediation." *Journal of Finance* 32, no. 2 (1977): 371–387.

López, Teresa. "AEPD (Spain) - AEPD PS-00508-2022 (gdprhub.eu)." https://gdprhub.eu/index.php?title=AEPD_(Spain)_-_AEPD_PS-00508-2022.

Lundqvist, Björn. "Competition and Data Pools." *Journal of European Consumer and Market Law* 7, no. 4 (2018): 146–154.

Lundqvist, Björn. *Regulating Access and Transfer of Data: Global Competition Law and Economics Policy*. Cambridge University Press, 2023.

Lundqvist, Björn. "Turning Government Data into Gold: The Interface Between EU Competition Law and the Public Sector Information Directive." *International Review of Intellectual Property and Competition Law* 44 (January 2013): 79–95. https://doi.org/10.1007/s40319-012-0007-0.

Lundqvist, Björn, and Murati, Erion. "Collaborative Platforms and Data Pools for Smart Urban Societies and Mobility as a Service (MaaS) from a Competition Law Perspective." In *Smart Urban Mobility – Law, Regulation, and Policy*, edited by Michèle Finck, Matthias Lamping, Valentina Moscon, and Heiko Richter, 191–226. Springer, 2020.

Lynskey, Orla. "Deconscturcting Data Protection: The 'Added-Value' of a Right to Data Protection in the EU Legal Order." *International & Comparative Law Quarterly* 63, no. 3 (2014): 569–597. https://doi.org/10.1017/S0020589314000244.

Maggiolino, Mariateresa. "Is the DMA (un)fair?" *Journal of Antitrust Law Enforcement* 12, no. 2 (July 2024): 267–272. https://doi.org/10.1093/jaenfo/jnae022.

Maggiolino, Mariateresa, and Laura Zoboli. "Smart Mobility and Technological Compatibility from an Antitrust Perspective." In *Smart Urban Mobility – Law, Regulation, and Policy*, edited by Michèle Finck, Matthias Lamping, Valentina Moscon, and Heiko Richter, 227–241. Springer, 2020.

Manley, Maria Isabel, and Strachan Grant. "Regulatory Data Protection." In *Navigating European Pharmaceutical Law*, edited by Maria Isabel Manley, and Marina Vickers, 255–276. Oxford University Press, 2015.

Mantelero, Alessandro. "The Future of Consumer Data Protection in the E.U. Re-Thinking the 'Notice and Consent' Paradigm in the New Era of Predictive Analytics." *Computer Law & Security Review* 30, no. 6 (December 2014): 643–660. https://doi.org/10.1016/j.clsr.2014.09.004.

Margoni, Thomas, Charlotte Ducuing, and Luca Schirru. "Data Property, Data Governance and Common European Data Spaces." *Computerrecht: Tijdschrift voor Informatica, Telecommunicatie en Recht* 3, no. 116 (April 2023): 202–211.

Martens, Bertin, and Néstor Duch-Brown. *The Economics of Business-to-Government Data Sharing*. EU Science Hub, 2020. https://joint-research-centre.ec.europa.eu/publications/economics-business-government-data-haring_en.

Mauro, Francesca, and Debora Stella. "Brief Overview of the Legal Instruments and Restrictions for Sharing Data While Complying with the EU Data Protection Law." In *Current Trends in Web Engineering*, edited by Sven Casteleyn, Peter Dolog, and Cesare Pautasso, 57–68. Springer International Publishing, 2016.

McSweeny, Terrell, and Brian O'Dea. "Data, Innovation, and Potential Competition in Digital Markets – Looking Beyond Short-Term Price Effects in Merger Analysis." *CPI Antitrust Chronicle* 2 (February 2018): 1–7.

Mezzanotte, Francesco. "Access to Data: The Role of Consent and the Licensing Scheme." In *Trading Data in the Digital Economy: Legal Concepts and Tools,* edited by Sebastian Lohsse, Reiner Schulze, and Dirk Staudenmayer, 159–187. Nomos/Hart Publishing, 2017.

Micheli, Marina, Marisa Ponti, Massimo Craglia, and Anna Berti Suman. "Emerging Models of Data Governance in the Age of Datafication." *Big Data & Society* 7, no. 2 (September 2020). https://doi.org/10.1177/2053951720948087.

Mitchell, Andrew D., and Neha Mishra. "Regulating Cross-Border Data Flows in a Data-Driven World: How WTO Law Can Contribute." *Journal of International Economic Law* 22, no. 3 (September 2019): 389–416. https://doi.org/10.1093/jiel/jgz016.

Mitchell Andrew D., and Neha Mishra. "WTO Law and Cross-Border Data Flows: An Unfinished Agenda." In *Big Data and Global Trade Law*, edited by Mira Burri, 83–112. Cambridge University Press, 2021.

Montagnani, Maria Lillà, and Antonia von Appen. "IP and Data (Ownership) in the New European Strategy on Data." *European Intellectual Property Review* 43, no. 3 (2021): 156–163.

Mylly, Ulla-Maija. "Transparent AI? Navigating Between Rules on Trade Secrets and Access to Information." *International Review of Intellectual Property and Competition Law* 54 (May 2023): 1013–1043. https://doi.org/10.1007/s40319-023-01328-5.

Nottingham, Mark. "Playing Fair in the Privacy Sandbox: Competition, Privacy and Interoperability Standards." (February 2021). http://dx.doi.org/10.2139/ssrn.3891335.

Ohlhausen, Maureen K., and Alexander P. Okuliar. "Competition, Consumer Protection, and the Right [Approach] to Privacy." *Antitrust Law Journal* 80, no. 1 (2015): 121–156.

Ohm, Paul. "Broken Promises of Privacy: Responding to the Surprising Failure of Anonymization." *UCLA Law Review* 57 (2010): 1701–1777.

Prüfer, Jens, and Christoph Schottmüller. "Competing with Big Data". *Journal of Industrial Economics* 64, no. 4 (February 2021): 967–1008. https://doi.org/10.1111/joie.12259.

Purtova, Nadezhda. "The Law of Everything. Broad Concept of Personal Data and Future of EU Data Protection Law." *Law, Innovation and Technology* 10, no. 1 (April 2018): 40–81. https://doi.org/10.1080/17579961.2018.1452176.

Ranchordás, Sofia. "Does Sharing Mean Caring? Regulating Innovation in the Sharing Economy." *Minnesota Journal of Law, Science & Technology* 16, no. 1 (Winter 2015): 414–475.

Reichel, Jane. "The European Strategy for Data and Trust in EU Governance: The Case of Access to Publicly Held Data." *CERIDAP* 4 (October 2023): 129–158. https://ceridap.eu/the-european-strategy-for-data-and-trust-in-eu-governance-the-case-of-access-to-publicly-held-data/.

Reimsbach-Kounatze, Christian. "Enhancing Access to and Sharing of Data: Striking the Balance between Openness and Control over Data." In *Data Access, Consumer Interests and Public Welfare*, edited by German Federal Ministry of Justice and Consumer Protection, and Max Planck Institute for Innovation, 27–68. Nomos, 2021.

Richter, Heiko. "Exposing the Public Interest Dimension of the Digital Single Market: Public Undertakings as a Model for Regulating Data Sharing." *Max Planck Institute for Innovation and Competition Research Paper* 20, no. 03 (March 2020): 1–29. https://dx.doi.org/10.2139/ssrn.3565762.

Rosati, Eleonora. "Originality in a Work, or a Work of Originality: The Effects of the *Infopaq* Decision." *Journal of Copyright Society U.S.A* 58, no. 4 (2011): 795–817.

Rubinstein, Ira S., and Woodrow Hartzog. "Anonymization and Risk." *Washington Law Review* 91, no. 2 (2016): 703–760.

Sappa, Cristiana. "What Does Trade Secrecy Have to Do with the Interconnection- Based Paradigm of the Internet of Things?" *European Intellectual Property Review* 40, no. 8 (2018): 518–523.

Schepp, Nils-Peter, and Achim Wambach. "On Big Data and its Relevance for Market Power Assessment." *Journal of European Competition Law & Practice* 7, no. 2 (February 2016): 120–124. https://doi.org/10.1093/jeclap/lpv091.

Schneider, Giulia. "Data Sharing for Collaborative Research under Art. 101 TFEU: Lessons from The Proposed Regulations for Data Markets." (2021). https://ssrn.com/abstract=3823191.

Sokol, Daniel D., and Roisin Comerford. "Does Antitrust Have a Role to Play in Regulating Big Data?" In *The Cambridge Handbook of Antitrust, Intellectual Property, and High Tech*, edited by Roger D. Blair and Daniel D. Sokol, 293–316. Cambridge University Press, 2017.

Stucke, Maurice E. "The Relationship Between Privacy and Antitrust." *Notre Dame Law Review Reflection* 97, no. 5 (2022): 400–416.

Stucke, Maurice E., and Allen P. Grunes. "No Mistake About It: The Important Role of Antitrust in the Era of Big Data." *Antitrust Source* (April 2015). https://ir.law.utk.edu/cgi/viewcontent.cgi?article=1777&context=utklaw_facpubs.

Swire, Peter. "Protecting Consumers: Privacy Matters in Antitrust Analysis." *The Centre for American Progress*, October 19, 2007. https://www.americanprogress.org/article/protecting-consumers-privacy-matters-in-antitrust-analysis/.

Thouvenin, Florent. "Informational Self-Determination: A Convincing Rationale for Data Protection Law?" *JIPITEC* 12, no. 4 (2021): 246–256. http://nbn-resolving.de/urn:nbn:de:0009-29-54098.

Tombal, Thomas. "GDPR As Shield to a Data Sharing Remedy." (February 2020). https://ssrn.com/abstract=3516718.

Tombal, Thomas. *Imposing Data Sharing among Private Actors: A Tale of Evolving Balances*. Kluwer Law International, 2022.

Tombal, Thomas. "The Rationale for Compulsory B2B Data Sharing and Its Underlying Balancing Exercises." *Revue du Droit des Technologies de l'information* 84 (January 2022): 5–26.

Tosoni, Luca. "Article 4(5). Pseudonymisation." In *The EU General Data Protection Regulation (GDPR): A Commentary*, edited by Christopher Kuner, Lee A. Bygrave, Christopher Docksey, and Laura Drechsler, 132–137. Oxford University Press, 2020. https://doi.org/10.1093/oso/9780198826491.003.0011.

Trakman, Leon L., Robert Walters, and Bruno Zeller. "Is Privacy and Personal Data Set to become the New Intellectual Property?" *International Review of Intellectual Property and Competition Law* 50 (September 2019): 937–970.

Trudel, Pierre. "Privacy Protection on the Internet: Risk Management and Networked Normativity." In *Reinventing Data Protection?,* edited by Serge Gutwirth, Yves Poullet, Paul Hert, Cécile Terwangne, and Sjaak Nouwt, 317–334. Springer, 2009.

Van Alsenoy, Brenda, Eleni Kosta, and Jos Dumortier. "Privacy Notices versus Informational Self-Determination: Minding the Gap." *International Review of Law, Computers & Technology* 28, no. 2 (July 2013): 185–203. https://doi.org/10.1080/13600869.2013.812594.

Van Eechoud, Mireille. "A Serpent Eating Its Tail: the Database Directive Meets the Open Data Directive." *International Review of Intellectual Property and Competition Law* 52 (April 2021): 375–378. https://doi.org/10.1007/s40319-021-01049-7.

Weber, Rolf H. "Information at the Crossroads of Competition and Data Protection Law." *Zeitschrift für Wettbewerbsrecht* 12, no. 2 (September 2014): 169–183. https://doi.org/10.15375/zwer-2014-0204.

Yan, Xingyu, and Huaiwen He. "Fine-tuning the *Ex-Ante* Approach to Regulating Data Combination Practices." *Journal of Competition Law & Economics* 18, no. 4 (December 2022): 881–904. https://doi.org/10.1093/joclec/nhac005.

Zanfir-Fortuna, Gabriela. "Article 13 Information to Be Provided Where Personal Data Are Collected from the Data Subject." In *The EU General Data Protection Regulation (GDPR): A Commentary*, edited by Christopher Kuner, Lee A. Bygrave, Christopher Docksey, and Laura Drechsler, 413–433. Oxford University Press, 2020. https://doi.org/10.1093/oso/9780198826491.003.0044.

Zarsky, Tal Z. "Incompatible: The GDPR in the Age of Big Data." *Seton Hall Law Review* 47 (August 2017): 1005–1009.

Zech, Herbert. "Data as a Tradeable Commodity." In *European Contract Law and the Digital Single Market: The Implications of the Digital Revolution*, edited by Alberto De Franceschi, 51–80. Intersentia, 2016. https://doi.org/10.1017/9781780685212.004.

Zech, Herbert. "A Legal Framework for a Data Economy in the European Digital Single Market: Rights to Use Data." *Journal of Intellectual Property Law & Practice* 11, no. 6 (June 2016): 460–470. https://doi.org/10.1093/jiplp/jpw049.

Zieliński, Marcin. "Business-to-Business Data Sharing within the EU Digital Market (2019–2021): Categorization of Data and Actors Involved in Data Sharing Operations." (May 2023). http://dx.doi.org/10.2139/ssrn.4462295.

Zoboli, Laura. "Fueling the European Digital Economy: A Regulatory Assessment of B2B Data Sharing." *European Business Law Review* 31, no. 4, (2020): 663–692.

Zoboli, Laura. "Il segreto commerciale e le politiche europee in materia di dati" *Annali Italiani del Diritto d'Autore, della Cultura e dello Spettacolo* 32 (2023): 232–261.

Zuboff, Shoshana. *The Age of Surveillance Capitalism: The Fight for a Human Future at the New Frontier of Power*. PublicAffairs, 2019.

Reports and Policy Papers*:*

ALI-ELI Principles for a Data Economy: Data Transactions and Data Rights, 2019, 28. https://europeanlawinstitute.eu/projects-publications/publications/ali-eli-principles-for-a-data-economy-data-transactions-and-data-rights/.

American International Group (AIG). *The Data Sharing Economy: Quantifying Tradeoffs that Power New Business Models*. Family Office Exchange, 2016. https://www.familyoffice.com/knowledge-center/data-sharing-economy-quantifying-tradeoffs-power-new-business-models-part-3-series.

Anzini, Martin, and Anne-Carine Pierrat. *Data Pools as Information Exchanges between Competitors: An Antitrust Perspective*, Centres for European Policy Network, 2020. https://www.cep.eu/fileadmin/user_upload/cep.eu/Studien/cepInput_Data_pools/cepInput_Data_Pools_as_Information_Exchanges_between_Competitors_An_Antitrust_Perspective.pdf.

Cattaneo, Gabriella, Giorgio Micheletti, Mike Glennon, Carla La Croce, and Chrysoula Mitta. *The European Data Market Monitoring Tool. Final Study Report.* Publications Office of the European Union, 2020. https://digital-strategy.ec.europa.eu/en/library/european-data-market-study-update.

Communication from the Commission "Towards a common European data space" COM(2018) 232 final, 9–10.

EPSC, Strategic Note, Entering the Data Economy, EU Policies for a Thriving Data Ecosystem, Issue 21, 2017, 5–7.

European Commission, Artificial Intelligence for Europe COM(2018) 237 final.

European Commission, Directorate-General for Communications Networks, Content and Technology, Patric Wauters, Anna Siede, Diana Cocoru, Florian Linz, Martina Barbero, and David Osimo. *Study on Emerging Issues of Data Ownership, Interoperability, (Re-) usability and Access to Data, and Liability: Final Report.* Publications Office of the European Union, 2018. https://data.europa.eu/doi/10.2759/781960.

European Commission, Directorate-General for the Information Society and Media, Wendy Carrara, Sander Fischer, Eva van Steenbergen, and Wae San Chan. *Creating Value Through Open Data: Study on the Impact of Re-use of Public data Resources.* Publications Office of the European Union, 2020. https://data.europa.eu/doi/10.2759/328101.

European Commission, Directorate-General for Justice and Consumers, Hans Graux, Geert Somers, Stefan Van Camp, Sophie Morel, Facundo Herrera, George Maridis, Debora Di Giacomo, and Solene Vassot, *Study on Model Contract Terms and Fairness Control in Data Sharing and in Cloud Contracts and on Data Access Right: Final Report.* Publications Office of the European Union, 2022. https://data.europa.eu/doi/10.2838/174720.

European Commission: Directorate-General for Justice and Consumers, Giorgio Monti, Thomas Tombal, and Inge Graef. *Study for Developing Criteria for Assessing "Reasonable Compensation" in the Case of Statutory Data Access Right – Study for the European Commission Directorate-General Justice and Consumers – Final Report.* Publications Office of the European Union, 2022. https://data.europa.eu/doi/10.2838/19186.

European Commission: European Innovation Council and SMEs Executive Agency, Alfred Radauer, Martin Bader, Tanya Aplin, Ute Konopka, Nicola Searle, Reinhard Altenburger, and Christine Bachner. *Study on the Legal Protection of Trade Secrets in the Context of the Data Economy – Final Report*. Publications Office of the European Union, 2022. https://data.europa.eu/doi/10.2826/021443.

European Commission. *Guidance on Sharing Private Sector Data in the European Data Economy Accompanying the Document Communication on 'Towards a Common European Data Space'*. Commission Staff Working Document. SWD(2018) 125 final.

European Commission, *Staff Working Document on Common European Data Spaces*. Published in Brussels on 23.2.2022, SWD(2022)45 final. https://digital-strategy.ec.europa.eu/en/library/staff-working-document-data-spaces (Accessed January 25, 2024).

European Commission Communication. *A European Data Strategy*. Published in Brussels on 19.02.2020. COM/2020/66 final.

European Data Protection Board (EDPB). *Guidelines 3/2019 on Processing of Personal Data through Video Devices*. January 29, 2020. https://edpb.europa.eu/sites/default/files/files/file1/edpb_guidelines_201903_video_devices.pdf.

European Data Protection Supervisor (EDPS). *EDPS Guidelines on the Concepts of Controller, Processor and Joint Controllership under Regulation (EU) 2018/1725*. November 7, 2019, 9–10, https://edps.europa.eu/sites/default/files/publication/19-11-07_edps_guidelines_on_controller_processor_and_jc_reg_2018_1725_en.pdf.

European Economic and Social Committee. *TEN/699 Guidance on the free flow of non-personal data*, EESC-2019-03048-00-00-PA-TRA (2018).

Feasy, Richard, and De Streel, Alexandre. *Data Sharing for Digital Markets Contestability: Towards a Governance Framework*. Centre on Regulation in Europe (CERRE), 2020. https://cerre.eu/publications/data-sharing-digital-markets-competition-governance.

Groupement Français de l'Industrie de l'Information, Paris, 'Position Paper, Key Issues for Successful PSI Policies in Europe: Improve the Articulation with GDPR and Enhance Data Quality' (2018).

IDC & Open Evidence. *Final Report, European Data Market* (February 2017) SMART 2013/0063, 123.

Impact Assessment Accompanying the document Proposal for a Directive of the European Parliament and of the Council on the re-use of public sector information' SWD(2018)127 32.

Jacques Crémer et al. *Competition Policy for the Digital Era*. European Commission, Publications Office of the European Union, 2019.

Krämer, Jan, Daniel Schnurr, and Sally Broughton Micova, *The Role of Data for Digital Markets Contestability: Case Studies and Data Access Remedies*. Centre on Regulation in Europe (CERRE), 2020. https://cerre.eu/publications/data-digital-markets-contextability-case-studies-and-data-access-remedies/.

Martens, Bertin, Alexandre de Streel, Inge Graef, Thomas Tombal, and Néstor Duch-Brown. *Business-to-Business Data Sharing: An Economic and Legal Analysis*. EU Science Hub, 2020.

McKeever, Brice, Solomon Greene, Graham MacDonald, Peter A. Tatian, and Deondre' Jones. *Data Philanthropy. Unlocking the Power of Private Data for Public Good*. Urban Institute, 2018. https://www.urban.org/research/publication/data-philanthropy-unlocking-power-private-data-public-good.

McKinsey & Company, Michael Chui, Mark Collin, and Mark Patel. *Internet of Things: Catching up to an Accelerating Opportunity*. McKinsey & Company, 2021. https://www.mckinsey.com/business-functions/mckinsey-digital/our-insights/the-internet-of-things-the-value-of-digitizing-the-physical-world.

OECD & Eurostat. *The Measurement of Scientific, Technological and Innovation Activities in Oslo Manual 2018, Guidelines for Collecting, Reporting and Using Data on Innovation*, 20 (4th Edition, OECD & Eurostat, 2018).

Organisation for Economic Cooperation and Development (OECD). *Enhancing Access to and Sharing of Data: Reconciling Risks and Benefits for Data Re-Use Across Societies.* OECD Publishing, 2019. https://doi.org/10.1787/276aaca8-en.

Organisation for Economic Cooperation and Development (OECD). *Guidelines on the Protection of Privacy and Transborder Flows of Personal Data.* 23 September 1980. https://www.refworld.org/docid/3dde56854.html.

Richter, Heiko. *Access to Private Sector Data for the Common Good: A Critial Review of Chapter V of the Proposed Data Act.* Centre on Regulation in Europe (CERRE), 2023. https://cerre.eu/wp-content/uploads/2023/02/Data_Act_B2G_data_sharing.pdf.

Legal texts

Australia-Singapore Digital Economy Agreement (SADEA). https://www.dfat.gov.au/sites/default/files/australia-singapore-digital-economy-agreement.pdf.

Charter of Fundamental Rights of the European Union [2012] OJ C326/391.

Convention for the Protection of Human Rights and Fundamental Freedoms, ETS No. 005.

Convention for the Protection of Individuals with regard to Automatic Processing of Personal Data, ETS No. 108 and Protocol amending the Convention for the Protection of Individuals with regard to Automatic Processing of Personal Data, CETS No. 223. The modernized convention in the article is referred to as Convention 108+.

Directive 95/46/EC of the European Parliament and of the Council of 24 October 1995 on the protection of individuals with regard to the processing of personal data and on the free movement of such data [1995] OJ L281/31.

Directive 2003/98/EC of the European Parliament and of the Council of 17 November 2003 on the re-use of public sector information [2003] OJ L 345/90.

Directive 2013/37/EU of the European Parliament and of the Council of 26 June 2013 amending Directive 2003/98/EC on the re-use of public sector information [2013] OJ L 175/1.

Directive 2019/1024/EU of the European Parliament and of the Council of 20 June 2019 on open data and the re-use of public sector information [2019] OJ L 172/56.

Regulation (EU) 2016/679 of the European Parliament and of the Council of 27 April 2016 on the protection of natural persons with regard to the processing of personal data and on the free movement of such data, and repealing Directive 95/46/EC (General Data Protection Regulation) in OJ L 119, 4.5.2016, pp. 1–88.

Regulation (EU) 2018/1807 of the European Parliament and of the Council of 14 November 2018 on a framework for the free flow of non-personal data in the European Union, in OJ L 303, 28.11.2018, pp. 59–68.

Regulation (EU) 2022/868 of the European Parliament and of the Council of 30 May 2022 on European data governance and amending Regulation (EU) 2018/1724 (Data Governance Act), in OJ L 152, 3.6.2022, pp. 1–44.

Regulation (EU) 2022/1925 of the European Parliament and of the Council of 14 September 2022 on contestable and fair markets in the digital sector and amending Directives (EU) 2019/1937 and (EU) 2020/1828 (Digital Markets Act), in OJ L 265, 12.10.2022, pp. 1–66.

Regulation (EU) 2022/2065 of the European Parliament and of the Council of 19 October 2022 on a Single Market For Digital Services and amending Directive 2000/31/EC (Digital Services Act), in OJ L 277, 27.10.2022, pp. 1–102.

Regulation (EU) 2023/2854 of the European Parliament and of the Council of 13 December 2023 on harmonised rules on fair access to and use of data and amending Regulation (EU) 2017/2394 and Directive (EU) 2020/1828 (Data Act), in OJ L, 2023/2854, 22.12.2023.

United States-Mexico-Canada Agreement (USMCA). https://ustr.gov/sites/default/files/files/agreements/FTA/USMCA/Text/19-Digital-Trade.pdf.

Index

Note: Page numbers in **bold** indicate tables in the text, and references following "n" refer notes.

9781032163710